FORT WAYNE DURING THE CANAL ERA, 1828-1855

Indiana Historical Collections
Volume XLVI

Allen County–Fort Wayne Historical Society

VIEW OF FORT WAYNE, 1855

FORT WAYNE DURING THE CANAL ERA 1828-1855

A Study of a Western Community in the Middle Period of American History

By Charles R. Poinsatte

INDIANA HISTORICAL BUREAU

1969

PREFACE

A number of years ago when I undertook this task one might have needed a justification for writing a scholarly work about a single western town during a comparatively brief period in its history. Since then the publications of the school of urban historians, especially those interested in the West such as Richard C. Wade, have made any apology unnecessary. These have focused their attention on the over-all picture, taking as representative examples the larger western communities such as Pittsburgh, Louisville, St. Louis, and Cincinnati. Other urban historians such as Blake McKelvey and Leland D. Baldwin have dealt with a particular phase of municipal development or have given a comprehensive account of their cities' histories, but one usually finds these works deal only with the larger cities. However, the small communities as well as the larger cities deserve to be studied for while the former were urban in spirit, at the same time they were still close enough to their rural neighbors to be influenced by them. On the other hand, unlike the six urban communities included in Merle Curti's study of Trempealeau County, Wisconsin,[1] Fort Wayne was of sufficient size not to be dominated by the surrounding rural area.

Essentially this is a history of Fort Wayne during the years when the Wabash and Erie Canal played a most significant role in its development. Yet I have not attempted to give a detailed account of every political, social, and economic event in the city's history during this era but rather to stress how Fort Wayne might be viewed as a microcosm in testing some of our conclusions about the West during the Middle Period in American history. For a study such as this Fort Wayne has

[1] Merle Curti, *The Making of an American Community* . . . (Stanford University Press, 1959).

certain advantages. Most of the issues that faced the man of the West and even the nation as a whole can be found working themselves out on a small scale at Fort Wayne. These included the problems of internal improvements, immigration, Indian removal and the declining fur trade in the Old Northwest, banking, land policy, commercial, industrial, and agricultural expansion as well as the religious and cultural developments in the West. For example, every student of American history knows of the western demand for internal improvements, but we may see here in one instance how and why this demand materialized, what type of individual took the leadership, what results a canal produced both in its construction and completion in respect to a particular city and its environs. Again, we are familiar with the purpose and method of the Indians' removal, but what effect did this policy have upon the life of a community, one dependent on the Indian trade? What factors attracted settlers to come to a small town in the West? How did the Irish and German immigrants fare in a town such as Fort Wayne? At what point did industry assume a role equal to commerce? Did cultural and political leadership in an essentially rural region come from the countryside or the town? Finally, what factors led one town to succeed while others fell by the wayside, for there were many "paper towns" even in Allen County. I do not pretend to answer these and other questions on a national scale, but only throw some light on the larger issues from the small segment of American society that made up Fort Wayne in the years from 1828 to 1855.

Earlier nineteenth century historians of the Fort Wayne region have dealt with the local history at times in detail and certainly, considering the available sources, with diligence, but not always with accuracy. Suffering from provincialism and antiquarianism, usually such works are too laudatory, and they make no attempt to relate the community's development to the sectional or national picture of the period. The interplay of religious, social, and economic developments and rivalries are usually ignored. It is the hope that the present work succeeds to some extent in these respects.

As far as possible, I have relied on primary sources. The extent and variety of such material for local history is greater than the uninitiated may imagine. The local newspapers of the period were usually available on microfilm at either the Fort Wayne Public Library or in the Indiana State Library at Indianapolis. While there were certain gaps, especially in the 1830s, over-all the newspapers furnished an abundance of material. Government documents were employed whenever possible. Municipal records were of value especially after the incorporation of the city in 1841. The original returns of the Seventh Census for Wayne Township, which are available on microfilm at Indiana University and the Indiana State Library, furnished accurate statistics on the city's industrial and commercial growth. Of special value in the questions dealing with the fur trade and the Indian trade, land and many other matters were the W. G. and G. W. Ewing and Allen Hamilton manuscript collections at the Indiana State Library, as well as the John Tipton Papers which have been published in part as Volumes 24-26 of the *Indiana Historical Collections.* The Susan Man and Hugh McCulloch Papers in the Lilly Library at Indiana University contain a wealth of material that has been virtually untouched. The same applies to the American Home Missionary Society Papers in the Hammond Library at the Chicago Theological Seminary. These in addition to other sources, such as those at the University of Notre Dame Archives, furnished valuable insights into the religious and social developments of the city. While the Samuel Hanna collection in the Fort Wayne–Allen County Historical Museum is voluminous, almost all of these documents deal with legal transactions and therefore, apart from indicating Hanna's ownership of great tracts in northern Indiana, are not particularly serviceable. On the other hand, many miscellaneous letters and documents in the Museum were of great use. Finally, certain citizens of Fort Wayne have made available to the writer material hitherto used sparingly, if at all, by previous writers. In this regard, I would like to thank in particular Mr. Peter Certia, Mrs. Bessie Roberts, and the late Charles Ross McCulloch.

I also want to extend my sincere gratitude to the archivists and librarians of the Indiana State Library, the Fort Wayne–Allen County Historical Museum, the Fort Wayne Public Library, the Chicago Theological Seminary, and the libraries and archives at Indiana and Notre Dame universities, especially to Miss Elfrieda Lang at the former university and the late Reverend Thomas T. McAvoy, archivist at Notre Dame, as well as to the many county and city officials who have been of assistance. I owe a special debt of gratitude to the late Dr. Aaron Abell, whose assistance was of immeasurable value and whose encouragement was appreciated deeply. Finally, I wish to express my deep appreciation to Dorothy Riker and Mrs. Shirley McCord of the Historical Bureau whose diligence has saved me from numerous errors and whose suggestions have proved extremely beneficial.

ST. MARY'S COLLEGE
NOTRE DAME, INDIANA

CHARLES R. POINSATTE

CONTENTS

ILLUSTRATIONS

MAPS

CHAPTER I

EARLY HISTORY: OUTPOST OF INDIAN DIPLOMACY AND TRADE

In my opinion, the savages themselves are the most christianized, and least savage of the two classes now congregated here.

The history of the Old Northwest is intimately related with the great system of natural waterways interlacing the Ohio-Mississippi Valley. These waterways provided the means by which the early explorers and traders traversed this region. It was only natural that portages and meeting points along this great network of rivers should hold unique positions of importance. This is particularly true of the early history of Fort Wayne (known to the Indians as Kiskakon or Kekionga and to the French and English as Fort Miami). The story of Fort Wayne begins as the history of the Maumee-Wabash portage. Located at the confluence of the rivers St. Joseph and St. Mary's, which together form the Maumee or Miami of Lake Erie, Fort Wayne is situated at the northeast starting point of the seven-mile portage to the Little River (see map, page 30). Twenty-two miles southwest of Fort Wayne, the Little River joins the Wabash which, in turn, empties into the Ohio and then into the Mississippi. For almost two hundred years, from the mid-seventeenth century until the mid-nineteenth century, the Maumee-Wabash portage was a vital overland link that tied together the great waterway systems of the St. Lawrence and Mississippi. In other respects the site of Fort Wayne was also at the "crossroads." From this point the traveler could journey northeast up the St. Joseph River into the present state of Michigan, or turn southeast up the St. Mary's River into the central portion of the present state of Ohio. Herein lies the significance of the words of Little Turtle, the great Miami chief, who once called the site of Fort Wayne, "that glorious gate . . . through which all the good words of our chiefs had to pass from the north to the south, and from the east to the west."[1]

The French fur traders and military established a post at this site sometime early in the eighteenth century.[2] During the French, British, and American occupation of the region, forts were maintained here as outposts of defense and diplomacy in the Indian country. The site of Fort Wayne figured prominently in the Indian wars between 1783 and 1795, and again in the War of 1812. The fort built here by Anthony Wayne in 1794 and its replacement continued to be garrisoned until 1819, and the Indian agency established here in 1802 was continued until 1828. In addition, an Indian trading house was in operation for ten years, from 1802 to 1812. On annuity payment days as many as a thousand Indians would flock to the site.[3] Situated in the center of the valuable Maumee-Wabash fur-producing region, the Indian villages at the headwaters of the Maumee had from the beginning attracted the fur trader, whether French, English, or American.

In a previous study the author has attempted to give a comprehensive background of the French and British occupation of the site of Fort Wayne and has stressed its importance in the

[1] Speech of Little Turtle at the Treaty of Greenville, 1795, in *American State Papers, Indian Affairs* (2 vols. Washington, D. C., 1832-34), 1:576.

[2] Although La Salle apparently knew of the portage as early as the 1670s, the first French post seems to have been established there by Jean Baptiste Bissot, Sieur de Vincennes, sometime between 1702 and 1719. Pierre-Georges Roy, *Sieur de Vincennes Identified* (Indiana Historical Society *Publications,* Vol. 7, No. 1, Indianapolis, [1919]), 71-72; Charles Poinsatte, A History of Fort Wayne, Indiana, from 1716 to 1829. A Study of Its Early Development as a Frontier Village (Unpublished M. A. thesis, University of Notre Dame, 1951), 6-9.

[3] Gayle Thornbrough (ed.), *Letter Book of the Indian Agency at Fort Wayne, 1809-1815* (Indiana Historical Society *Publications,* Vol. 21, Indianapolis, 1961), 10-12, 233-34; Nellie A. Robertson, "John Hays and the Fort Wayne Indian Agency," in *Indiana Magazine of History,* 39 (1943):227. William Wells represented the Federal government among the Miami before the agency was officially established.

early days of American settlement.[4] The decline of the fur trade together with the purchase of the surrounding Miami lands in 1826 and the removal of the Indian agency in 1828 combined to bring to a close the frontier phase of Fort Wayne's development. The second period, that of the more permanent commercial development, was about to dawn. Plans were being formulated for the construction of the Wabash and Erie Canal with Fort Wayne as a focal point. It is with this transitional period that the present study begins.

After the departure of the military garrison in 1819, the Indian agency occupied quarters within the stockade. In 1823 a Federal land office was established at the former military post to handle the sale of land ceded by the Miami and Wea in 1818. In 1824 Fort Wayne was selected as the seat of the newly created Allen County which included almost all of northeastern Indiana.[5] The selection was due in part to a realization of its potentialities but equally as much to the fact that it was virtually the only settlement in this region of Indiana. With a population numbering around two hundred in 1825, it was by far the largest community in the county.[6]

There are a number of eyewitness accounts relating to Fort Wayne during this period for almost every traveler through

[4] Poinsatte, A History of Fort Wayne, from 1716 to 1829.

[5] Robertson, "John Hays and the Fort Wayne Indian Agency," in *Indiana Magazine of History,* 39:225. An act of May 8, 1822, created the land office but it was not opened until the following year. U. S. *Statutes at Large,* 3:701-2. Allen County was formed by act of December 17, 1823, effective April 1, 1824. *Revised Laws of Indiana,* 1823-24, pp. 109-11; George Pence and Nellie C. Armstrong, *Indiana Boundaries, Territory, State, and County* (*Indiana Historical Collections,* Vol. 19, Indianapolis, 1933), 226.

[6] Accurate estimates of Fort Wayne's population at this time are difficult to obtain because of the transitory character of some of its people. However, a permanent population of at least two hundred may be safely assumed. Allen Hamilton to Absalom Peters, December 10, 1828, in Papers of the American Home Missionary Society, Hammond Library, Chicago Theological Seminary; *Valley of the Upper Maumee River* (2 vols. Madison, Wis., 1889), 1:38; O. H. Smith, *Early Indiana Trials and Sketches . . .* (Cincinnati, 1858), 169.

northern Indiana was obliged to stop at this lone village. In general these accounts dwell upon the difficulties in reaching Fort Wayne and upon the virgin nature of the land in its immediate vicinity. The country around Fort Wayne was described in 1819 as being "very fertile" and the situation of the village "commanding and healthful."[7] Thomas Scattergood Teas, a scholarly young adventurer who visited Fort Wayne in 1821, wrote: "The settlement at this place consisted of about 30 log cabins and two tolerably decent frame houses. . . . The inhabitants are nearly all French Canadians. The fort stands at the lower end of the village. . . ."[8]

From the fort a cart track angled down to the river bank and boat landing, the bustling center of the town's traffic in furs; and three embryonic roads, boggy and stump filled, led respectively northeast to Detroit, northwest to Fort Dearborn and Lake Michigan, and southeast to Fort Recovery, Ohio.

One of the keenest observers was James Riley, a civil engineer who had been sent to Fort Wayne to survey the lands ceded by the Indian treaties of 1818 as well as the government reserve. Riley's most interesting letter was written from Fort Wayne during the time of the annuity payments to the Indians in 1820. It was addressed to Edward Tiffin, Surveyor General. After speaking highly of the natural advantages of the site of Fort Wayne, Riley urged that the government land be offered for sale as soon as possible, thereby establishing "a cordon of hardy and *respectable settlers*."[9] Riley described the situation then existing in the following terms:

[7] See, for example, various accounts in Harlow Lindley (ed.), *Indiana as Seen by Early Travelers (Indiana Historical Collectons,* Vol. 3, Indianapolis, 1916), 135, 143, 241-43, 246-55; Poinsatte, A History of Fort Wayne, from 1716 to 1829, pp. 144-51, quotation on p. 146.

[8] Lindley (ed.), *Indiana as Seen by Early Travelers,* 250.

[9] Riley to Tiffin, November 14, 1820, quoted in Louis A. Warren, "Captain James Riley, Mariner-Author-Surveyor," in *Old Fort News,* 10:no. 4 (December, 1946):6.

There are now, in its [Fort Wayne's] immediate vicinity, more than 40 families of *"squatters"* and traders, besides a great number of young men, each with his *bundle,* or shop, of goods and trinkets; all of whom are depredating on the public lands, for timber for their numerous buildings, for fire-wood, &c. &c.; and as they have no interest in the soil, and little hope of being able to purchase the land when sold, a system of waste and destruction is going on, and is apparently entered into by all; . . . There are now assembled, as I should judge, at least *one thousand* white persons from Ohio, Michigan, Indiana, and New York, whose object is stated to be that of trade with the Indians, in order to carry off some of their specie, paid them by the Government. They have brought whiskey in abundance, which they pretend to deposit with the agent, until he shall have finished his business with the Indians; but yet contrive to deal out large quantities from their deposits *in the woods,* so that the savages are kept continually drunk, and unfit for any business.[10]

Anyone who could transport to Fort Wayne enough kegs of whiskey, blankets, shawls, and other Indian goods could set up a store. The Indian customers were plentiful and for the most part gullible. Canoes lined the river banks after the hunting season, when the Indians brought in their great loads of peltries. As Riley indicated, many of the whites who traded with the Indians were a transient and rather worthless lot. Nevertheless the opportunities also attracted some energetic men who, mingling with the original French population, remained to stamp their names upon the small settlement.

These settlers included James Barnett, a native of Pennsylvania, who was with Harrison's army at Fort Wayne in 1812

[10] *Ibid.,* 7. Riley may have exaggerated the number of traders present. The Indian agent estimated there were about eleven hundred Miami present. A thousand dollars worth of beef and flour were issued to them while they waited for the payment, which had been delayed a month while the agent hauled the sum of over $18,000 in silver dollars from Cincinnati to Fort Wayne. Robertson, "John Hays and the Fort Wayne Indian Agency," in *Indiana Magazine of History,* 39:227-28. Isaac McCoy, who also witnessed the payment, wrote that the Indians had "no sooner received their money from the government than scenes of drunkenness ensued . . . which lasted for many days." Isaac McCoy, *History of the Baptist Indian Missions . . .* (Washington, D. C., 1840), 84-85.

and who returned in 1818 as a permanent resident and trader; Paul Taber and his sons, Cyrus and Samuel, and his daughter, Lucy, all of whom came in 1819; Francis Comparet, who came in 1820, and established, together with Alexis Coquillard and Benjamin Kercheval, a post for John Jacob Astor's American Fur Company at Fort Wayne; Dr. William Turner, a former post surgeon, who returned to Fort Wayne in 1819 and later served for a short time as Indian agent; and James Aveline who with his family came from Vincennes to Fort Wayne.[11] Among the settlers who came to Fort Wayne in 1819 was Samuel Hanna, Indian trader and pioneer merchant, land speculator, judge, legislator, canal builder, railroad entrepreneur, and banker. In many respects, Samuel Hanna was to become Fort Wayne's most active citizen as the small community grew from a mere village to a city during his lifetime. Hanna was definitely a product of the American frontier. Born October 18, 1797, in Scott County, Kentucky, into a large family, he was taken by his parents to a farm near Dayton, Ohio, in 1804. Here he helped to clear the land and secured what formal education was available. While still in his teens, he traveled throughout the area as a postrider. Through no fault of his own, he failed in his first business endeavor as a merchant in Piqua, Ohio, while still only nineteen. He then taught for a brief time before securing, together with his brother, Thomas, a government contract to furnish supplies during the treaty negotiations with the Indians at St. Mary's, Ohio, in 1818. Using the experience and the profit he had made from this contract, Hanna, while yet only twenty-two, came to Fort Wayne to establish a trading post in partnership with his brother-in-law, James Barnett. He immediately erected a

[11] *The John Tipton Papers,* edited by Nellie A. Robertson and Dorothy Riker (3 vols. *Indiana Historical Collections,* Vols. 24-26, Indianapolis, 1942), 1:360-61n, 535n-36n; Bert J. Griswold, *The Pictorial History of Fort Wayne, Indiana* . . . (2 vols. Chicago, 1917), 1:241, 243, 247, 254.

small log building on the site which later became the northwest corner of Barr and Columbia streets.[12] As Hanna's means accumulated, he extended his mercantile operations to other places: Lafayette, where he was for many years in business with his brother, Hugh; and South Bend, where he financed the operations of his wife's brother, Colonel Lathrop M. Taylor.[13] Hanna also served as an associate judge of the circuit court and was repeatedly elected as a member of the state legislature while the canal issue was being agitated. However, Hanna was not so much a politician as a builder with great business sagacity. A Presbyterian in religion, he exemplified in his personal life the Calvinistic virtues of industry and frugality. He especially claimed credit for his economy during the early stages of his business career and often declared that "he never expended one dollar for any personal pleasure or luxury until he was worth over fifty thousand."[14]

In 1822 the family of Alexander Ewing came to Fort Wayne from Troy, Ohio. The Ewing family consisted of Alexander Ewing, an old Pennsylvania trader, his wife, Charlotte, three daughters, and four sons—Charles, who became president judge of the Eighth Judicial Circuit of Indiana, Alexander, who later became a prosperous Cincinnati merchant, and George W. and William G., who became associated with their father in the trading establishment. Until the father's death in 1826, the business operated under the name of "A. Ewing and Sons."

[12] G. W. Wood, *The Life and Character of Hon. Samuel Hanna* (Fort Wayne, 1869), 5-10, 15. Early accounts of Hanna's life state that he was an agent of the American Fur Company; however, evidence indicates that while he sold furs to the company he never served as their agent. See J. Crooks to B. B. Kercheval, Fort Wayne, September 1, November 2, 1821; J. Crooks to J. Hedges, Fort Wayne, January 3, 1822; Crooks to Abbott, March 3, 1822, in American Fur Company Letter Book, Vol. 2, photostats in Chicago Historical Society Library.

[13] Concerning Hanna's role in the founding of South Bend, see Bert Anson, The Fur Traders in Northern Indiana, 1796-1850 (Unpublished Ph. D. thesis, History Department, Indiana University, 1953), 105, 107, 121.

[14] Wood, *Samuel Hanna,* 10.

After that the firm was called, "W.G. & G.W. Ewing." The Ewings became widely known for their real-estate and fur-trading operations, the latter on a scale that eventually made them rivals of the American Fur Company in the Great Lakes region. At the height of their business activity, the Ewings had branch houses in Logansport, Lagro, and Peru, Indiana, and posts in Missouri, Iowa, Michigan, Kansas, Wisconsin, and Minnesota. Hugh McCulloch who came to know the Ewing brothers well, later was to write, "Enterprising, laborious, adventurous men they were, but so devoted to business, so persistent in the pursuit of gain, that they had no time to enjoy the fruits of their labors. I have rarely met their equals in business capacity or general intelligence; very few have I known who had less real enjoyment of life."[15]

In a sense these newcomers such as the Ewings, Hanna, and Barnett, were rivals of the earlier established French families. At first, however, the American traders worked through or with the more experienced French traders in dealing with the Indians.[16] The rivalries were also lessened by intermarriage between the two elements. G. W. Ewing, for example, married a daughter of Louis Bourie. John P. Hedges, another American trader, also married into the Bourie family. Eventually, having gained experience and having greater capital, the American traders usually outdistanced the French, who often became their agents by the latter part of the twenties.

The establishment of the government land office in 1823 brought to Fort Wayne Samuel C. Vance as the first register of the land titles and Joseph Holman as receiver of the public moneys. Since Holman also engaged in the Indian trade,[17] much of the clerical work connected with the office came under

[15] Hugh McCulloch, *Men and Measures of Half a Century . . .* (New York, 1888), 106.

[16] Anson, Fur Traders in Northern Indiana, 77.

[17] *John Tipton Papers,* 1:332n, 385.

the direct supervision of Allen Hamilton, a young man who accompanied Holman and Vance as their assistant. Hamilton later became one of the foremost merchants in the Fort Wayne area and would also play a leading role in civic matters. He was born in Tyrone County, Ireland, in 1798 of Protestant parents. Having received a fairly good education in business, he came to America in 1817 after the financial failure of his father. Here he hoped to retrieve the family wealth and in this respect he was quite successful in the years that followed his arrival at Fort Wayne. As a trader, he became a good friend of the Miami, and in particular their chief, Richardville, whom he served as a business adviser. In this manner he was generally able to obtain choice land sites from the Indians in exchange for his services and for payment of their debts. Hamilton at times secured land in partnership with John Tipton, the Indian agent at Fort Wayne. With rare insight regarding land values and through his general business acumen, Hamilton eventually amassed a small fortune.[18]

The act that set up the land office at Fort Wayne also provided that all public lands for which the Indian title had been extinguished and which had not been granted to or secured for the use of any individual or individuals or appropriated and reserved for any other purpose were to be opened for sale. The site of the fort and an additional thirty acres on which the public buildings were located were withheld by the government in order that the Indians assembling for councils or annuity payments might have a place for encampment.[19] On

[18] *Ibid.*, 1:607n. Hugh McCulloch estimated Hamilton's estate to be worth at least a million dollars. McCulloch, *Men and Measures of Half a Century,* 105. Hamilton had twelve children by his wife, the former Emerine Holman. Among the descendants of this union have come such scholars as Edith Hamilton, Greek scholar and playwright, Alice Hamilton, first woman professor at the Harvard Medical School and a pioneer in industrial and occupational medicine, and Holman Hamilton, American historian.

[19] U. S. *Statutes at Large,* 3:701-2; *John Tipton Papers,* 1:332n-33n.

October 22, 1823—the thirty-third anniversary of Harmar's defeat on this same spot, and the twenty-ninth anniversary of the dedication of Wayne's fort—the government land sale was opened at the fort. John T. Barr from Baltimore, Maryland, and John McCorkle from Piqua, Ohio, combined their resources to purchase the tract which is known as the Original Plat of the town. John Barr's firm, "Barr and Campbell," was engaged in merchandising in many parts of Ohio and Pennsylvania.[20] Barr's business activities in the West led him into land speculating. Judging from his instructions to his agent in Fort Wayne, Barr hoped to profit both from the selling of lots in the new town and from selling goods to the white settlers.[21] Thus he represented a composite of eastern merchant-financier and land speculator. John McCorkle, on the other hand, was interested in the Indian trade at Fort Wayne. Undoubtedly he also had land speculation in mind when he purchased the original plat with Barr. However, of the twenty Indian traders licensed in 1821-22 by the government agent to trade in the Fort Wayne region, McCorkle had by far the greatest amount of capital invested.[22] Unlike Barr, McCorkle was a westerner, born in Piqua, Ohio, in 1791. As a young man, he soon became engaged in the Indian trade and like Hanna and others profited from supplying goods for the government treaty negotiations with the tribes. He had gained considerable experience in promoting the development of new towns both in his hometown of Piqua and in laying out the new town of St. Mary's, Ohio, in 1821. More than likely McCorkle had dealt with Barr for some time prior to 1824, since Barr's firm was actively

[20] Henry Rudisill to John Barr, Fort Wayne, January 16, 1830, Rudisill Letterbook, in possession of the Hahn family (1964); *Valley of the Upper Maumee River*, 2:36-37 (sketch of Rudisill).

[21] See numerous entries in the Rudisill Letterbook.

[22] *House Executive Documents*, 18 Congress, 1 session, No. 7; Anson, The Fur Traders in Northern Indiana, 81.

promoting business in southwestern Ohio. It is not surprising, therefore, to learn that the two men came to the Fort Wayne land sale together, traveling down the St. Mary's River from Ohio in a bateau. For the original tract they paid twenty-six dollars per acre, an extremely high price for undeveloped western land at that time.[23] Barr and McCorkle took immediate steps to plat and survey their property which today includes that part of downtown Fort Wayne bounded on the north by the Nickel Plate Railroad, on the east by Barr Street, on the south by Washington Boulevard, and on the west by the alley between Calhoun and Harrison streets. Altogether the plat consisted of 118 lots with four north-and-south streets and five east-and-west streets.

One reason why Barr and McCorkle paid such a relatively high figure was their belief that the townsite would continue to be of great value as a place of Indian trade, and for a few years their judgment seemed to be more than vindicated, as the capitalization of the fur traders operating from Fort Wayne in 1827 far surpassed the combined capitalization of those operating from Detroit and Chicago.[24] However, by the late 1820s the situation was changing due to the purchase of the greater part of the Indian lands in northern Indiana in the treaty with the Miami and Potawatomi in 1826 at Mississinewa. As late as that year the northern third of the state was held by less than three thousand Indians while the southern two thirds was

[23] John McCorkle to William McLean, February 7, 1828, *John Tipton Papers*, 2:18n; Register of Receipts, Fort Wayne Land Office, 1823-36, in Archives Division, Indiana State Library. Alexander Ewing purchased eighty acres immediately west of the Barr and McCorkle tract, while the heirs of William Wells purchased the tract between the forks of the St. Mary's and St. Joseph rivers. The latter tract had been set aside for Wells by Congress in 1809 and was thus pre-empted at the minimum price of $1.25 an acre. The Barr and McCorkle plat was immediately adjacent to the government Indian agency and therefore more valuable than the "Wells pre-emption."

[24] Anson, The Fur Traders in Northern Indiana, 95.

settled by one hundred times as many whites. Thus the pressure of the whites, who lusted for the rich land north of the Wabash-Maumee line, led to an inexorable demand for Indian removal. Fort Wayne as a central point along this line of the Maumee and Wabash rivers, and at the edge of the white civilization, held a unique and paradoxical position. The traders at Fort Wayne—the Ewings, Hamilton, Hanna, Barnett, William N. Hood, Comparet, Coquillard, and others—were making a handsome profit in their dealings with the Indians. As long as the Indian agency remained at Fort Wayne, and as long as the Indians remained in this area and received ever-increasing annuities, these men would profit. Removal of the Indians, as William G. Ewing pointed out, would deprive the area of many thousands of dollars distributed annually.[25]

On the other hand, there was another factor, especially important at Fort Wayne, which made the cession of the Indian lands very desirable. The craze for internal improvements had struck Indiana in the 1820s. The most discussed and most promising project was the proposed Wabash and Erie Canal, for which the portage at Fort Wayne was the focal point. Many of the traders at Fort Wayne were able through their astuteness (or in some cases "fraud") in business with Indians to acquire valuable property along the route of the proposed canal. Nevertheless the Indians still held the territory north of the Wabash and Maumee, and their removal was necessary for the work to be able to proceed. To a great extent it became a question of which interest was more powerful, the Indian traders and fur companies or the larger group of land speculators, townsite promoters, merchants, and settlers of the Wabash and Maumee valleys.[26] It was inevitable that the latter group should win out, but in the final analysis the Treaty of 1826 with the

[25] *John Tipton Papers,* 1:13.

[26] Poinsatte, A History of Fort Wayne, from 1716 to 1829, p. 177.

Miami went a long way in placating many of the Fort Wayne Indian traders largely at the expense of both the government and the Indians. That an agreement was reached with the Miami was due to a great extent to the work of John Tipton, Indian agent at Fort Wayne since 1823.[27] Tipton had more than an official interest in the negotiations since he had already acquired personal possession of lands along the proposed canal route.

By this time the procedure in negotiating Indian treaties had become fairly stereotyped. The Indians were gathered together by commissioners who made liberal promises of good things to come. At the meeting place preparations were made for feeding great numbers of people; traders were instructed to attend with attractive selections of goods, barrels of whiskey were imported, and every precaution was taken to satisfy the appetites and desires of the Indians. At the proper time the commissioners in charge assembled the braves, to whom was read a stilted and pompous message from the Great White Father in which the Indians were upbraided for their depredations, drunkenness, and other misconduct, and reminded of the forebearance, generosity, and friendliness of the whites. At this point the Indians were asked what lands they would surrender and if they would move farther west.

Neither the Miami nor the Potawatomi wanted to give up their lands in 1826, but after food and whiskey had been consumed and goods given out to the value of $61,588, they showed signs of weakening. However, it was apparent that the government commissioners could get nowhere unless they could secure the support of the traders. The latter were concerned to have their claims—sometimes two or three times the actual amount of credit they had extended to the Indians—allowed and paid for out of the annuities. They also wished to gain

[27] *Ibid.,* 162-64.

control of more desirable land through the treaty, thus obtaining it without the land being put up at public auction as was the legal procedure.[28]

Collusion and fraud were usually present in the treaty negotiations. Almost all of the leading statesmen of the day recognized this fact. As one student of the period points out,

> Calhoun . . . connived at it [fraud]. Jackson . . . had little sympathy for Indians; when engaged in making Indian treaties, he was surrounded by questionable characters. Jackson himself said that corruption of Indian chiefs was a *sine qua non* to successful negotiation. President Van Buren, in the face of indubitable proof of a fraudulent treaty, ratified it. The American Fur Company secured senatorial consent to a treaty favorable to its own interest through Senator Benton, a giant of his day.[29]

Thus there had grown up in the administration of Indian affairs a method of passing Indian lands to the whites without subjecting them to the land laws of the United States. The statutory method of land disposal was for the Indians to cede land to the United States; the land would then be surveyed, divided into sections, and sold at auction to the highest bidder. Any remaining sections were sold for $1.25 an acre. This method was fair and democratic. The non-statutory method of land disposal worked in this way: trader and Indian agents, who generally co-operated closely with one another, would include in the Indian treaties provisions authorizing the patenting of certain lands to the chiefs, half-breeds, or ordinary members of the tribes. These individuals then conveyed their rights to traders in payment of real or imaginary debts before the treaty was signed or shortly thereafter. Although presidential approval for such conveyances was necessary, in most cases the approval could be secured easily, provided the agents would report that the Indians had received a fair price for their land.

[28] *John Tipton Papers,* 1:13-14.

[29] Rex Potterf, *Indian Treaties as the Basis for Land Titles* (An address delivered January 30, 1931, published by Fort Wayne Public Library, 1952), [12].

As the agents were either under obligation to the traders for support in treaty negotiations or were personally interested in some of the reserves, they could usually be induced to send in a favorable report even though the Indians might have bartered their holdings away for some trinkets or a few drinks.[30]

It is not surprising, therefore, to find the traders in full force at the treaty grounds in 1826, fighting for their interests. They worked through the chiefs and headmen of the tribes to whom they gave gifts and loans. To take care of the traders' claims, present and prospective, it was necessary to increase the annuities and agree to pay the Indian debts. In addition, goods to the value of $72,300 were distributed to the Miami at the treaty and during the next two years. For these stipulations the Indians surrendered an estimated 926,000 acres, the main part of which was along the Wabash and Maumee rivers. From this cession, the Miami were permitted to retain 81,800 acres for tribal villages and 13,920 for individual reserves.[31]

The treaty of 1826 secured the surrender of the land by the Indians but the enlarged annuities it provided would tend to lessen the desire for their ultimate removal. The frontier community of Fort Wayne could not be disdainful of payments of specie which ran as high as $100,000 in some years, as for example in the early 1840s.

It is no wonder that when the people of Fort Wayne learned that John Tipton had applied to the government officials to move the Indian agency from Fort Wayne, many protested vigorously. For some time Tipton had desired to remove the agency to a more central location in the Indian country. The exploitation of the Indians at Fort Wayne was reason enough,

[30] *John Tipton Papers,* 1:17-18.

[31] For the official account of the negotiations leading to the treaty, see *American State Papers, Indian Affairs,* 2:683-85, and *John Tipton Papers,* 1:576-92. The treaties signed at Mississinewa are in Charles J. Kappler (ed.), *Indian Affairs. Laws and Treaties* (2 vols. Washington, D. C., 1904), 2:195-201, and in U. S. *Statutes at Large,* 7:295-303.

but Tipton had to wait for a favorable opportunity to press his case. The attitude of the traders at the 1826 treaty gave him a plausible excuse to push the project of removal. In a letter written February 7, 1827, to Thomas L. McKenney, head of the Indian Office, Tipton listed seven reasons why the agency should be removed from Fort Wayne. Not only was it too remote from the Indians, argued Tipton, but it was also too close to numerous grogshops and to the traders who sold his wards whiskey, encouraged them to run up debts which must later be deducted from annuities, and cheated them in a hundred different ways.[32] Realizing there would be opposition to the removal of the agency, Tipton enlisted the aid of Lewis Cass, his immediate superior, members of the Indiana Congressional delegation, as well as prominent citizens in support of the move.

Upon learning of Tipton's proposal, the traders and other citizens of Fort Wayne put aside petty quarrels and joined in common defense to prevent the removal. A petition signed by 118 individuals of the town and county and forwarded to the Secretary of War, pointed out that they had purchased land and settled the same "under a belief that the agency would continue at Fort Wayne. . . . We think a removal . . . would not add any thing to the General Government or the Indians, and would materially injure all the present settlers of this country." They too sought the aid of Indiana's senators and representatives in Congress. John McCorkle, as a principal owner of real estate at Fort Wayne, wrote to Representative William McLean of Ohio:

> This settlement has been formed in consequence of the establishment of the agency at that place. Reserves were made for the use of the agent, thereby holding out a guarantee to the purchasers of public lands and property, that this agency would be continued at that place until the Indians should be removed from that

[32] *John Tipton Papers,* 1:651-52.

> country. Among others, I became a considerable purchaser of considerable public lands, for which I paid an extravagant price. . . . If a removal should take place, the *Indians,* as well as the inhabitants at Wayne, who have expended their all there will be greatly disobliged.[33]

In a letter to Senators James Noble and William Hendricks, Samuel Hanna presented a strong case for retention of the agency at Fort Wayne. The Indians did not want it removed; it was a central point, and the competition among the Indian traders gave the Indians the opportunity to purchase goods at a fair price. Letters from W. G. and G. W. Ewing to Congressman Oliver H. Smith contained similar arguments, and Smith was sufficiently convinced to write the Secretary of War to withhold the order for removal until the people in the area of Fort Wayne had the opportunity to present the *"whole"* facts.

Despite the opposition against removal, Tipton secured authorization on March 14, 1828, for the transfer to a site on the Wabash River in the Indian country. Rebuffed by this decision, Senator Noble presented on April 17 a motion calling upon President Adams for copies of all the recommendations for and remonstrances against the removal of the agency, as well as information on the exact location where it was to be removed, and who owned the site. The President complied with this request together with a letter from McKenney stating that he understood the agency was to be removed to a spot on the Wabash River between the mouths of Pipe Creek and the Eel River, and that the Indians owned the land. The documents in the case were ordered printed but no further action was apparently taken at this session or the following one.[34]

[33] *John Tipton Papers,* 2:18.

[34] *Senate Documents,* 20 Congress, 1 session, No. 189. On April 18 Senator Noble moved that the Senate recommend to the President that the agency remain at Fort Wayne until he was advised by the people through the members of the General Assembly that it should be removed. The motion was tabled. *Senate Journal,* 20 Congress, 1 session, 311.

Congressman Thomas H. Blake who had actively promoted the removal wrote Tipton that "the *agency* . . . is, in any event, fast at Eel River, fast as the rock of Gibralter, and I consider the other as certain, the distribution of the annuities there too unless you suffer those d--d rascally speculators in Ohio to breed civil war among your Indians, which is a matter *you will no doubt see well to.*"[35]

Tipton had a personal interest in securing the removal of the agency to a spot near the junction of the Wabash and Eel rivers. He and his friends were in the process of obtaining control of the Indian reserves there and shortly thereafter the town of Logansport was platted on one of the reserves.[36] Some of the Fort Wayne traders gravitated to the new town, among them Cyrus Taber and George W. Ewing. Whiskey soon became as plentiful at Logansport as it had been at Fort Wayne and the Indians were induced to overpurchase as often and were cheated as badly as they had been at the former location. One can hardly see what benefit had been attained by the removal of the agency other than the enhancement of Tipton's prestige and personal fortune.

In the long run, however, the Miami treaty of 1826 and the removal of the agency were to benefit Fort Wayne. Not only did the treaty secure some 926,000 acres of land wanted by actual settlers, but it also opened the way for the construction of the Wabash and Erie Canal. The treaty even looked forward

[35] *John Tipton Papers,* 2:32-34.

[36] The original plat of the town was laid out in April, 1828, on the reserve granted to George Cicott in the Potawatomi treaty of 1826. Part of the reserve adjoining the town plat was in Tipton's possession within two years. *John Tipton Papers,* 2:47n. One of the additions to the town was laid out on land that had been reserved to the Miami chief Richardville in 1826. He sold the land to Joseph Holman in 1827 for $500 and Tipton in turn secured the deed from Holman for $600 on April 3, 1828. In another transaction, Tipton, Allen Hamilton, and Cyrus Taber agreed to purchase and divide reserves belonging to Richardville, Little Charley, and Francis Godfroy, each receiving one third of the lands. *Ibid.,* 1:20-21; 2:24; 3:462-64.

to the building of the canal by stipulating that the Federal government had the privilege of securing, if necessary, a right-of-way for a canal through the remaining Indian reservations. Furthermore, through the various treaties many of Fort Wayne's leading citizens were able to gain valuable land along the route of the proposed canal thus stimulating them to promote energetically this important improvement.

While the change was not immediately apparent, the removal of the agency meant that the town would eventually secure a more stable and industrious type of settler than heretofore and that its growth would depend more upon its own natural advantages and industry than on the artificial boom of the annuity payments. Virtually every visitor to Fort Wayne at the time of the Indian payments had been disgusted by the orgies that attended them. While it is evident that the Indians were being degraded, it is clear that they were not always inferior to some of the early white settlers in the region. One spectator at the annuity payments wrote:

> Horse-racing, drinking, gambling, and every kind of debauchery, extravagance and waste, are the order of the day, and night, too; and in my opinion, the savages themselves are the most christianized, and least savage of the two classes now congregated here. Here the whites set examples to the Indians too indelicate to mention, and that cannot fail to produce in their minds disgust for the American character.[37]

Often this type of white squatter cheated the Indians in minor matters and sold whiskey illegally to them. Tipton distinguished between the traders in the address he gave at the Miami payment in 1828.

> . . . there is no man but him who knows can tell how difficult the task is to allow traders who will pursue a fair and friendly trade to attend these payments and keep out those wretched beings who go all lengths to get money. they stop at nothing. they form combinations with men who have me[a]ns to procure whisky and smugle

[37] Warren, "Captain James Riley," in *Old Fort News,* 10: no. 4:6.

into the country, if they can elude my vigilence and violate the law they plume themselves for dexterity in that disgracefull traffic in which no honest man will engage.[38]

In an effort to answer charges brought against him by some of the Fort Wayne traders in 1827, Tipton wrote to his superior:

Although it is improper for a man to speake of his neighbors faults and follies, yet boath self defence and truth Justifies the assertion that a majority of the Citizens of this village are of the lowest order of society, such as discharged soldiers and dishonourable men. . . . who have fled from the offended laws of their Country elsewhere and have stoped here on account of the quantity of money anually disbursed at this place. Their constant practice is to get money from the Indians by every artifice in their power.[39]

Disagreeable and unethical as it often was, the Indian trade had played an important role in the development of the village. While it was at Fort Wayne, the agency plus the fur trade had attracted such men as Samuel Hanna, Francis Comparet, Cyrus Taber, and the Ewings—men who remained to build a city.

[38] *John Tipton Papers,* 2:87.
[39] *Ibid.,* 1:662.

CHAPTER II

YEARS OF TRANSITION, 1829-1832

I know of no part of the west that affords so great inducements to the farmer as the vicinity of this place.

The years between 1829 and 1832 mark the beginning of Fort Wayne's transition from a small village situated about the fort and depending entirely on the fur and Indian trade to a town which was to become an important center of commerce and transportation. However, these years were indeed difficult ones for the citizens of Fort Wayne. The purchase of the Miami lands followed by the removal of the Indian agency threatened to cut off the primary source of income for the village of some two hundred and fifty permanent residents. According to Tipton's estimate in 1827, seven out of every ten families in Allen County depended on the Indian trade.[1] Any efforts that may have been made to re-establish the agency at Fort Wayne came to naught. All that remained was a subagency and even this was discontinued in 1830 rather than repair the public buildings in the stockade. That year Congress authorized the sale of the government reserve on which the agency and the old fort stood.[2]

A few weeks after the principal agency had been removed, Lewis G. Thompson, physician and land speculator at Fort Wayne, wrote Tipton: "Matters have not materially changed since you left us—this set of creatures here (for they are not

[1] John Tipton to Thomas McKenney, February 7, 1827, *John Tipton Papers,* 1:651.

[2] *Ibid.,* 1:332n-33n; 2:36n, 233; U. S. *Statutes at Large,* 6:448. In the 1840s, Allen Hamilton and Joseph Sinclear acted in the capacity of subagents at Fort Wayne.

fit to be call'd men) that were sent among us for the same purposes that flies were sent among horses; still keep buzzing about, as though they had lost their prey, and hardly knew where to light." Thompson thought of leaving Fort Wayne, at least temporarily, but was prevented "by the indisposition of several of my patrons." At any rate, he concluded, "I think best to stick hard by, and starve the d—l—."[3]

Others did leave, but those who remained did so on a mixture of hope and faith—hope that the canal would actually be initiated, and faith that its construction would bring all the economic blessings promised. In the meantime, they would try to get along as best they could. That the merchants still relied heavily upon government expenditures and hoped for new treaties with the Indians is evident from a letter of G. W. Ewing to Tipton in 1830 pleading for a delay in the Indian payments at Logansport until Ewing's goods would arrive from New York. Writing from New York, Ewing added:

> Since I arrived at this place I have learn[d]. that the appropriation Bill, relative to Treaties &c in our section of Country, has failed, and that consequently we shall have no Treaty this season, should this be the case I shall be one, among many others . . . who will deeply regret it. The embarrass[d]. condition of many of our citizens calls loudly for relief from some quarter and I can see no prospect for us unless it should be through some Treaty or Indian transaction. I have used every exertion to have our goods on as early as possible. All is now ready and I shall ship tomorrow. Judge Hanna is here, and our goods will go forward together. . . . To be absent, or out of goods at the time of the Payts. would be ruinous to us, as it is the Indian interest upon which we depend almost exclusively. . . .[4]

In the summer of 1832 W. G. Ewing reported that he had sold only $1,600 of Indian goods during the previous fall.[5]

[3] Lewis G. Thompson to Tipton, April 29, 1828, *John Tipton Papers,* 2:42.

[4] G. W. Ewing to Tipton, July 3, 1830, *ibid.,* 2:295-96.

[5] W. G. Ewing to Charles Ewing, September 5, 1832, Ewing Papers, Indiana State Library.

Closely linked to the decline in the Indian trade was the falling off of the fur trade during this same period.[6] This was due only indirectly to the cession of land by the Indians inasmuch as the Indians were becoming accustomed to living more and more from the government annuities rather than by trapping. This situation had been developing for some time, and the fur traders were already coming to rely more on white settlers for trapping. However, by the late 1820s there were not yet enough whites to produce a large supply of furs. Another reason assigned by the fur traders as partially responsible for their misfortune was the epidemic of cholera in London and New York in the early 1830s, another indication of how close the tie was between the western traders and their markets in the East. As we shall note later, the fur trade in the region of northern Indiana was far from dead and would experience a definite revival in the late 1830s, but during the period in which we are now concerned its slump only added to the economic woes of Fort Wayne.

Actually the reasons for the community's plight and the cure were quite evident at the time. William Barbee, an Ohio merchant, after commiserating with the Ewings over the loss of the annuity payments at Fort Wayne and over the town's "pecuniary embarrassments," pointed out that the Indian trade had been declining for some years and must at any rate soon disappear. He added that if the "country [had] been filled by agriculturists before this happened, the town would not have felt the depression." Fort Wayne's salvation, he concluded, lay in the rapid commencement by the state of the Wabash and Erie Canal. Railroads he considered too visionary.[7]

[6] Anson, Fur Traders in Northern Indiana, 154; report of the Secretary of War to the President, February 8, 1832, in U. S. *Senate Documents,* 22 Congress, 1 session, No. 90, p. 4.

[7] William Barbee to W. G. Ewing, November 17, 1831, Ewing Papers.

In general agreement with Barbee's opinion was James Chute, the newly arrived Presbyterian minister. He reported to the American Home Missionary Society, "The inhabitants have heretofore depended wholly upon the Indian trade, & neglected the cultivation of the land." However, he went on to say, "I know of no part of the west that affords so great inducements to the farmer as the vicinity of this place. . . . This place will undoubtedly exert a most powerful influence upon the surrounding country."[8] Later in the same letter, Chute made it clear that the above predictions were based on the assumption that communications with the East would be improved.

Despite its natural advantages, it was evident that Fort Wayne's future lay in the development of internal improvements and the rapid settlement and cultivation of the fertile river valleys, the agricultural output of which would find a natural market in Fort Wayne.

For some time prior to 1829, the more forward-looking and enterprising citizens of the village had seriously advocated the incorporation of the town as a means toward attaining these ends. They advanced the following arguments: (1) the number of inhabitants was sufficient for and warranted incorporation; (2) such action would serve to stabilize conditions at Fort Wayne by providing a system of local government and needed ordinances, thereby attracting additional settlers; (3) by incorporating, the citizens could gain more unity of action for important undertakings, in particular the canal. Throughout the summer of 1829 the question was debated, but by Septem-

[8] James Chute to Absalom Peters, September 20, 1831, American Home Missionary Society Papers, Hammond Library, Chicago Theological Seminary. Chute complained that because of its isolation the cost of living was extremely high at Fort Wayne, twice that of Columbus, Ohio, his previous mission. This situation of course further contributed to the economic distress of the townspeople, who, heretofore, had often purchased such items as salt and woolen goods very cheaply from the Indians. The latter had obtained these supplies with their annuities.

ber the opposition gradually ebbed. At a mass meeting on the seventh of that month, after a brief discussion, a two-thirds majority of those assembled voted in favor of incorporating the town of Fort Wayne.[9] In the following week the first board of trustees was elected, consisting of Hugh Hanna, younger brother of Samuel Hanna, John S. Archer, William G. Ewing, Dr. Lewis G. Thompson, and John P. Hedges. They were to serve only one year and had the power of appointing the town officers—assessor, treasurer, collector of taxes, marshal, and supervisor of the streets. That these positions could not be considered political plums is clear from the fact that the town marshal received only $2.00 a year for his services, while the assessor was paid an annual salary of $5.00. With such small incentives, it is not surprising that the officers were negligent in the keeping of records. A special auditing committee in 1832 reported that "The records of 1829 and 1830 were well made up, with the exception that there was no expose made of the receipts and expenditures during these years."[10]

In purely local matters the trustees set to work to carry out such mundane but important actions as the draining of swamps and the clearing of underbrush. Vigilance committees were appointed for this purpose. In 1836 the town trustees considered "means to drain the cellars and remove the nuisance of dead matter in this corporation."[11] However, funds for such undertakings were as usual insufficient. The total amount of taxes received, for example, in 1831 was only $91.12½.[12] The question of local transportation being all important, the regulatory power of the trusteeship was employed in 1830 to establish a ferry service across the St. Mary's River. A monopoly for this

[9] Robert S. Robertson (ed.), *History of the Maumee River Basin* (Vols. 2-3 of 3 vols. Indianapolis, *c.* 1905), 2:95.

[10] Records of the Town Trustees, May 8, 1832, Fort Wayne City Hall.

[11] *Ibid.*, June 10, 1836.

[12] *Ibid.*, March 1, 1832.

privilege was granted to Zenas Henderson, but the rates were fixed by the trustees, and Henderson was subject to a heavy fine if he violated the provisions of the license. There seems to have been little doubt in this western community that such police power fell within the scope of the town government.

While the maintenance of a ferry and the clearing of the streets of stumps and seasonal mudholes helped to facilitate the town's local transportation, the greater problem remained of bringing Fort Wayne into closer and easier contact with other western communities and with the East. This was not to be an easy task. All the accounts of the period concerning Fort Wayne's relatively isolated position are in agreement. The most officially documented of these is that of John Spencer, receiver of public moneys in the Fort Wayne Land Office from 1832 to 1840. In 1852 Spencer petitioned Congress to be reimbursed for the heavy expenditures he had made in transporting the specie received for government lands. Spencer secured numerous affidavits proving that as late as 1836 the country around Fort Wayne was almost an unbroken wilderness. One of the most expressive of the affidavits was that of a blunt old mule driver, Amos Compton, who testified that he lived on the road leading to Piqua about thirteen years and traveled it probably more than any other man; that in doing so he frequently had to leave the road and take a zigzag course to avoid swamps and streams. In traveling with a wagon, he sometimes had to cut a trail through the woods for ten or twelve miles; at other times they had to stop and build bridges. Sometimes travel was so slow that they could not reach a settlement by evening and had to spend the night in the woods.[13]

Henry Rudisill, postmaster at Fort Wayne from 1831 to 1841, testified that the weekly mail between that town and

[13] *Letter of Col. John Spencer, Late Receiver of the Land Office at Fort Wayne, Indiana . . .* (New York, 1852), 44-45.

Winchester was very irregular on account of the bad roads and high waters, while Thomas Tigar described his bad experiences in trying to transport a printing press from Indianapolis to Fort Wayne.[14]

Coming from Toledo in 1835, the Reverend Daniel G. Jones found the overland trip to Fort Wayne as costly as the trip from New York City to Toledo. He wrote it was utterly impossible to get through except by horseback.[15]

A particularly low region to the southeast along the Piqua road cost many travelers the loss of their livestock or goods. This section was aptly termed by the townspeople "the Bloody Murrain." Outside of a few isolated farms around the town, the country was still in a state of wilderness. In 1830-31, because of the severe winter, travel was almost entirely abandoned; the town itself was infested by wolves.

If possible, therefore, the traveler to Fort Wayne in 1830 came by the rivers, still the chief arteries of communication as they were a century before in the day of the *coureur de bois*.The canoe and pirogue remained dominant on the rivers. Pirogues packed with furs at Fort Wayne were floated down the Maumee, at times even unattended. For heavier freight the keelboat was employed. Upstream, these boats were propelled strictly by manpower as six to seven men would shove the boats up the river with long poles. The "Maumee River Line" of keelboats owned and operated by two Fort Wayne men, John Barber and Patrick Ravenscraft, carried freight to Toledo.[16]

[14] *Ibid.,* 39-40. See also Rudisill to John Barr, January 2, 1830, in Rudisill Letterbook.

[15] Letter to Absalom Peters, October 29, 1835, in American Home Missionary Society Papers.

[16] Statement of Alexander C. Comparet, in *Reminiscences of Old Fort Wayne, 1906,* compiled by Lura Case Woodworth, Carolyn Randall Fairbank, and Martha Brandriff Hanna (Fort Wayne—Allen County Public Library [1953]), [17-18].

Even in the winter the rivers provided the easiest means of travel, by use of sleigh. Usually the Maumee remained frozen until April as the dense forest of timber along the banks and the frozen brush kept the ice from moving out except by a freshet. The June freshet was awaited with confidence, and the shippers were seldom disappointed. In preparation for it, the keelboats were loaded in advance with grain and other products.[17] Occasionally during periods of high water steamboats came up the Maumee from Lake Erie. Their arrival was an occasion for merriment, but the steamboat could not be employed successfully on the Maumee beyond Defiance, Ohio. In the minds of the townspeople the canal remained the only solution to the transportation problem.

It is outside the scope of this study to dwell at length on the various problems and debates in Congress and in the Indiana legislature concerning the canal.[18] Who first conceived the idea of linking the Wabash and Maumee rivers by a canal is merely a matter of speculation, for the advantages to be gained were so apparent that as one writer states, "The lengthening and shortening of the portage with the changes in the seasons must have suggested the scheme to every traveler over

[17] McCulloch, *Men and Measures of Half a Century,* 41-42. According to McCulloch, "in 1835 the rise of the upper Wabash was so much later than usual that some of the owners of the flat-boats became discouraged, and sold the corn with which they were laden at six cents a bushel. But the river did not fail. The rain fell, the waters rose, and in a few days the purchasers of the corn were richly compensated for what they called their 'trust in Providence.'"

[18] While there have been general works on the canals such as Carter Goodrich's recent study, *Canals and American Economic Development* (Columbia University Press, 1961), and Alvin F. Harlow's *Old Towpaths* (1926), there has been no detailed study published of the entire history of the Wabash and Erie Canal. Willis Richardson's master's thesis on the subject, written in 1925, is available only in typescript in the Indiana State Library. The best published monograph on the canal is Elbert J. Benton's *The Wabash Trade Route in the Development of the Old Northwest (Johns Hopkins University Studies in Historical and Political Science,* Series 21, Nos. 1-2, Baltimore, 1903).

this swampy pass, whether French or English."[19] During and following the American Revolution, the strategic and commercial value of the portage was recognized by the military and by both the legislative and executive branches of the government.[20] Article IV of the Ordinance of 1787 provided that this portage should be reserved as a free route to be used in common by all citizens.[21] A stipulation to this effect in Wayne's treaty with the Indians at Greenville in 1795 was eloquently contested by Little Turtle, but in the end the Miami chief was forced to acquiesce.[22] Washington pointed out the importance of the site on more than one occasion. One of his fondest hopes was to connect the Ohio River with the Atlantic coast. After an investigation of western topography, he wrote in 1785 to his future secretary of war, Henry Knox, suggesting that the Maumee-Wabash portage was the most feasible point for water communication between the Ohio and Lake Erie.[23] Other statesmen and writers of the period likewise entertained ideas of a canal at Fort Wayne.[24] During his surveys of government lands in 1819-20, James Riley undertook on his own initiative the examination of the portage route to determine the practicality of uniting the waters of the Wabash and Maumee with a canal. He apparently was the first to offer concrete evidence that a canal was practical.[25]

[19] Benton, *The Wabash Trade Route,* 32. Little Turtle claimed that the portage brought his tribe, the Miami, as much as $100 in one day. *American State Papers, Indian Affairs,* 1:576.

[20] Concerning the military significance of the portage site, see Poinsatte, A History of Fort Wayne, from 1716 to 1829, Chapters I-IV.

[21] Article IV of the Northwest Ordinance.

[22] *American State Papers, Indian Affairs,* 1:576.

[23] William Henry Smith (ed.), *The St. Clair Papers. The Life and Public Services of Arthur St. Clair . . .* (2 vols. Cincinnati, 1882), 2:181; John C. Fitzpatrick (ed.), *The Writings of George Washington . . .* (39 vols. Washington, D. C., 1931-44), 28:11, 168.

[24] Benton, *The Wabash Trade Route,* 33-34.

[25] Warren, "Captain James Riley," in *Old Fort News,* 10:no. 4:4-6.

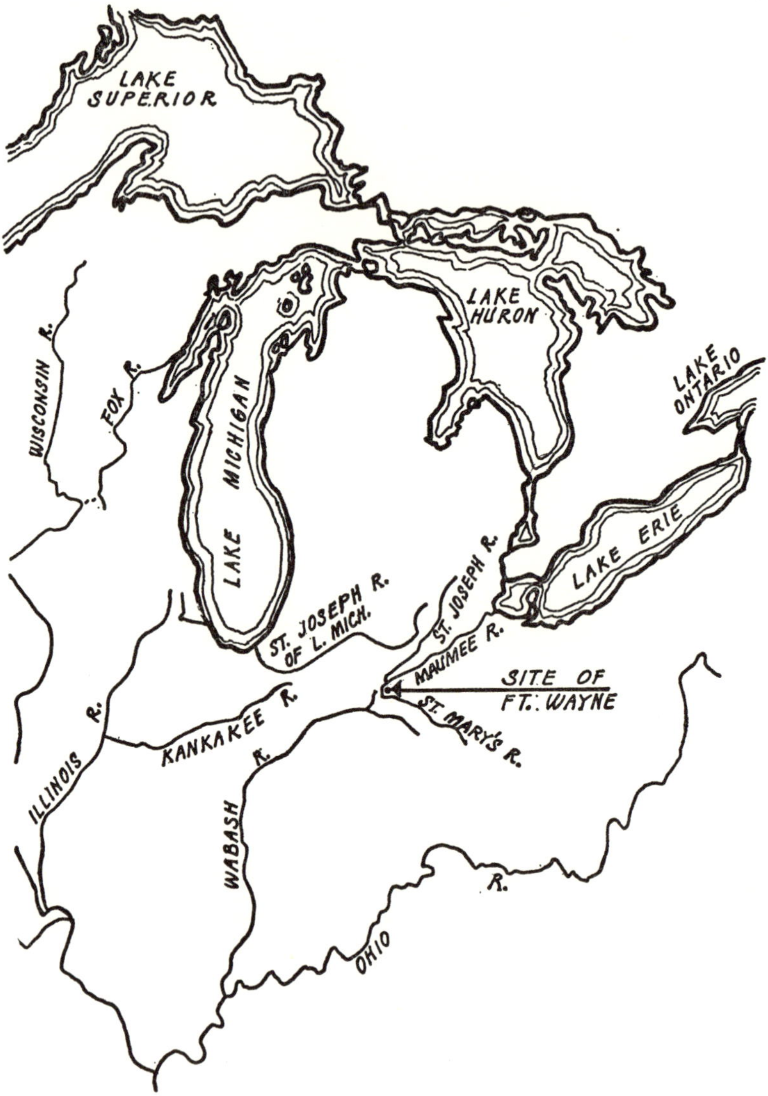

PORTAGE AT FORT WAYNE IN RELATION TO RIVER ROUTES

A canal connecting Lake Erie with the Wabash River had been brought to the attention of the Indiana legislature at various times. However, the state was in no financial position to undertake such a project even though the original estimates were far below the final cost. As late as 1826 the state's revenue amounted to only $33,000, barely enough to cover expenditures.[26]

It was evident to the citizens of Fort Wayne as well as to others interested in the project that Federal aid would be necessary if the canal were ever to be built. And to obtain the desired aid it would be necessary for those interested to work together politically and present a united front. Samuel Hanna was one of the main leaders in pushing the project. Having made frequent trips to New York, he was in a position to understand its importance to the future growth of Fort Wayne. This was likewise true of other merchants in the town, particularly Allen Hamilton, another vigorous supporter of the canal. John Tipton, as Indian agent, was very active in promoting the work as was David Burr, who was soon to remove from Jackson to Cass County.[27]

Jonathan Jennings, one of Indiana's three representatives in Congress, had been one of the commissioners at the 1818 treaty with the Indians held at St. Mary's, Ohio, and was no doubt well acquainted with the possibilities of a canal connecting the waters of the Maumee and Wabash. He first introduced a bill looking toward Federal aid in January, 1823, but it was tabled and not until the following session was a bill passed. This called for Indiana to begin construction within

[26] *Messages and Papers relating to the Administration of James Brown Ray, Governor of Indiana, 1825-1831,* edited by Gayle Thornbrough and Dorothy Riker (*Indiana Historical Collections,* Vol. 34, Indianapolis, 1954), 158, 192.

[27] Benton, *The Wabash Trade Route,* 39n; Wood, *Samuel Hanna,* 16. Burr, a native of Connecticut, first lived at Salem, Indiana, where he was postmaster from 1817 to 1821.

three years and to complete the work in twelve years, and was rejected by the Indiana legislature.[28] Indiana did benefit however from another act of this session which appropriated money for surveys for possible canals in the West.[29]

Members of the Indiana General Assembly were, however, pushing the canal project. A Senate committee, of which John Ewing of Vincennes was chairman, made a report in February, 1825, in which they recommended that action be taken to open a canal between the Wabash and the Maumee; that they try to obtain a land grant from the Federal government; and that the President take steps to extinguish the Indian titles to lands along the Wabash.[30] In 1826, as we have noted, the last of these recommendations was consummated by the treaty with the Miami and Potawatomi. In the same year Samuel Hanna was elected for the first time by the voters of Allen and Randolph counties to serve in the Indiana House of Representatives. In the House and later in the Senate, he was to play a leading role in pushing for state action on construction of the canal.

With completion of the Erie Canal in 1825, the arguments for furnishing an outlet from Lake Erie to the Ohio River grew stronger. Ohio launched her canal program that same year, and in the succeeding years the people of Fort Wayne followed wistfully the news of the canal celebrations in the neighboring communities of that state.

In 1826 a corps of United States engineers under the direction of Colonel James Shriver was sent to survey the portage at Fort Wayne. All became ill and Shriver died. The following year Asa Moore continued the survey to the mouth of the Tippecanoe and then from the junction of the St. Joseph and

[28] Richardson, History of the Wabash and Erie Canal, 17-21.

[29] *Ibid.*, 20-21; U. S. *Statutes at Large*, 4:22-23; Benton, *The Wabash Trade Route*, 39.

[30] Indiana *Senate Journal*, 1825, pp. 168-76.

St. Mary's down the Maumee as far as the rapids, where he also died on October 4, 1828.[31]

Meanwhile, in Congress Jennings, John Test, and William Hendricks were continuing to press for Federal aid in construction of the canal in Indiana. Representatives from other areas in the Northwest were likewise exerting pressure for Federal aid for internal improvements in their neighborhoods. As Benton has pointed out, military as well as economic factors were important in securing final Congressional approval. "The experience of the Northwestern campaigns of the War of 1812 had demonstrated the futility of military operations with inadequate means of transporting troops and supplies. These expenditions were almost invariably failures due to defective transportation."[32] However, strictly political reasons also entered into the decision of Congress. "Sectional jealousies . . . compelled the national government to distribute its wealth in money and lands among the western states demanding canals and roads to counterbalance the Atlantic seaboard clamoring for harbors and ships."[33]

On March 2, 1827, Congress passed a significant act not only for the Wabash and Erie Canal but for all future internal improvements in the United States. For weeks a bill had been debated in the Senate granting Indiana three sections of land on each side of the route of the proposed canal. Finally this bill was amended to give the state alternate sections of land for five miles on each side of the canal.[34] Since the Federal government retained the right to the remaining sections of land, it was hoped that this land would at least double in value and thus

[31] *John Tipton Papers,* 1:561n, 781n.

[32] Benton, *The Wabash Trade Route,* 36. The military value of the canal was stressed by William Hendricks in his speech before the United States Senate on April 20, 1826. *Congressional Debates,* 19 Congress, 1 session, 591-98.

[33] Benton, *The Wabash Trade Route,* 37.

[34] Richardson, History of the Wabash and Erie Canal, 21-28; *Congressional Debates,* 19 Congress, 2 session, 310-18, 338.

the national government would be repaid for its grant. The amended bill further stipulated that the state of Indiana must begin construction of the canal within five years.

Given the support of the Adams administration and guided by the followers of Henry Clay's "American System," the bill passed the House and Senate in the last hours of the session.[35] This was most fortunate since the next Congress, composed largely of Jacksonian adherents, would have likely rejected the measure. It is a fair assumption that after Jackson took office in 1829, he would have vetoed such a bill as he did the extension of the Maysville Road. The act of 1827 was achieved in part as a result of direct demands by the citizens of the West, not only the farmers but also the land speculators and the merchants of small towns such as Fort Wayne.

On January 5, 1828, the Indiana General Assembly accepted the land grant and provided for the election of three commissioners who were to locate the route, make estimates of construction costs, and ascertain the value of the lands under the Congressional grant. To perform these tasks, they were to have the opportunity of studying the surveys made by the U. S. engineers; if these proved inadequate at any point, they were authorized to make additional surveys. An appropriation of $2,000 was to take care of their salaries and expenses for a two-year period.[36]

The commissioners—Samuel Hanna, David Burr, Robert John—met at Fort Wayne during the following summer, but had no equipment to carry out additional surveys which they deemed necessary. Samuel Hanna took matters in his own hands by journeying to New York in an incredibly rapid time for his day and returning with the necessary instruments. On the second day of their work, John Smyth, their only surveyor,

[35] *Congressional Debates,* 19 Congress, 2 session, 1496, 1512; U. S. *Statutes at Large,* 4:236.

[36] *Laws of Indiana,* 1827-28, pp. 10-12.

was stricken by fever, but Burr and Hanna, although inexperienced, completed the survey for a feeder canal from the St. Joseph River into the main line of the canal. Their report to the General Assembly was not printed, but judging from the remarks of the committees which received it, it was believed that the St. Joseph River would be able to supply an adequate amount of water for the summit level of the canal. The estimated cost of the work from the Indiana-Ohio line to the mouth of the Tippecanoe River was approximately one million dollars.[37]

Until this time, it was presumed that the eastern end of the canal would be confined within Allen County, as the navigable point of the Maumee was believed to be inside the county limits. But it was now discovered that it would be necessary to extend the canal into Ohio. This necessitated the appointment of a commissioner to meet with a representative of Ohio to work out an agreement whereby that state would build its portion of the canal and receive a portion of the land granted to Indiana.[38] Much of the time of the 1828-29 legislative session was spent in debate on the canal. The speaker of the House favored a railroad as did Governor Ray. The canal committees made lengthy reports in favor of proceeding with construction but were not able to obtain the needed legislation.[39] The debate was continued at the next session, when the canal advo-

[37] Wallace A. Brice, *History of Fort Wayne . . .* (Fort Wayne, 1868), 303-4; *Messages and Papers of James Brown Ray*, 379-81n; Indiana *Senate Journal*, 1828-29, p. 140. The site of Fort Wayne was determined to be the highest point in the valleys of the Wabash and Maumee rivers; it was 198 feet above Lake Erie, while east and west of Fort Wayne the land was lower. With an adequate water supply furnished by a system of locks, it was believed that canalboats coming from the East could be raised to the summit level and then similarly lowered on their westbound route down the Wabash Valley.

[38] *Laws of Indiana*, 1828-29, p. 147; Richardson, History of the Wabash and Erie Canal, 29-30.

[39] Indiana *House Journal*, 1828-29, pp. 169-91; Indiana *Senate Journal*, 1828-29, pp. 137-51.

cates finally won out and obtained a ratification of the compact with Ohio, the organization of a new board of canal commissioners, and the opening of sales of canal lands.[40] The new board, composed of David Burr, Jordan Vigus, and Samuel Lewis were to serve for three years; one was to have charge of land sales, one of canal funds, and the third was to handle the accounts. The land was to be offered for sale at one fourth in cash, the balance in 17 years, with interest at 6 per cent. Land sales were opened the following October at Logansport and Lafayette and continued until February 10, 1831; they proved to be a disappointment as the highest price received was $4.06 per acre, the lowest, $1.25.[41] The proceeds were not sufficient to begin construction.

Another disappointment was the failure of the Ohio legislature to ratify the agreement of the joint commission.[42] Again efforts were made in the Indiana legislature to drop the entire project; those who favored a railroad had gained sufficient strength to block further legislation in 1830-31. But the following summer the friends of the canal rallied their forces and at the next session, on January 9, 1832, an act was passed to permit the canal commissioners to borrow $200,000 with which to begin construction.[43] The five years which Congress had given in which to begin construction had almost run out! The canal was saved.

The citizens of Fort Wayne were jubilant and lost no time in calling a mass meeting at which time February 22 was selected as an appropriate date to break the first ground for the canal.

[40] *Laws of Indiana,* 1830-31, p. 13.

[41] Logan Esarey, *Internal Improvements in Early Indiana* (Indiana Historical Society *Publications,* Vol. 5, No. 2, Indianapolis, 1912), 90. The sales were resumed in 1832.

[42] *Ibid.*

[43] *Laws of Indiana,* 1831-32, p. 108. See below, pages 256-58, for some of the arguments for and against canals as compared with those for and against railroads.

The population of the town in 1832 was slightly over three hundred. With all the enthusiasm and pageantry they could display, on the appointed day the townspeople celebrated the fulfillment of almost ten years of effort. A procession headed by a military band and the national colors moved from the courthouse square across St. Mary's River to the point selected for the ceremony. Here after a good deal of oratory about the importance of the work being initiated, Jordan Vigus "struck the long-suspended blow—broke ground—while the company hailed the event with three cheers."[44] The procession then marched back into town where in the evening a parade (featuring a float representing a canalboat) as well as bonfires and the general illumination of all the homes and buildings by candles placed in the windows brought the memorable day to a close. Heretofore the canal had been a vague, uncertain dream, but now faith and hope had blossomed into reality.

[44] The account of the celebration was carried in the Logansport *Cass County Times,* March 2, 1832, and reprinted in the Fort Wayne *Times,* February 28, 1850, and in *Canal Celebrations in Old Fort Wayne* (Fort Wayne—Allen County Public Library, 1953), 7-34.

CHAPTER III

NEW HOPE—NEW PEOPLE

Come to this country. There is no better land.

Although the canal was auspiciously inaugurated in February, 1832, construction did not begin until the following June, and even then delays were encountered for various reasons. It has been stated that "the scarcity of good building material in Allen County for the locks and waterways proved the greatest obstacle."[1] However David Burr, writing in the summer of 1832, put his finger on the pulse of the problem—the lack of an adequate labor supply. As a leading promoter of the canal Burr was quite concerned about the delay, and according to him "the Indian war [the Blackhawk War] & fear of the Cholera has prevented people from coming here at all."[2] On the frontier one could not encounter two more powerful deterrents against enticing settlers or laborers. In fact, while contemporary opinions vary considerably, Fort Wayne seems to have been a healthier place than many of its neighboring communities in Ohio were prepared to admit. Burr had no reason to falsify the true picture when he wrote to Tipton in the same letter that there had not been "a single case of sickness this season" in Fort Wayne.[3] Nevertheless, for a long time

[1] *The Wabash-Erie Canal* (Fort Wayne—Allen County Public Library, 1952), [4].

[2] David Burr to John Tipton, August 7, 1832, *John Tipton Papers,* 2:676.

[3] *Ibid.* In the fall of 1834, James Chute wrote from Fort Wayne: "Though we have been exempt from the cholera, yet other diseases have been very prevalent & swept many of our citizens into the world of the spiritual. . . . This amount of sickness is not usual in this country. Heretofore it has been very healthy; but in the early part of summer floods of rain fell, & exceptionally hot weather immediately succeeded. . . ." Chute to Absalom Peters, September 25, 1834, American Home Missionary Society Papers, Hammond Library, Chicago Theological Seminary.

after the canal construction began Fort Wayne seemed to have a poor reputation regarding the salubrity of its climate. In part this was due to the usual rivalries between western communities, but it was also due to the fact that since labor was scarce throughout the western states the canal contractors from other areas deliberately spread such rumors.[4]

The question of health would remain in dispute, but the threat of an Indian war soon passed. It is true that for a while during the summer of 1832 the danger appeared grave enough to cause settlers north of Fort Wayne to flee to the town for refuge.[5] Once more it appeared as if Fort Wayne was to become an outpost of defense against the Indian. Although Black Hawk's warriors never really threatened northeastern Indiana, the war eventually helped to seal the fate of the remaining Indians in this region. Pressure for their complete removal became increasingly strong even from the area around Fort Wayne, once the stronghold of the Indian traders. As we shall note later, these views, coinciding as they did with the Federal policy of these years, eventually triumphed.

Despite the difficulties encountered some progress was made on the canal during the summer of 1832. In June Jesse L. Williams was appointed chief engineer and came to Fort Wayne in the same month.[6] Williams represented the dynamic spirit of youth on the frontier. Born of Quaker parents in 1807 in North Carolina, he moved with his family to Cincinnati where he learned the rudiments of canal construction from men such as David S. Bates and Nathan S. Roberts who had just helped to complete the Erie Canal. Before coming to Indiana Williams had been employed as chief engineer on one section of the Miami Canal then being built in Ohio. Although

[4] Harlow, *Old Towpaths,* 270.

[5] H. Herman Schauinger, *Stephen T. Badin, Priest in the Wilderness* (Milwaukee, Wis., 1956), 232.

[6] Recollections of Jesse Williams, in Fort Wayne *News-Sentinel,* June 8, 1874.

sharply criticized at a later date by various land speculators for his selection of the route of the Wabash and Erie Canal,[7] Williams apparently performed his task efficiently. Hugh McCulloch said of him:

> Few of our civil engineers have surpassed Mr. Williams in engineering skill, and I have never known his equal in industry and endurance. His labors as chief engineer of the Wabash and Erie Canal, and other public works in Indiana, were prodigious, but he never failed to be equal to them. Week after week and month after month, every day except Sunday, on which he always rested, he could be found upon the line of the public works, usually in the saddle, and, in the evening, and until midnight at his desk.[8]

When Indiana undertook the extensive system of public works in 1836 Williams was appointed chief engineer of the state with some 1,300 miles of proposed canals, turnpikes, and railroads to oversee. He moved to Indianapolis at this time and remained until the entire program collapsed in 1839. In 1841 he again became chief engineer of the Wabash and Erie Canal and returned to Fort Wayne where he participated in civic and banking matters and took an active part in the formation of the First Presbyterian Church. Throughout his life, however, his primary interest remained internal improvements. In 1854 Williams was selected to supervise the construction of the Fort Wayne and Chicago Railroad.[9]

With the arrival of Williams in June, 1832, a contract was made by the commissioners for the construction of fifteen miles

[7] John Tipton to Jesse L. Williams, December 12, 1835, *John Tipton Papers,* 3:187-88.

[8] McCulloch, *Men and Measures of Half a Century,* 107.

[9] Fort Wayne *Journal-Gazette,* October 10, 1886; Esarey, *Internal Improvements in Early Indiana,* 93. From 1864 to 1869 he served as director of the Union Pacific Railroad by appointment from President Lincoln, resigning in the latter year when he discovered the secret relationship between the Union Pacific and the Crédit Mobilier. His report to the Secretary of the Interior showing that the construction of the road would have been possible at a figure greatly below the original estimates and subsidies was later used in the investigation of the Crédit Mobilier. Fort Wayne *Journal-Gazette,* October 10, 1886.

of canal. In the succeeding November, four miles, including an important dam across the St. Joseph River, were put under contract. This dam was one of the most important achievements in building the canal. An enormous undertaking for its day, the dam was constructed

by men working with hand tools, horses and mules. The purpose of this dam was the creation of a lake to impound a water supply for the summit section. Water was introduced into the main line by means of a feeder canal. The dam, begun in 1832, was not completed until 1834; floods repeatedly delayed its construction. When completed, the dam was a huge mass of forest trees, sand and gravel; it rose 17 feet above the river bed and was 230 feet long between abutments. These abutments were 25 feet high, 20 feet wide, and 110 feet long.[10]

The abutments and the site of the dam may still be traced in old Robison Park and on the farm of the author's father, which was formerly one of Chief Richardville's reserves. Since the area has returned largely to a state of nature, the modern mind cannot conceive of the prodigious labor required for its construction. Thus by the end of the year 1832 nineteen miles were under construction, and in January, 1833, the commissioners were directed to let the balance of the section from the Aboite River to Huntington.[11]

With the awarding of the contracts by the commissioners, local enthusiasm mounted. Meetings were called to promote the rapid construction of the canal. Not without some misgiving Reverend James Chute noted the change, "the general inquiry is, how shall I make my fortune? Some are for taking contracts, some for speculating in land, and others for estab-

[10] *The Wabash-Erie Canal,* [6]; *Messages and Papers relating to the Administration of Noah Noble, Governor of Indiana, 1831-1837,* edited by Dorothy Riker and Gayle Thornbrough (*Indiana Historical Collections,* Vol. 38, Indianapolis, 1958); Indiana *Senate Journal,* 1832-33, pp. 72-74.

[11] Speech of Hugh McCulloch, July 4, 1835, in Indianapolis *Indiana Journal,* September 18, 1835.

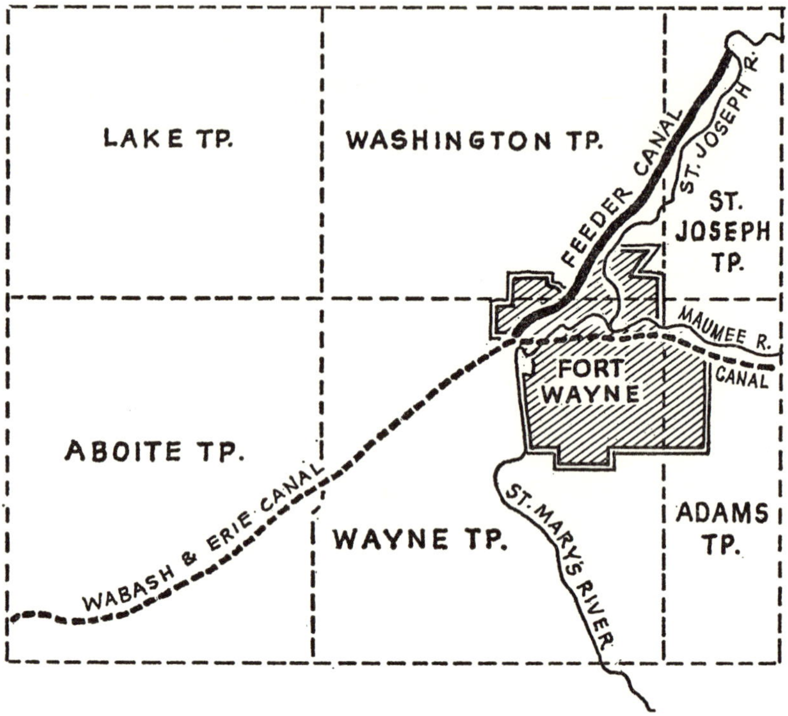

WABASH AND ERIE AND FEEDER CANALS AT FORT WAYNE

lishing groceries & *selling whiskey*."[12] To this Chute added that while the town "holds out every inducement for men of enterprise . . . when men emigrate, we want they should bring with them *virtue*. Of infidelity we have a sufficient stock, & some to spare, we would willingly exchange it for a more valuable commodity."[13] Generally more optimistic was David H. Colerick, a capable lawyer who had settled in Fort Wayne in 1829, and who was now filled with a new spirit of enthusiasm. "Since the canal letting, the place wears a new and very cheering aspect—men now have come to resolves and determinations —to press forward and be acting—New fields are now thrown open for industry and enterprize—all appears to be in creditable motion—except a few excrescences we have welded on our little village, some lean and hungry moral assassins—who have become literally diseased in all the vices of the human heart— and who are great draw backs on the pleasure harmony and happiness of this little community."[14]

While the latter comments appear to have been motivated in part because of political differences, both this and the previous letter point up not only the change in spirit following the beginning of the canal but also the possibility of a growing distinction between the old and new elements in Fort Wayne's citizenry. The fact was that Fort Wayne was attracting new settlers. Allen County as a separate unit was first included in the Federal census of 1830. In that year it had a population of approximately one thousand. Ten years later, when the sixth Federal census was taken, there were 5,942 living in Allen County. The population of Wayne Township, including Fort Wayne, numbered 2,080.[15] By checking the average popu-

[12] James Chute to Absalom Peters, March 12, 1832, American Home Missionary Society Papers.

[13] *Ibid.*

[14] David Colerick to John Tipton, June 9, 1832, *John Tipton Papers,* 2:623.

[15] U. S. Bureau of the Census, *Compendium of the Seventh Census* (1850), 224.

lation of the other townships in the county, one might assume that the population of Fort Wayne must have been slightly over 1,500.[16]

These figures reveal only the statistical growth of the town. It may be asked, "What manner of men were these settlers? What was their background? What impelled them to settle in a village of a frontier area?" In 1829 Rebecca Ward, a young Quakeress who had recently moved to Fort Wayne, wrote to a friend who was growing tired of Newport, Rhode Island, and thinking of moving to New Jersey, "Come to this country. There is no better land. There are many things different from what we have been accustomed to, yet if I was . . . about to get married, I should not live in New Jersey, but you must all consider these things for yourselves."[17] In 1831 a young college graduate, Hugh McCulloch of Kennebunk, Maine, had determined to move to the West. He had come to this decision calmly and firmly and now with enthusiasm born of assurance he wrote to a former classmate both to explain his own action and urge his friend to share this new adventure.

What then shall I speak of? The West? Aye, the West—the growing prosperous West—the land of broad rivers and rich prairies; and, as some say, of knaves and pickpockets—of visionaries dreaming of eminence and fortune, and bankrupts who have been removed thither to get rid of the impolite calls of their creditors.

Between you and me, my friend, I have almost concluded to make this same west the place of my future abode. You know also that it is not a characteristic of mine to be visionary. I have weighed the advantages and disadvantages of a removal in opposite and equally poised scales. I have considered the matter dispassionately, deliberately, seriously, and have come to the conclusion that

[16] *Ibid.; Sixth Census of Enumeration of the Inhabitants . . . as Corrected at the Department of State* (1840), 347. This estimate of slightly over 1,500 would seem to agree with the population figure given for Fort Wayne in 1838 in J. B. Colton's *The State of Indiana Delineated: Geographical, Historical, Statistical & Commercial . . .* (New York, 1838), 13.

[17] Rebecca Ward to Daniel Puckett, September 1, 1829, Lewis G. Thompson Papers, Allen County—Fort Wayne Historical Society Museum.

it will be decidedly for my interest to bid adieu to New England, and to the mournful ditty of 'over the hills and far away,' set my face toward the setting sun. The prospects of Lawyers in New England are by no means cheering enough to satisfy *me*. The profession, even now, groans with the number of its supernumerary incumbents. The people here are becoming more and more enlightened, and, as I think, less and less fond of litigation. I can make a living in my profession in Boston—I can do the same in Maine. But this is not enough. I shall never be satisfied with it, until I am confident that I can do no better. I have no strong desire to be rich, but I am determined not to die *poor* if it can possibly be avoided. The western states are increasing with almost unparalleled rapidity.

The expenses of living there are much less than in Massachusetts. The people are more ignorant, and consequently are more inclined to litigation, and more apt to get entangled in the intricacies of the law. Professional men are more scarce, and are looked upon as persons of considerable importance.—These are some of the reasons which induce me to think of bidding adieu to the land of my birth. I would not be misunderstood. I do not expect that a young man can there obtain legal or political elevation without the possession of uncommon powers of mind, or vigorous untiring labor. But I do think that his prospects as a Lawyer or a Politician . . . would be better there than in New England.

Have you concluded to remain in Kennebunk? I hope not. It is no place for a man of any degree of energy. You can live there it is true. But are you contented, satisfied, happy? Are you willing to say here I am settled for life—here I must stay, rust, die. No my friend, quit Kennebunk and go with me to the West.[18]

The young would-be lawyer who wrote the above letter was destined to play a large role in the history of Fort Wayne and then his nation, serving the latter as Secretary of the Treasury under three presidents—Lincoln, Johnson, and Arthur. Born in 1808, Hugh McCulloch was the son of a wealthy New England shipowner who lost most of his fortune during the War of 1812. Educated at Saco Academy and Bowdoin College (attending the latter in the same years as Hawthorne), McCul-

[18] Hugh McCulloch to Robert Smith, Boston, November 11, 1831, McCulloch Papers, Lilly Library, Indiana University, quoted in Raymond J. Reece, "Hugh McCulloch Moves West," in *Indiana Magazine of History*, 32 (1936): 95-96.

loch then studied law in Boston. Here he also improved himself culturally by attending debates, concerts, sermons, and public addresses.[19] Although his doctor had advised him to move West for his health, McCulloch, then twenty-three, had already reached this decision, apparently independent of this counsel.[20] As one may judge from the above letter Hugh McCulloch was an educated New Englander, stamped with the Yankee traits of industriousness and logic; yet, despite the fact that he "considered the matter dispassionately," one feels the overtones of romanticism then associated with the westward movement. Needless to say, his opinions regarding the better opportunities for a lawyer to advance in the West might seem disparaging to Westerners (not to mention the legal profession), but who is to deny that the individual with ability could and did advance more rapidly in the West.

McCulloch left Boston in April, 1833, armed with letters of introduction from such men as Daniel Webster and the Reverend John Pierpont, one of Boston's leading Unitarian ministers. Traveling by way of the Ohio McCulloch arrived at Cincinnati where he was advised by a lawyer of Vigo County, Indiana, to settle in that state. After spending a few weeks in Madison, Indiana, McCulloch was admitted to the Indiana bar and had almost determined to remain in one of the southern counties of the state. Indianapolis he felt "had nothing to recommend it" other than the fact that it was the state capital; none of the "incipient towns of the West" appeared "so utterly forlorn."[21] However, McCulloch was advised by General Tilgh-

[19] McCulloch, *Men and Measures of Half a Century*, 16-32, 35.

[20] In respect to his health, the West proved beneficial. Although ill to the point of death immediately after his arrival in Fort Wayne, McCulloch recovered sufficiently to live until 1895—87 years! In 1837 he wrote to his fiancé that he was enjoying better health than he had ever had. McCulloch to Susan Man, McCulloch Papers.

[21] McCulloch, *Men and Measures of Half a Century*, 71.

man A. Howard, United States District Attorney, not to settle in southern Indiana.

> There are some nice fellows in the southern counties, [General Howard argued] but the people generally have come from Kentucky, Tennessee, or the Carolinas; they are good enough people in their way, but having been raised in the States in which slavery exists, they are not enterprising; their ways are not your ways . . . Go north. But [replied McCulloch] northern Indiana is mostly a wilderness . . . No matter if it is a wilderness, [Howard answered] it will not long be a wilderness. It is . . . the most inviting country I have ever seen, and it will soon be filled by people from New York and New England—the right kind of people to develop it . . . a canal is being built which will unite the Wabash with Lake Erie.[22]

Young McCulloch accepted this advice and traveled horseback from Indianapolis to Logansport, then to South Bend and La Porte before turning eastward toward Fort Wayne. As he neared its vicinity he found the country "a magnificent wilderness, mostly covered with lofty trees of almost countless varieties," and although he came from the port of Kennebunk, he discovered in his "exhilaration of spirits" that "there is more music in the singing of birds than in the roar of the sea."[23]

When McCulloch arrived at Fort Wayne late in June, 1833, he found the town "had little to recommend it but its site which . . . was commanding and picturesque."[24] A surveyor, Lazarus Wilson, in the previous month had likewise found the town "handsomely situated on the south bank of the St. Mary's river—down which it extends eastward, to the old Fort."[25] While Wilson seemed impressed by the number of Indians still to be found in the town,[26] McCulloch was more

[22] *Ibid.*, 78.

[23] McCulloch describes his journey from Indianapolis in *ibid.*, 79-95.

[24] *Ibid.*, 98.

[25] Lazarus B. Wilson to Mary Barbee, April 6, 1833, quoted in Alma W. Wilson, "An Early Indiana Surveyor—Lazarus B. Wilson," in *Indiana Magazine of History*, 10 (1914):50.

[26] *Ibid.*

impressed by the character of its white settlers, men like Samuel Hanna, Allen Hamilton, the Ewings, Samuel Lewis, Dr. Lewis Thompson, Jesse L. Williams, Robert Brackenridge, Marshall S. Wines, John Spencer, Francis Comparet, and John Bourie. McCulloch did not praise all these figures unstintingly, yet he could write fifty years later, "Since then I have seen a good deal of the world. I have been thrown among people of all grades; I have been brought into social and business relations with men standing high in public esteem; but the men of whom I have spoken, after a lapse of more than half a century, stand out before me in bold relief as remarkably intelligent, enterprising, far-seeing, and withal kind-hearted, generous men."[27]

Only a few days after his arrival in Fort Wayne McCulloch was called upon to deliver a Fourth of July oration. Happy to find this Bostonian tradition so strong in the little community, McCulloch responded with a patriotic address worthy of the occasion. During the ceremonies, however, he contracted a chill followed by a fever from which he did not fully recover until October. Since during his prolonged illness Fort Wayne had given indications of rapid growth both in population and business as a result of the increased tempo of the canal work, McCulloch was induced to remain. Furthermore, as he stated, the question "had been decided by the emptiness of my purse."[28] Although successful as a lawyer in his first year in Fort Wayne and elected judge of the probate court during his second year, McCulloch was destined to find his career in banking. In October, 1835, he was appointed cashier and manager of the Fort Wayne branch of the recently chartered State Bank of Indiana, and served in this position until the expiration of the bank's charter almost twenty-two years later.

[27] McCulloch, *Men and Measures of Half a Century,* 108.
[28] *Ibid.,* 112.

In 1838 McCulloch married Susan Man of Plattsburg, New York. Two years previously Miss Man had come to Fort Wayne with Alida Hubbell, sister of Woolsey Hubbell who was employed as a teller in the bank. These two young ladies from New York had decided to open a girls' school somewhere in the West and had been persuaded to select Fort Wayne through the combined efforts of Samuel Hanna, Allen Hamilton, and Woolsey Hubbell. Susan Man found "the society [at Fort Wayne] a charming one for a small village."[29] There were frequent tea parties, rides on horseback, walks in the forest, sleighing parties, and visits in the various homes. There were times when she found the Hoosier habits a little crude; however, after eight years of marriage, Mrs. McCulloch returned to visit friends in New York City and concluded that while they had everything "the heart can wish . . . I should much prefer living in the way we do."[30] By then Susan Man's adjustment to the life of a small western village was complete, and it was with genuine regret and only out of a sense of duty to her country and her husband that Susan McCulloch moved to Washington in 1865.

Although the most famous, Hugh McCulloch was not the only settler to come to Fort Wayne from Kennebunk, Maine. In 1834 Captain Asa Fairfield and his brother Oliver arrived with the idea of investing in land nearby. Both of the Fairfields were seafaring men who for a number of years had followed a prosperous career as captain-owners of their own vessels.[31] There is no positive evidence, but apparently they were induced

[29] Susan Man McCulloch, "Recollections," MS in possession of McCulloch heirs.

[30] Susan McCulloch to Hugh McCulloch, July 24, 1846, McCulloch Papers.

[31] There is some evidence to indicate that the Fairfields acted as privateers in the War of 1812. It is known that they were captured by the British, Oliver being imprisoned for sixteen months and Asa for six. *Valley of the Upper Maumee River,* 1:213.

to consider Fort Wayne as a likely site for investment through the efforts of McCulloch who was the cousin of Mrs. Asa Fairfield. Hence, discouraged by the declining commercial profits, the Fairfield brothers sold out their interests in Kennebunk, hoping that the opportunities in the West would be greater. Asa Fairfield brought $30,000 with him.[32] Such an individual amount of capital had never been heard of before in the town. Allen Hamilton, who later died as a millionaire, told McCulloch that he would consider himself wealthy for life with such a sum.[33] With part of his capital Asa Fairfield purchased 240 acres of land immediately south of Fort Wayne. In 1835 the two brothers returned to Kennebunk in order to bring their families to Allen County. On their return trip westward they were accompanied by another brother Charles Fairfield and his family. While Oliver Fairfield soon became engaged in the bakery business, Asa and Charles undertook the task of clearing and farming their land. Shortly after his arrival Asa Fairfield ordered constructed the first boat to operate on the Wabash and Erie Canal and for some time served as master of his own boat. It is likely that he had in mind such an enterprise when he first decided to settle in Fort Wayne. Asa Fairfield also invested part of his capital in the Fort Wayne branch of the State Bank, in which he became a director.[34]

Other New Englanders, such as Madison Sweetser and Royal W. Taylor, both from Vermont, came to Fort Wayne about the same time as McCulloch and the Fairfields.[35] Indeed, it was

[32] Griswold, *Pictorial History of Fort Wayne,* 1:321.

[33] McCulloch, *Men and Measures of Half a Century,* 105.

[34] Griswold, *Pictorial History of Fort Wayne,* 1:319-21. In Pittsburgh the group bought two carriages which were transported by boat to Fort Wayne. These vehicles, the first of their kind in the town, were viewed as signs of progress by the citizenry.

[35] Sweetser's family had moved to Ohio from Vermont. He first came to northern Indiana as a canal contractor, but shortly thereafter became a merchant in Fort Wayne. Taylor became one of Fort Wayne's most successful merchants.

becoming apparent by the mid-1830s that the native American-born population of Fort Wayne was to consist more and more of settlers from the North. Hugh McCulloch's adviser, General Howard, was correct in his view. It is true that southern settlers had never been in the majority at Fort Wayne; nevertheless, prior to 1830, men such as the Hannas from Kentucky, Samuel Lewis and Smalwood Noel from Virginia, Jonathan McCarty and John Tipton from Tennessee, and Henry Cooper from Maryland had established themselves at Fort Wayne. A good percentage of those more prominent Fort Wayne men who did come from the South before and after 1830 were Federal political appointees. Neither Samuel nor Hugh Hanna held any Federal office; Tipton was Indian agent; Samuel Lewis came to Fort Wayne as subagent and then became canal commissioner; Joseph Holman, a native of Versailles, Kentucky, was the first receiver of public moneys at the Fort Wayne land office. In 1830 Holman, an Adams appointee, was replaced by Jonathan McCarty, a Jacksonian Democrat from Tennessee. When McCarty was elected to Congress in 1831 from the Fort Wayne district he was followed in office by Colonel John Spencer, a native of Kentucky. In 1840 James W. Borden, originally from South Carolina, became receiver. Of those who held the office of register in the land office, Robert Brackenridge, who served from 1830-34, William Polke, 1841-43, and Samuel Brenton, 1843-44, were all natives of Kentucky.[36]

By 1850 out of the 12,964 native-born Americans living in Allen County only 562 or 3.32 per cent were from the South. Of the native-born settlers from northern states who settled in Allen County prior to 1850, only 3.22 per cent came from

[36] For appointments to the land office, see U. S. Senate, *Executive Proceedings*, Vols. 3-6, Index. Jonathan McCarty, although from the South originally, favored the antislavery cause while in Congress, specifically favoring the abolition of slavery in Washington, D. C.

New England. Actually the 397 settlers coming directly from New England numbered less than those from the South (562). As might be expected the great majority (12,005 or 71 per cent in 1850) of Allen County's settlers came from the Middle Atlantic and North Central states including Indiana. Almost half (5,327) were native-born Hoosiers.[37] As early as the 1830s many of the American-born settlers of Fort Wayne were coming from the four states of Ohio, Pennsylvania, New York, and New Jersey. In his famous essay Frederick J. Turner stated, "The men of the frontier had closer resemblances to the Middle region than to either of the other sections."[38] Certainly the development of Fort Wayne bears testimony to the validity of this statement. A listing of the settlers from the above mentioned states would be copious, however, it may be pointed out that three of Fort Wayne's earliest mayors came from New York (Franklin Randall, Henry Sharp, and George W. Wood), while another (Merchant Huxford) came from Ohio, and a fifth mayor (Henry Lotz) was a native of Pennsylvania. Three of Fort Wayne's first newspaper editors were from New York.[39] In the field of medicine almost all of the pioneer doctors at Fort Wayne came from or studied in one of the three states—New York, Pennsylvania, and Ohio.[40] During her first decades Fort Wayne received five physicians from the medical schools at Philadelphia, New York City, and Fairfield, New York.

[37] Elfrieda Lang, Immigration to Northern Indiana, 1800-1850 (Unpublished Ph.D. thesis, Indiana University, 1950), 129, 182; Elfrieda Lang, "An Analysis of Northern Indiana's Population in 1850," in *Indiana Magazine of History,* 44 (1953):24-27.

[38] Ray Billington (ed.), *Frontier and Section. Selected Essays of Frederick Jackson Turner* (Englewood Cliffs, N. J., 1961), 54.

[39] Isaac De Groff Nelson, George W. Wood, and Peter P. Bailey. Of the other three editors during the period, two were born in Indiana and the third was an English immigrant.

[40] Dr. Lewis G. Thompson, one of Fort Wayne's earliest physicians, was from Kentucky. In the late 1830s and throughout the 1840s, German doctors also came to Fort Wayne.

Among these were Dr. James Ormiston and Dr. Lewis Beecher, graduates of the college of physicians and surgeons of Fairfield, and Dr. John Evans, who although a native of Kentucky, studied in Philadelphia under the well-known Dr. Benjamin Rush. In the 1840s the Ohio schools began to furnish Fort Wayne with medical graduates. Ohio also contributed the town's first druggist, Merchant Huxford, in 1833. In the same year Miss Susan Clark who taught the first private school for young children arrived from Ohio. As previously mentioned, Miss Hubbell and Miss Man, the other two women teachers of the 1830s, were natives of New York. In 1822 Charles Ewing from Pennsylvania settled in Fort Wayne as the town's first lawyer. Thereafter, although there were exceptions such as Henry Cooper from Maryland and Hugh McCulloch and William Coombs from Maine, most of the town's leading attorneys came from the Middle Atlantic and North Central states. David H. Colerick, one of the most famous of the lawyers and political figures of Allen County from 1829 until 1887, was a native of Washington, Pennsylvania.

Naturally the Middle Atlantic and North Central states gave to Fort Wayne citizens other than those in the professional classes. Many of the merchants and craftsmen who came in the 1830s hailed from these states. Jacob Fry of Pennsylvania established a tannery in 1834. The opportunity presented by the canal construction brought Marshall S. Wines, canal contractor from New York. In 1832 one of Fort Wayne's most noted pioneer merchants, Peter Kiser (or Keiser), located permanently here. Born in Ohio of German parents, Kiser had visited Fort Wayne frequently before he decided to remain as a butcher and merchant. Although illiterate he came to wield a political influence almost as large as himself—over 300 pounds. He was elected to the state legislature in 1847 where he was active in promoting the free school system of Indiana.

With the possible exception of the Ewings, the most important settler from Pennsylvania was Henry Rudisill. Born in Lancaster, Pennsylvania, in 1801, this English and German-speaking pioneer had gradually moved westward with his family. Having learned the trade of a merchant by the time he was seventeen, Rudisill became an agent for John Barr, the Baltimore merchant who was one of the original proprietors of Fort Wayne. After representing Barr's firm in both Chillicothe and Lancaster, Ohio, Rudisill was sent in haste to Fort Wayne following the sudden death of John McCorkle, Barr's partner in the purchase of the original plat.[41] Rudisill and his wife (Elizabeth Johns) made the hurried journey in the last two weeks of December, 1829. From the beginning Rudisill labored diligently in the interests of his employer,[42] and it was high time that someone safeguard Barr's property as Rudisill discovered upon his arrival. Some squatters had already started to farm Barr's land, consequently destroying much valuable timber, while others were actually building shops on the proprietor's town lots without any apparent permission.[43] Furthermore, McCorkle's various agents had failed to keep accurate accounts, and Rudisill found it almost impossible to ascertain the names of the purchasers and the exact amounts due to Barr for those lots already sold. When he did determine the amount due he then faced difficulties in collecting the sum since specie was scarce at Fort Wayne, especially from 1828 to 1833.[44]

Rudisill was very careful to solicit advice from Barr in almost every matter. Judging from Rudisill's complaints, Barr often neglected to give his agent precise instructions.[45] Whether this helps to explain Barr's eventual failure we can-

[41] See above, p. 10.

[42] Rudisill wrote regularly to Barr and copied these letters in his own "Letterbook," which is in the possession of his heirs.

[43] Rudisill to Barr, January 2, 1830, Rudisill Letterbook.

[44] Rudisill to Barr, January 16 and 23, 1830, Rudisill Letterbook.

[45] Rudisill to Barr, February 20 and March 6, 1830, Rudisill Letterbook.

not be certain; perhaps he was already involved in too many financial difficulties to pay particular attention to Rudisill's problems. Whatever the case, in 1834 Barr was forced into bankruptcy and disposed of his remaining 189.16 acres at Fort Wayne, the land having been mortgaged in 1831 to Stephen Gerard, the well-known financier of Philadelphia.[46]

In his first letters to Barr, Rudisill constantly mentioned the scarcity of commodities and available labor at Fort Wayne.[47] Despite these problems Rudisill wrote shortly after his arrival, "I am well pleased with Fort Wayne and the Country around it the Citizens appear to be very attentive and obliging to Strangers."[48] Although young, Rudisill had a good deal of experience in meeting the difficulties of frontier merchandising. He immediately set out to improve his situation by requesting a stock of approximately $3,000 worth of goods from his employer's eastern stores to use in trading.[49] Later he was to take the lead in constructing both flour and sawmills within the vicinity of Fort Wayne.

To remedy the high cost of labor as well as to find efficient workers to clear Barr's lands and to answer the need for skilled craftsmen, Rudisill suggested the importation of German immigrants directly from Baltimore. In his second letter to Barr he urged his employer

> to hire some Germans from Germany and send them out to me German Emigrants are frequently arriving in Baltimore and would be glad of such an opportunity, you can hire them much lower than the Americans and I think they are more to be depended on you can hire a good stout young man for 60 or 90 dolrs. a year if you could get whole familys it would be better I know Persons in Ohio who have hired them for [illegible] 100 dolrs. a year. their women are good in [the] Corn field before I left Lancaster I was informed that a Brickmaker of that Class of People could be had

[46] Joseph G. Young, Piqua, to Allen Hamilton, February 15, 1834, Allen Hamilton Papers, Indiana State Library.

[47] Rudisill to Barr, January 2, 8, and 16, 1830, Rudisill Letterbook.

[48] Rudisill to Barr, January 2, 1830.

[49] Rudisill to Barr, March 6, 1830.

in Baltimore he was represented to me as an Excellent workman his name I could not learn but he lives with a Mr. Klinfetter near Fish Market I for my Part would Prefer to have hands of the above description they are more industrious and temperate than our americans they will also make good Citizens of a Town Hirelings are very high here and to hire them in Ohio and bring them out they find out that their wages are not so high [and] they become dissatisfied the young men I have with me are good strong hands but I contracted with them only through a year. . . .[50]

Within two weeks Rudisill renewed his request, this time adding, "I wish you by all means if you possibly can to send me the Germans I would prefer the Wurtembergers as they are the most industrious and temperate it is difficult to get good hands here or in Ohio."[51] Rudisill was determined to have German labor and thus by the end of his first month in Fort Wayne broached the subject for a third time. "I feel very anxious to hear from you concerning the Germans I would rather have 3 of them than 6 of our common hands."[52]

Judging from the above statements Rudisill seemed to be motivated chiefly by economic considerations but it appears that he also hoped to attract a large number of German Lutherans to settle in Fort Wayne. Wurtembergers were not only "the most industrious and temperate" in the eyes of Rudisill, they were also Lutheran in which faith Rudisill was an ardent believer. As Barr directed westward those Germans whom he could persuade to set out for Fort Wayne through promises of work and land, Rudisill took charge of them upon their arrival in the frontier community. By 1837 Rudisill had a nucleus of twenty-three German families with which to organize the first Lutheran congregation in Fort Wayne.[53]

Although at times he differed with Jacksonian policies, Rudisill, until his death in 1858, remained almost as firm in his political faith in the Democratic party as he did to his

[50] Rudisill to Barr, January 8, 1830.

[51] Rudisill to Barr, January 16, 1830.

[52] Rudisill to Barr, January 30, 1830.

[53] See below, p. 162.

religious convictions of Lutheranism. Appointed to replace Allen Hamilton in 1831 as postmaster at Fort Wayne, he held the position until the Whigs took office in 1841. Undoubtedly Rudisill had a great influence over the German vote as it remained consistently Democratic.[54] However, it would be wrong to assume that Rudisill's influence was paramount in this respect. Other factors such as German antagonism to the nativist element in the Whig party were to prove equally if not more important.[55]

Neither is it correct to conclude that it was only through Rudisill's efforts that the Germans began to settle in and around Fort Wayne. As early as 1822 John Siebold, a German Lutheran, came to Fort Wayne as a day laborer and soon became an independent farmer. Two years later Martin Bargus, a skilled carpenter, arrived having followed what would become the classical route of German immigrants to Fort Wayne until the canal was completed—from New York City to the Erie Canal, by lake to Detroit, ox team from Detroit to the Maumee, and pirogue down the Maumee.[56]

Even after 1830 Henry Rudisill's role was somewhat secondary to the other factors which induced German settlement. These factors were the nature of the soil which was extremely good around Fort Wayne, the comparatively easy route from New York to the mouth of the Maumee, but above all, the Wabash and Erie Canal. What Carl Wittke has said concerning the German immigrant in general may apply very specifically to those who came to Fort Wayne.

> The German farmer usually was shrewd in selecting the best farming country available and, as a rule, preferred wooded areas, a sign of superior soil. He was also interested in accessibility to the mar-

[54] This was true even during the Civil War, although there was a sizeable minority of Germans who were Republicans.

[55] See below, pp. 188, 231, 268.

[56] Bargus, a Catholic, was married to a German girl; their child was the first child born of German parents in northern Indiana.

kets and usually did not gamble on the chance development of a railroad or canal, which might suddenly drive up the value of his land . . . The German farmer was essentially conservative, a hard worker, a careful investor, and anything but a speculator.[57]

The soil around Fort Wayne was fertile and heavily wooded. When the Germans started to come in greater numbers the canal was becoming a reality, and thus it would not only furnish an all water route to Fort Wayne for the immigrants, but it also gave them the assurance that their goods would be marketed once they were established. The German craftsman, moreover, found work in a community which held out the promise of a sound economic future. Some came to work on the canal. These men were skilled and often served as carpenters or stonemasons in the construction. Many were employed as unskilled diggers, but these positions were more often filled by the Irish.

The fact is that the period with which we are presently concerned, the early 1830s, witnessed the greatest influx of Irish immigrants into the Fort Wayne region. In the decade prior to 1830 only twelve Irish immigrants settled in the whole region of northern Indiana.[58] Of these first Irish settlers Allen Hamilton from Ulster was the only noteworthy figure to locate in Fort Wayne. As mentioned previously, he was fairly well educated and soon laid the basis of a remarkably successful career. In 1829 Allen Hamilton financially assisted his younger brother, Andrew, in coming to the United States. The young man was anxious to leave Ireland as he expected civil war to break out at any time over the question of the Catholic franchise,[59] and he was generally convinced that there was

[57] Carl Wittke, *We Who Built America. The Saga of the Immigrant* (New York, 1939), 208.

[58] Elfrieda Lang, "Irishmen in Northern Indiana before 1850," in *Mid-America,* 36:190.

[59] Andrew Hamilton, Irvinestown, North Ireland, to Allen Hamilton, April 7, 1829, Hamilton Papers, Indiana State Library.

"not a worse country in the world than Ireland at the present."[60]

As this conviction grew in the minds of an increasing number of Irish, many willingly began to emigrate to the United States during the 1830s. The great majority remained in the East; however, by 1840 there were 456 Irishmen in northern Indiana, Allen County containing the greatest number, 114. By 1850, when the Irish were faced with the choice of emigration or starvation, there were 424 Irish immigrants living in Allen County alone, almost twice the number (249) living in La Porte County, the next most Irish populated county of northern Indiana.[61]

Certainly the construction of the canal, beginning as it did at Fort Wayne, was the primary reason for the Irish settlement. It is well known that with the meager funds, if any, the Irish immigrants brought with them to America, few could afford to journey westward. Thus if these impoverished people were ready to labor with pick and shovel for $10 a month and risk their lives in a constant fight against malaria, canal construction offered the opportunity for a new life. On the other hand, the severe labor shortage at Fort Wayne necessitated the importation of workers. Advertisements appeared in various papers similar to the following:

Cash for Canal Hands.

We wish to employ laborers on the Wabash and Erie Canal, 12 miles west of Fort Wayne.

The situation is healthy and dry. We will pay $10 per month for sober and industrious men.[62]

MURRAY & VERMILYA

[60] Andrew Hamilton, Jr., New York, to Allen Hamilton, August 1, 1829, Hamilton Papers.

[61] Lang, "Irishmen in Northern Indiana before 1850," in *Mid-America,* 36:190. In 1840 there were 114 Irishmen living in Allen County compared to 77 in Cass County, the next most Irish populated county.

[62] Indianapolis *Indiana Journal,* August 4, 1832; Indiana *House Journal,* 1833-34, pp. 163-64.

Agents for the Wabash and Erie Canal were also sent to New York, Pennsylvania, and Ohio, where they recruited principally among the Irish and, to a lesser extent, German immigrants. In exchange for a lien on the immigrant's wage the agent often advanced the transportation costs to Indiana. At the same time pseudo-agents were ready to exploit those Irish who hoped to find work on the canal. On one occasion the Fort Wayne *Sentinel* reported:

> A number of stone-cutters, chiefly Irish, and many with their families, have arrived here the past week, from New York on their way to Lafayette to work on the canal. . . . They were engaged by G. M. Nash . . . who advertised in the New York papers and by bills posted . . . that he was authorized by Messrs. Moorehead & Co. of Lafayette to engage them to work on the canal. Nash got $6.50 from each and gave them passage to Toledo. From Toledo, Moorehead & Co. would give them passage to Lafayette, where their fares would be returned. The Company denies all knowledge of Nash and needs no stone-cutters since the locks are made of wood. These families are to be pitied. Induced by high wages, now [they have] . . . no money and no jobs.[63]

A very attractive inducement to many Irish and German immigrants was the offer of the canal's trustees to sell 40, 80, or 160 acres of land at favorable rates to canal construction laborers.[64] After 1842 the state often paid the workers in scrip of various types which it had issued to finance the building of the canal. It was agreed that this scrip could be used to purchase canal lands; however, its value fluctuated considerably, and often the canal workers sold it as low as 48 cents on the dollar.[65] Nevertheless, in 1832 the monthly wage of $10 offered at Fort Wayne was about the average canal workers received

[63] Fort Wayne *Sentinel,* August 27, 1842.

[64] Annual Report of the trustees of the Wabash and Erie Canal to the General Assembly, December, 1847, in Indiana *Documentary Journal,* 1847, pt. 2, no. 6, p. 205. Also see Wittke, *We Who Built America,* 192.

[65] Nathan O. Ross to W. G. Ewing, February 10, 1845, Ewing Papers, Indiana State Library; Fort Wayne *Sentinel,* September 2, 1843; Lang, "Irishmen in Northern Indiana before 1850," in *Mid-America,* 36:192.

through the various states of Pennsylvania, Ohio, and Indiana. As competition for the labor supply grew more intense prior to 1837, the rate advanced to $13 a month and at times even higher. In addition to their wages the workers were supplied with food and drink. The demand for provisions, of course, benefited the merchants of Fort Wayne. Soon whiskey which had been a principal item in the Indian trade took on a renewed value. James Chute, the Presbyterian minister, used all of his influence to prevent "the use of ardent spirits on the [canal] line."[66] He secured the complete co-operation of Jesse L. Williams and the canal commissioners in drawing up the early canal contracts which stated, "the party of the first part [William Rockhill, contractor] shall not permit any workmen in his employ while they are engaged in constructing this Section [at Fort Wayne] to drink distilled spirits of any kind under the liability of forfeiting this contract at the option of the party of the Second part [Samuel Lewis, Canal Commissioner]."[67] For a time, according to Chute, the commissioners did enforce this provision.[68] Perhaps this helps to explain the early shortage of canal laborers at Fort Wayne, for by 1834 Chute admitted that "in some instances [the contractors] have broken over, being too much influenced by the character of their workmen."[69] Considering the conditions under which the laborers worked it was almost impossible to maintain such a provision. In the case of the Irish, not only were they accustomed to whiskey, but the beverage was considered as "the one specific" for malaria, "and every gang of workmen boasted a 'jigger boss' whose duty it was to carry a large tin pail of

[66] James Chute to Absalom Peters, December 17, 1832, American Home Missionary Society Papers.

[67] Canal contract between William Rockhill and Samuel Lewis, June 4, 1832, Miscellaneous Papers, Allen County—Fort Wayne Historical Society Museum.

[68] Chute to Peters, December 17, 1832.

[69] Chute to Peters, January 27, 1834. By the summer of 1835 Chute had grown quite discouraged. Chute to Peters, July 8, 1835.

whisky along the line and issue a small drink or jigger whenever it seemed needed. His judgment was the only limit or guide."[70] When it was pointed out to a former "jigger boss" that the workmen must have been perpetually drunk, he replied "You wouldn't expect them to work on the canal if they were sober, would you?"[71]

There was almost as much truth as jest in the above statement. While there has been a tendency to exaggerate the number who died from malaria and cholera,[72] still the hardships were great and death was frequent. The first recorded burial at Fort Wayne by the missionary priest Stephen Badin was that of an Irish canal laborer, Richard Doyle, who "died suddenly."[73] Often in the decade 1833-43 the priests at Fort Wayne and along the canal line were called to attend the dying or bury the dead.[74] After one epidemic Father Louis Mueller informed his bishop that fifty of his parishioners in and about Fort Wayne had been carried away by the fever.[75] Half-obliterated markers along the route of the canal still bear mute testimony of the hazards of construction near Fort Wayne.

In addition to their fondness for whiskey the Irish brought with them the political and religious animosities that rent their homeland. Bloody affrays between the Corkonians and Fardowns (Ulstermen) had already occurred at Williamsport, Maryland, and elsewhere in the East. These factions soon carried their feud to the region between Fort Wayne and Lafayette. By July, 1835, the situation had reached the break-

[70] Lafayette *Journal,* September 23, 1899.

[71] *Ibid.*

[72] It has been said that one Irishman died for each six feet of canal built. *The Wabash-Erie Canal* (Fort Wayne—Allen County Public Library), [14].

[73] *Biographical Sketch of Rt. Rev. Julian Benoit, by a clergyman of the Episcopal Household* (n.p., 1885), 10.

[74] *Ibid.,* 6.

[75] Mary Salesia Godecker, *Simon Bruté de Rémur, First Bishop of Vincennes* (St. Meinrad, Ind., 1931), 371.

ing point. During the daytime work on the canal was frequently interrupted when rumors circulated that one party was marching to attack the other, while at night the families left their huts to sleep without fire in the woods out of fear of being burnt or murdered.[76] The two factions were determined to honor the anniversary of the Battle of the Boyne (July 12, 1690) in a fitting manner by engaging in an open conflict. Consequently, on July 10, 1835, some six to eight hundred Irishmen began to assemble near Lagro. Only the quick intervention of the Fort Wayne, Logansport, and Huntington militia, together with the diplomacy of David Burr and Father Simon Lalumiere, prevented bloodshed.[77]

In the summer of 1833 about one thousand men were working on the canal near Fort Wayne,[78] and in the following two years between one and two thousand men labored between Fort Wayne and Huntington.[79] Naturally many of these men were transitory workers. Father Badin was well aware of this when he urged the immediate building of chapels at Fort Wayne and along the canal line "because as soon as the work is done in one section of the country the Catholic hands move to another section."[80] Nevertheless, many laborers did settle permanently. There is a great deal of evidence to indicate that many of these men were accompanied by their families and thus were prepared to accept permanent residence in a town

[76] David Burr to Governor Noah Noble, December 30, 1835, in *Messages and Papers of Noah Noble*, 419-23.

[77] *Ibid.* According to Burr, the Irish were extremely determined, "in very orderly array, well armed, and not a noisy or a drunken man amongst them." See also Godecker, *Simon Bruté de Rémur*, 345.

[78] James Chute to Absalom Peters, September 12, 1833, American Home Missionary Society Papers; Simon Bruté to Frederick Resé, March 4, 1835, University of Notre Dame Archives.

[79] Harlow, *Old Towpaths*, 267.

[80] Stephen Badin to John B. Purcell, September 23, 1834, University of Notre Dame Archives.

or area that they felt was suitable.[81] Of the 1,766 Irish settlers in northern Indiana by 1850, 53 per cent were listed as farmers, 26 per cent as laborers and 21 per cent as artisans or professional men.[82] It is reasonably safe to assume that many of the latter two groups were employed in Fort Wayne since the canal was completed by then and Fort Wayne was by far the most important town in this region of the state.

Taking advantage of their opportunities some of these men prospered. It is somewhat misleading to point to the fact that by 1850 the average real estate wealth of the 424 Irish settlers in Allen County was $563.72 and that the total value of their real estate holdings was $239,020, the highest of the 21 counties in northern Indiana, as these figures include the property of Allen Hamilton.[83] The latter held real estate valued at $110,000 and was the wealthiest Irish immigrant in the state. However, we may point to John Roche as an outstanding, although exceptional, example of a former canal laborer who succeeded. John Roche came in the mid-thirties and by 1842 was superintendent in charge of canal repairs. His Catholicism helped him in winning the friendship of the last Miami chief, Francis Lafontaine, who also was a Catholic. The latter accepted Roche as a partner in his trading establishment at Huntington and named Roche as one of the administrators of his estate. By 1860, Roche was joint owner (with Hugh McCulloch) of 1,800 acres of land southwest of Fort Wayne and was closely connected with the banking affairs of the city. He died in 1894 leaving an estate worth $500,000.[84]

[81] Burr to Governor Noble, December 30, 1835, *Messages and Papers of Noah Noble,* 420, 421.

[82] Lang, "Irishmen in Northern Indiana before 1850," in *Mid-America,* 36:193.

[83] *Ibid.* Even excluding Hamilton's wealth, the Irish in Allen County generally fared better than their fellow countrymen in other northern Indiana counties through which the canal passed.

[84] George I. Reed (ed.), *Encyclopedia of Biography of Indiana* (2 vols. Chicago, 1895), 1:170-72.

Unlike the German immigrant, the Irish settler in Fort Wayne rarely proceeded directly to his ultimate destination. A typical case is that of Maurice Cody. Born in County Cork he emigrated to the United States in 1825. He first worked in New York and then went to Pennsylvania and Maryland. In 1834, acompanied by his uncle and two brothers, he came overland from Maryland to Fort Wayne.[85] Again unlike the Germans, the number of Irish who came to Fort Wayne tended to level off after 1840 whereas the Germans came in increasing numbers.

The appearance of these two groups beginning in the early 1830s plus the increasing numbers of native Americans, especially those from the Middle Atlantic states, served to add new elements to the earlier French, Indian, and native American population at Fort Wayne. By the summer of 1835 the factor responsible to a great extent for this growth—the canal—was opened as far as the Little Wabash River at Huntington, Indiana, some twenty-five miles from Fort Wayne. To commemorate the occasion three boats brought the citizens of Huntington to Fort Wayne where with the local citizenry they joined in celebrating the Fourth of July. Some five hundred people were taken by boat to the feeder dam, after which they returned to the town to hear an address by Hugh McCulloch. Naturally this speech was filled with many of the patriotic expressions of the time, still one may sense yet today the new spirit of nationalism that was emerging in such a western town as Fort Wayne. And as we read it again today it seems only proper that the spokesman for this spirit was the young McCulloch, the new citizen of the West and representative of that generation of Americans which would fight to preserve the nation.

McCulloch dealt at length with the questions of slavery and abolition, stating in part:

[85] Griswold, *Pictorial History of Fort Wayne,* 1:319.

We trust that we may soon be freed from the gross inconsistency of styling ourselves the friends of the rights of man while we hold within our own borders millions of human beings in absolute and degrading servitude. We feel that this is a blot upon our national banner. Would to God that we were able to wash it out! We commiserate with the blacks in their deplorable situation. We would gladly extend to them all the aid in our power to improve their condition, to strike off their chains, and to let in upon their minds the light of knowledge and of liberty. But we can extend no aid to those measures that seem to us only calculated to excite sectional discord and to aggravate the servitude of the slave without accomplishing any permanent good . . . slavery is never to be abolished in America either by exciting the slave to rebellion or by heaping reproach upon his master.[86]

For McCulloch the issues of slavery, sectionalism, and internal improvements were linked. Therefore, when he came to speak of the Wabash and Erie Canal he forcibly expressed the belief that through the promotion of such internal improvements the national government would help to eradicate sectionalism.

The history of our country is an argument in favor of internal improvements—an argument which no intellect can misunderstand and no sophistry weaken. The objections which are sometimes raised to appropriations being made by the government to aid the states in carrying such improvements into operation are, it seems to me, the result of narrow views and illiberal policy. They are founded principally upon the opinion that such appropriations, inasmuch as it will be difficult, if not impossible, to make a satisfactory distribution of them among the states, will give rise to jealousy and will be creative of endless bickerings and strife. But is there not good reason to believe that sectional feelings are in some measure kept alive by the very absence of such improvements, and that railroads and canals, extending their benefits through large tracts of country, will tend to overcome and destroy them? In my judgment, such improvements, although carried into operation in the different states through the assistance of the general government, are calculated to destroy local prejudice and to unite our whole country in the bands of national attachment. Whatever tends

[86] Speech of Hugh McCulloch, July 4, 1835, printed in Indianapolis *Indiana Journal,* September 18, 1835, also in *Canal Celebrations in Old Fort Wayne,* 23, 24.

to bring the people of the different states together and creates a community of interests among them acts directly and powerfully to make them liberal in feeling and national in character.[87]

Looking back over the last three years undoubtedly the townspeople could conclude with McCulloch,

that the commencement of the Canal was the right way to improve the country. It was the right way to make the donated lands valuable to the state, to attract to them the attention of emigrants, and to make the wilderness of which so much had been said the very [heart?] of the state.

. . . .

We look upon this Canal as the first link . . . in a chain of improvements which will one day . . . extend from Lake Erie to the Mississippi.[88]

[87] *Canal Celebrations,* 32-33.
[88] *Ibid.,* 31, 32.

CHAPTER IV

TRIAL AND TRIUMPH, 1835-1843

The stir and bustle of our wharves makes Fort Wayne appear like quite a seaport town.

Undoubtedly the people of Fort Wayne who listened to the speech of Hugh McCulloch on July 4, 1835, would have been less optimistic had they known the problems that were to face the canal builders during the next eight years. Only a pessimist would have dared suggest that not until July 4, 1843, would they celebrate the completion of the canal from Lafayette, Indiana, to Lake Erie.

During the years 1832-35, while the canal was moving principally westward from Fort Wayne, Ohio had delayed beginning its section of the improvement. By the agreement of 1829 with Indiana, Ohio had pledged to complete the Wabash and Erie Canal as far eastward as surveys would indicate this to be necessary. However, the Ohio legislature did not formally ratify the agreement until 1834 and then delayed awarding construction contracts until 1836. Apart from the usual regional differences within the state regarding internal improvements, the most important reasons for this inaction were: (1) a scarcity of funds, (2) the sparse settlement of northwestern Ohio, (3) a boundary dispute between Ohio and Michigan over the Toledo region, and (4) fear that the Wabash and Erie Canal would serve the interests of northern Indiana much more than it would serve those of Ohio.

For a short time some of the citizens of Fort Wayne also thought it would be better if Ohio did not build its portion of the canal since they hoped that the Maumee River could be improved for steamboats, and thus Fort Wayne would be the point of deposit and exchange.[1] These hopes failed to materialize when it was discovered that the rapids of the lower Maumee plus the shallow water at times in the upper Maumee made the river unsuitable for heavier boats. Soon the people of Fort Wayne, not understanding Ohio's position, looked upon the hesitation of their neighboring state as "unnecessary and prejudicial" to their interest.[2]

To the west of Fort Wayne construction costs were higher than anticipated. However, any doubts about the completion of the canal were quickly forgotten in 1836 in part because of Ohio's action and also because the state of Indiana that year pledged its resources to a massive program of internal improvements including turnpikes and railroads as well as canals. This "Mammoth Internal Improvement Bill" calling for appropriations of $13,000,000 has been both criticized as a "mad act" and ably defended by historians.[3] Our concern is with Fort Wayne which in the long run was probably more hurt than helped by the bill insofar as Indiana scattered its small resources on various projects throughout the state instead of concentrating them on the Wabash and Erie Canal. However the immediate effect on Fort Wayne seemed beneficial because according to the plan the Wabash and Erie Canal constituted "the main artery or trunk" for the other improvements.[4] Moreover, according to the act a railroad or canal was envisioned from Fort Wayne northwestward to Michigan City on Lake

[1] Henry Rudisill to John Barr, February 6, 1830, Rudisill Letterbook.

[2] Benton, *The Wabash Trade Route,* 50.

[3] See Harlow, *Old Towpaths,* 268, and Benton, *The Wabash Trade Route,* 51-55. Harlow writes, "By that mad act Indiana placed her neck in a yoke of debt which was destined to gall her for half a century and to humiliate her in the eyes of the world." Benton's principal argument is that the routes were carefully and well selected, giving as proof the fact that eventually successful railroads were built along these same routes. Poor financial management and haste, he claims, were the main errors.

[4] Benton, *The Wabash Trade Route,* 53.

Michigan.[5] This meant that Fort Wayne, being on two improvements, would be the principal inland town between Lake Erie and Lake Michigan.

It is no wonder that optimism prevailed in 1836-37 as the canal by the latter year stretched westward from Fort Wayne to Peru, and to the east work was actually started in Ohio. The eyes of the nation seemed turned toward Indiana. "Eastern newspapers made scornful comparisons between her magnificent spirit of enterprise and the somnolence of Massachusetts."[6] In the center of all the activity was Fort Wayne.

Then came the Panic of 1837 with all its disastrous effects upon the internal improvement programs of the western states. Work stoppages forced Ohio to virtually suspend her operations in 1838, but Indiana struggled on until the fall of 1839.[7] By then conditions had reached their low point. As late as September M. S. Wines, the contractor for the portion of the canal a few miles east of Fort Wayne, was trying to push forward the work "just as if nothing had befallen our finances. In fact [he added] it is impossible for me to stop without money." Nevertheless he had decided to get rid of his canal property in the event the construction of the canal was permanently discontinued.[8] Work came to a standstill by the end of the season, and throughout 1840 the picture at Fort

[5] *Laws of Indiana,* 1835-36 (general), p. 9.

[6] Harlow, *Old Towpaths,* 269.

[7] In that year the Morris Canal and Banking Company of New York along with several other firms failed. The dealings of the Morris Company with Milton Stapp and Dr. Isaac Coe, canal fund commissioners, had been highly irregular, and when the company collapsed they owed the state over two million dollars for internal improvement bonds which they had purchased on credit. See *Messages and Papers relating to the Administration of David Wallace, Governor of Indiana, 1837-1840 (Indiana Historical Collections,* Vol. 43, Indianapolis, 1963), 30, 260n.

[8] M. S. Wines to Jesse L. Williams, September 29, 1839, Fort Wayne—Allen County Historical Museum.

Wayne seemed hopeless. In February Susan McCulloch wrote to her mother:

Our business men begin to feel the pressure and will probably soon feel it worse for the State owes the Contractors on the Canal and they owe both the merchants and the poor laborers who have done all the work. The state will not pay and the contractors cannot pay their hands off nor their honest debts. (So much for the doings of Martin the First [President Van Buren] . . .)I wish he had to see the sufferings of the poor Irish and Germans on our canal lines and hear some of it too.[9]

In the same month Alexander Rankin, the Presbyterian minister at Fort Wayne, reported that money had virtually disappeared in the area and that "not one in ten is able to meet his engagements . . . all eyes were turned to the legislature for some relief; but they have spent the winter in wrangling about party politicks."[10] By September Rankin reported to his superior that it had been impossible to collect his salary for the past year.[11]

The following year, however, saw a renewal of hope as Indiana received a grant of additional land to extend the canal to Terre Haute, and Ohio started construction once again. In place of cash, Williams had paid the contractors with certificates or drafts on the fund commissioners and by action of the legislature in 1841 these could be used for payments on canal lands. The following year provision was made to pay for construction in canal scrip.[12] The scrip used east

[9] Susan McCulloch to Mrs. Frederick Halsey, February 15, 1840, McCulloch Papers, Lilly Library, Indiana University. Inasmuch as Mrs. McCulloch's husband was in charge of the only Fort Wayne bank at this time, her comments on the financial conditions should bear considerable weight.

[10] Alexander Rankin, Fort Wayne, to Milton Badger, February 29, 1840, American Home Missionary Society Papers, Hammond Library, Chicago Theological Seminary.

[11] Rankin to Badger, September 3, 1840.

[12] U. S. *Statutes at Large,* 5:414; *Laws of Indiana,* 1840-41 (general), pp. 199-200; 1841-42 (general), pp. 24-25.

of the Tippecanoe River to the Ohio border became known as "White Dog"; that west of Lafayette was called "Blue Dog." "Blue Pup," a shin plaster, which could be used to buy "Blue Dog" also came into circulation.[13] This scrip was made receivable for principal and interest on canal lands as well as for canal tolls and water rents on the Wabash and Erie Canal. It varied considerably in value. It has been stated that many merchants along the canal line were ruined because they had accepted the scrip at par value.[14] There is no evidence to indicate that this was the case among the more experienced merchants at Fort Wayne. According to an account by A. C. Comparet, the establishment owned by his father and Peter Kiser was very careful in accepting scrip. Other firms such as that of Allen Hamilton also knew its real value and when possible used it to pay off their debts for canal lands.[15] The Ewings bought "White Dog" from the canal workers through the company's agents.[16] In reality the canal workers appear to have fared the worst from being paid in scrip, but some of the more clever laborers used the opportunity to their own advantage. Michael Hedekin, one of the Irish workers at Fort Wayne, bought the scrip at attractive discounts and, although he came to Fort Wayne in 1834 a poor man, by 1843-44 he was able to construct the Hedekin House, one of Fort Wayne's best hotels. The Fort Wayne *Sentinel,* a paper which generally favored the laboring man and farmer, said that "Blue Pup," considered the most variable of all scrip, benefited only "currency mongers."[17] Local situations also provided the clever speculator with opportunities. When the Fort Wayne branch of the State Bank temporarily refused to accept state scrip,

[13] Fort Wayne *Sentinel,* September 2, 1843.

[14] *Laws of Indiana,* 1841-42 (general), pp. 24-25; Harlow, *Old Towpaths,* 275.

[15] "Reminiscences of A. C. Comparet," in *Old Fort News,* 18:no. 4—19:no. 5:6-7.

[16] Nathan O. Ross to W. G. Ewing, February 10, 1845, and Memo on purchase of "White Dog" at 48½ cents, April 8, 1845, Ewing Papers.

[17] Fort Wayne *Sentinel,* March 4, 1843.

a local panic occurred, with some customers offering the currency to the merchants at 25 per cent of its value. The *Sentinel* warned its readers to hold on to their scrip.[18] This incident led the editor the following week to come out against the issuance of any more scrip even if used to extend the construction of the canal.[19]

Whatever may be said against this means of financing the completion of the canal to Lafayette, it must be admitted that it was largely through the use of the scrip that the canal was completed to that town late in 1841. With this accomplishment enthusiasm mounted again in Fort Wayne. Up to this time traffic on the canal had been almost entirely local, but early in 1841 the Wabash and Erie Transportation Company owned by Samuel Mahon, Lewis G. Thompson, and Francis Comparet advertised that they would "commence running at the opening of the navigation on the Wabash and Erie Canal a Daily Line of boats for passengers and freight from Lafayette, Indiana, to a point 6 miles beyond the Indiana State line; making 146 miles."[20] Two weeks later the "Good Intent Line" announced that it would also offer regular service from Lafayette to the state line "at prices sufficiently low to assure the public that this line is not got up to carry on the extortion so long practiced by the old Line."[21] In November, the *Sentinel* reported, "Canal boats now run heavily laden with merchandize from the east for this and other places down the canal. The stir and bustle of our wharves makes Fort Wayne appear like quite a seaport town."[22]

A month later a boat loaded with thirty-five thousand hoop poles left Fort Wayne for New Orleans. The cargo was owned by Fort Wayne citizens and the boat was not to be unloaded

[18] Fort Wayne *Sentinel,* March 19, 1842.
[19] *Ibid.,* March 26, 1842.
[20] *Ibid.,* April 10, 1841.
[21] *Ibid.,* April 24, 1841.
[22] *Ibid.,* November 6, 1841.

until it reached New Orleans. Fort Wayne was indeed the center of the increasing traffic on the canal as the state auditor's report revealed; almost half the tolls for the year 1841 were collected at Fort Wayne.[23] However, the total amount of tolls collected since the beginning of operation, only $13,060.21, indicated that the canal could not be successful without being completed to the eastern terminus at Lake Erie.

Ohio had renewed her efforts in 1841 and there was expectation that the work would be finished within a year. The farmers of the Fort Wayne region responded by sowing more cash crops, especially wheat, in the spring of 1842,[24] and were rewarded by the appearance of a number of eastern commission agents, one of whom sought twenty thousand bushels of wheat from the Fort Wayne area.[25]

With increasing confidence the *Sentinel* stated, "Some may perhaps smile at the idea of [eastern] goods ever being sold in Fort Wayne at a lower rate than in Cincinnati, or think it visionary to talk about wholesale stores here supplying our northern neighbors with goods . . . , [the canal] must be the quickest and cheapest route [from New York]."[26] Although the summer of 1842 proved to be an exceptionally dry season, there was a surplus of water power at Fort Wayne.[27] This also was an encouraging sign for future industry. By the end of the summer a number of canalboats started to arrive from Buffalo in preparation for the fall harvest.

Altogether 1842 was a year of hopeful anticipation. Even though Ohio failed by a few miles to finish her section of the canal,[28] 1843 loomed as *the* year during which all expectations

[23] Fort Wayne *Sentinel*, January 8, 1842.

[24] *Ibid.*, April 30, 1842.

[25] *Ibid.*, May 14, 1842.

[26] *Ibid.*, March 26, 1842.

[27] *Ibid.*, September 10, 1842.

[28] There was still a short distance east of Defiance which had to be completed.

would be fulfilled. Even heavy spring rains which threatened the banks of the canal did not dampen the enthusiasm as Fort Wayne at the central point made preparations for celebrating its opening from Lafayette to Lake Erie. The canal was opened to traffic from the lake in April, and on May 13 all the citizens of the town were invited to the American House to make the arrangements for the celebration on July 4. A grove on the farm of Colonel Thomas Swinney was selected as the site for the ceremonies.[29] Preparations were made to feed twenty thousand guests.[30] All homes prepared to receive the out-of-town visitors. Invitations were sent to such notables as George Clinton, Martin Van Buren, Winfield Scott, Henry Clay, Daniel Webster, John McLean, and a number of other civic leaders from New York, Ohio, and Indiana.[31] Lewis Cass accepted an invitation to be the honored speaker. As a former Superintendent of Indian Affairs in Indiana and Michigan and an explorer, he had traversed the Maumee-Wabash valleys frequently in the early part of the century.

> On Saturday . . . the guests began to arrive; and by Sunday evening, the taverns were overflowing. On Monday afternoon the canalboats began to line our wharves and continued without intermission through the night to land the passengers. . . . Each boat was met on its arrival by the reception committee, who took the passengers to the houses which they were to make their homes during their visit. . . .
>
> Throughout the forenoon, visitors from the interior of the country, remote from the canal line, flocked in by hundreds on horseback or in wagons and vehicles of every description. We have not learned the exact number of canalboats present; they extended in a double tier the whole length of the city, from the upper to the

[29] Fort Wayne *Sentinel,* June 3, 1843.

[30] *Ibid.,* June 24, 1843.

[31] The *Sentinel* printed all the replies, some of which were quite lengthy; naturally all were laudatory. As might be expected, Webster's was the most eloquent and expressed once again his spirit of nationalism. *Ibid.,* July 15, 1843.

lower basin. Being mostly decorated with flags, they gave to our wharf a very interesting appearance.[32]

The celebration began at sunrise, fittingly, with a twenty-six gun salute from the old fort. Accompanied by a number of bands (of which the German Band seemed to be the most distinguished in their uniforms) the procession moved out of the city to Swinney's grove. The oration by Lewis Cass, which was long and lacked continuity, must have tired his audience of around fifteen thousand people.[33] The historic day closed with numerous toasts and feasting for all.

Well might the citizens of the town have taken pride "on the final accomplishment . . . for which they [had] so long, so sedulously, and so perseveringly labored."[34] Equally well might they have taken hope "that the darkest hour in the day of [their] depression [had] passed away."[35] No one realized that within a decade they would consider the canal as inadequate for their needs and would anxiously await the coming of the first railroad.

[32] Fort Wayne *Sentinel,* July 15, 1843; *Canal Celebrations in Old Fort Wayne,* 50-51. The only incident which marred the reception of the distinguished visitors was the unfortunate accident which befell Lewis Cass. "A local poet had written some grandiloquent lines and it was part of the ceremony that these verses should be read to the statesman as he disembarked. The gangplank was not securely stayed and while General Cass stood listening to the phrases . . . the plank slipped and down went the thriftiest of trimmers. He came up moist but fervid and won Indiana to his presidential plans." Lafayette *Journal,* September 25, 1899.

[33] For the complete address, see Fort Wayne *Sentinel,* July 15, 1843, reprinted in *Canal Celebrations in Old Fort Wayne,* 54-79. The essential ingredient in the long address was the then prevalent spirit of "Manifest Destiny."

[34] Letter of Martin Van Buren, June 5, 1843, as quoted in Fort Wayne *Sentinel,* July 15, 1843, and *Canal Celebrations,* 102-3.

[35] Letter of Daniel Webster, June 9, 1843, as quoted in Fort Wayne *Sentinel,* July 15, 1843, and *Canal Celebrations,* 107-8.

CHAPTER V

A DECADE OF ECONOMIC DEVELOPMENT AND PHYSICAL GROWTH

The vast crowds of land buyers and speculators seemed to fill the village and cover the wilderness in this section of the country.

Despite the many problems encountered before the canal was opened to Lake Erie, from the very beginning of its construction in 1832 the waterway materially aided Fort Wayne. The years immediately following 1832 provided financial opportunities for old and new settlers alike. William Rockhill, who came to Fort Wayne in 1823 and had purchased a large tract of land lying west of the city, secured in 1832 a contract from Samuel Lewis, canal commissioner at Fort Wayne, for the construction of certain sections of the middle division of the canal.[1] Rockhill benefited not only from the contract but from the fact that the sections to be built were within the very close vicinity of his property, thus enhancing its value. In 1834 Samuel and Hugh Hanna received profitable contracts for the building of canal sections west of Fort Wayne.[2] As mentioned before, the opportunity to participate in these contracts attracted Marshall Wines, a New York canal builder, to settle in Fort Wayne in 1832. Wines co-operated closely with Jesse L. Williams in the maintenance of the feeder canal at Fort Wayne and in the construction of sections east of the town

[1] Canal contract between William Rockhill and Samuel Lewis, June 4, 1832, in Fort Wayne—Allen County Historical Museum.

[2] Leola Hockett, "The Wabash and Erie Canal in Wabash County," in *Indiana Magazine of History*, 24(1928):296.

as far as Defiance, Ohio.[3] Wines also purchased property east of the town surrounding the site where the Indiana Technical College now stands. Here, adjacent to his land between the Maumee River and the north side of the canal, he later erected a three-and-a-half-story flour mill which represented an investment of $6,000.

Actually Wines's mill was antedated by a number of water-powered mills within the vicinity of Fort Wayne. One of the first of these was a gristmill erected by Samuel Hanna and James Barnett in 1827, on the left bank of the St. Mary's River in what is now Foster Park, at that time several miles south of the town. A few years later the mill was sold to Louis Davis and then to Asa Fairfield.[4] Since most of Samuel Hanna's mill operations were of short duration, one can conclude that he entered into them for purposes of speculation. Like the other Indian traders, Hanna had secured choice sites for mills. Since the early traders were more likely to have capital, they often developed these sites and then sold out to men interested in such investments.[5]

Late in 1830 Henry Rudisill and his father-in-law, Henry Johns, built a flour mill on the west bank of the St. Joseph River almost three quarters of a mile north of the village. Rudisill had the financial backing of John T. Barr in Baltimore, yet many people of the area gave freely of their labor in

[3] Marshall Wines to Jesse L. Williams, September 3, 1836, and September 29, 1839, in Fort Wayne—Allen County Historical Museum, photostatic copies in possession of the author. In addition to Wines, a number of other contractors arrived in 1832-33, but most of them did not settle permanently in Fort Wayne. Concerning their arrival, see James Chute to Absalom Peters, December 17, 1832, American Home Missionary Society Papers, Hammond Library, Chicago Theological Seminary.

[4] Roy M. Bates, "The Water-Powered Mills of Allen County, Indiana," in *Old Fort News,* 7:no. 1 (February, 1942):18. Apparently the mill of Hanna and Barnett was the first to be constructed after the War of 1812. An earlier mill built in 1802 was destroyed by the Indians during the war. *An Early Mill at Three Rivers* (Fort Wayne—Allen County Public Library, 1953).

[5] Anson, The Fur Traders in Northern Indiana, 217.

order to construct this mill and the necessary dam.[6] This type of co-operative enterprise was welcomed by the citizens inasmuch as before the construction of these early mills all meal, flour, and cracked corn had to be brought from Ohio thus contributing extensively to the high price of food in Fort Wayne. These grist mills also encouraged farmers to settle in the region, as they now had an opportunity to market their surplus products.

Other than those two mills there had originated prior to 1832 but few enterprises not directly connected with the Indian trade. These included a brickyard, a tannery, two blacksmith shops, a cooper shop, and a bakery. Excluding merchandising, the most important industry of the town was the processing of the furs for shipment East and the manufacturing of jewelry and trinkets for the Indian trade by a French silversmith, Jean Baptiste Bequette; his articles were used in the Indian trade west of Fort Wayne by the Ewings and others.[7]

The decade following 1832 saw a considerable rise in the industrial interests at Fort Wayne. In a sense it was a transitional period which witnessed the beginning of the transformation of the town's economic life from one based almost entirely upon trade to one depending more and more on manufacturing. As the immigrants continued to settle the area the demands for industrial products became more pronounced. Since transportation costs still limited the manufactured products of the East, the scene was set for local manufacturers to provide for the needs of the area served by Fort Wayne. For example, some time prior to June, 1834, David Coles had erected a sawmill on the Maumee,[8] while in the same year

[6] Bates, "The Water-Powered Mills of Allen County," in *Old Fort News*, 7:no. 1:15.

[7] The Ewing Papers contain numerous receipted bills for work sold to the Ewings.

[8] Fort Wayne *Sentinel*, June 14, 1834.

Horney Robinson constructed another sawmill on a small tributary of the Little Wabash River a few miles southwest of the town. Much of the mill's output was shipped to Fort Wayne by way of the canal to be used in the many new buildings being erected in this period of the town's expansion. By 1835 Allen County could boast of its first steam-powered mill erected by Benjamin Sunderland. The boiler for this mill had to be dragged by eight yoke of oxen from Dayton, Ohio.[9]

In 1834 James Chute noted that "mechanics particularly would find the most flattering prospects" at Fort Wayne.[10] Skilled labor was in demand for that same year the town and the surrounding area were able to support the following new enterprises—a tailoring shop; the cabinet making business of Tinkham, Ebbert, and Rhinehart; Henry Work and Isaac Cron, tanners and shoemakers; Comparet and Coquillard who besides their fur trading were brewers of "good strong Beer"; Jacob Fry's tannery; a marble works owned by James Humphrey; Oliver Fairfield's bakery; and a gunsmith and bell making shop.[11] The year 1835 saw the appearance of Fort Wayne's first established butcher shop owned by Peter Kiser as well as an additional brewery, and shoemaking and blacksmith shops. During the following year, John Cochrane built the first planing mill.

By the spring of 1837 the canal had reached Logansport and a new industry directly related to the increasing navigation on the canal took firm root in Fort Wayne—that of canalboat construction. Although F. P. Tinkham built the town's first canalboat in 1834, the first boat yards were those of Barthold

[9] Bates, "The Water-Powered Mills of Allen County," in *Old Fort News,* 7:no. 1:7; Griswold, *Pictorial History of Fort Wayne,* 1:333, 607-8.

[10] James Chute to Absalom Peters, March 17, 1834, American Home Missionary Society Papers.

[11] Fort Wayne *Sentinel,* June 14, 1834.

and Sons and James W. Deneal.[12] Later Francis Comparet and his sons constructed boats for the Mahon brothers who operated a line on the canal.[13] By the late 1840s the firm of Ellsworth and Rippe were building most of the packet and freight boats for the canal.

While the Panic of 1837 was to have disastrous results upon Indiana's program of internal improvements and to leave the merchants and landowners in grave difficulties, it had little permanent effect upon the growth of Fort Wayne industry. The industries that had originated in the town by 1837—flour and sawmills, tanneries, distilleries, for example—were, for the most part, very small concerns operated by various craftsmen who were manufacturing articles on a small scale and for a limited market. The manufacturing of the town was of course closely tied to agriculture. Basically the producers drew upon the surrounding farms for their raw materials, and for their market looked as much to the farmer as to the townsman. Most of the settlers who had arrived by 1837 proved to be permanent ones, and while at times their financial situation was difficult in the following years, the town's industry still had to expand to meet their normal requirements. That agricultural production grew considerably in the area surrounding Fort Wayne even during the depression years was revealed by the fact that the taxable acreage of Allen County increased from 58,717 in 1840 to 212,709 in 1841.[14]

Skilled workers continued to establish their shops in Fort Wayne during these years. Many of these craftsmen were German such as the Baker family from Hesse-Darmstadt. Kilian Baker built Fort Wayne's first wagons, while John, George, and Jacob Baker erected the first steam sawmill as well as initi-

[12] Fort Wayne *News-Sentinel,* March 15, 1872. Deneal had in his employ Captain John Whiteaker, who later became governor of Oregon.

[13] "Reminiscences of A. C. Comparet," in *Old Fort News,* 18:no. 4—19:no. 1:4; Griswold, *Pictorial History of Fort Wayne,* 1:340.

[14] Fort Wayne *Sentinel,* January 8, 1842.

ated the manufacture of plows in 1838. In the following year Jacob C. Bowser from Ohio, together with James Story, established a foundry and machine shop. Despite heavy losses from fire the first year the firm prospered and was enlarged often thereafter. The creation of the Bowser and Story foundry is significant inasmuch as it represents, although in a very small way, the beginning of heavy industry in Fort Wayne. Thereafter one can see promise of a type of manufacturing in Fort Wayne which would rise above the purely craft level.

By 1840 the census figures reveal that Fort Wayne had definitely assumed the leadership in industry throughout the northern third of Indiana. Of the state's 87 counties, Allen County ranked twenty-third in manufacturing and first among the northern counties in the state. The total amount of capital invested in manufacturing in Allen County amounted to $67,300.[15] Although Fort Wayne was not listed as a separate unit in the census, for all practical purposes the statistics for Wayne Township are really those of Fort Wayne, and Wayne was by far the most important of all the townships in Allen County. For example, of the 265 persons directly engaged in manufacturing and trades in the county, Wayne Township accounted for 238. The next ranking township employed only seven persons in manufacturing and trades. Of the 52 persons in Allen County who were engaged in commerce, 49 of these lived in Wayne Township. Of the 28 individuals in the county who were engineers or connected with the learned professions, 27 of these resided in Wayne Township.[16]

While the economic development of Fort Wayne corresponded with the general pattern of other mid-nineteenth century towns of the Northwest insofar as there was gradually substituted "the encouragement of manufacturing for an earlier

[15] United States Bureau of the Census, *Compendium of the Sixth Census* (1840), 290-97.

[16] *Ibid., Sixth Census of Enumeration of the Inhabitants* (1840), 347, 371.

emphasis on trade,"[17] commerce still retained a dominant role in the life of the community. However, important changes did occur also in the channels of trade. As we have noted previously, by 1832 the Indian and fur trade, while still vital to the community, was declining. With the inauguration of the canal and the influx of white settlers, the chance for profits elsewhere proved very tempting to the traders. As one authority has pointed out, "The canal with its land investments, lock sites, and trading locations offered the Indian traders a golden opportunity."[18] As the Indian trade lessened, merchants in Fort Wayne sold more goods to the whites. These articles (cloth, guns, iron instruments, salt, whiskey) were at first not so different as might be expected. The major difference was that the white settler preferred greater variety and bought more often but in smaller quantities. In other words merchandising was made more complex. Naturally, as Fort Wayne's life became richer in taste and culture, other luxury items such as silk, china, etc., were brought from the East or from Europe. The home of the Miami chief, Richardville, was furnished with carpets and draperies from Paris.[19]

Until Fort Wayne was linked by canal with Lake Erie, the shipping charge still remained a large item in the price of goods for the Fort Wayne merchant. The firm of Hamilton and Taber, for example, paid freight charges of $1,033.91 on a $5,529.20 consignment of merchandise from New York in 1840.[20] These costs meant that in general the older well-established merchants maintained their leading positions. In fact, since many new merchants did not have sufficient capital and were not known to eastern creditors, they had to secure the

[17] Bayrd Still, "Patterns of Mid-Nineteenth Century Urbanization in the Middle West," in *Mississippi Valley Historical Review,* 28 (1941-42), 189-90.

[18] Anson, Fur Traders in Northern Indiana, 228.

[19] Fort Wayne *Journal-Gazette,* September 2, 1958.

[20] Hamilton and Taber Account Book, entry for July 13, 1840, in Fort Wayne—Allen County Historical Museum.

approval of such men as Hanna, the Ewings, Comparet, and Hamilton, who were better known in the East. This situation led the above men into the commission business. Since Hanna, for example, went East regularly, he soon started buying for other Fort Wayne merchants. He became in a sense the underwriter for the small merchant.[21]

Like his counterpart in other towns of the Old Northwest, the Fort Wayne merchant-trader found the problem of a sufficient amount of reliable currency and credit a difficult one to solve. This was especially true at Fort Wayne in the period after 1831 as the Indian agency had been removed and there would be no major treaties with the Indians of the area for seven years. Still the country was developing rapidly and credit was needed to take advantage of the opportunities. Most of the money previously acquired by the traders was tied up in land. In fact, Hanna was considered for a time to be "land poor." Gold specie was rarely seen at Fort Wayne. Hugh McCulloch later stated, "I had been a banker for fourteen years before I handled or saw a dollar in gold except for the ten-thaler pieces which were brought into this country by German immigrants."[22]

In view of these facts, it is not surprising that although Allen County voted for Jackson in 1832, many of the citizens of Fort Wayne, especially the merchants, did not agree with his policies regarding the Bank of the United States. Even Rudisill, a staunch Democrat who had been appointed postmaster by Jackson, told McCarty, the Democratic representative from the Fort Wayne district, that the people of Fort Wayne were dissatisfied with his course in Congress. When asked why

[21] To Hanna was entrusted such tasks as bringing Bibles and religious tracts from the East. See James Chute to Absalom Peters, June 13, 1832, American Home Missionary Society Papers.

[22] McCulloch, *Men and Measures of Half a Century,* 119.

by McCarty, Rudisill answered candidly, "we want the bank."[23] To defend the interests of Tipton who was a candidate for re-election to the United States Senate, Colerick "told the people that Gen. Tipton did not belong to that party—which says Jackson—right or wrong—Jackson—Bank or no Bank and that you [Tipton] were only with Jackson, while Jackson was with the constitution and the sound policy of our country."[24] Earlier in the same year, Hanna had written to Tipton urging the latter to vote for the renewal of the Federal Bank's charter.[25] The Fort Wayne merchant could not follow the anti-bank policies of Jackson,[26] nor, on the other hand, could he be completely satisfied with the eastern control of credit. While he may have wished for a modification of the national banking system along lines of decentralization, he nevertheless saw the need for a *regulated* expansion of credit. To a great extent Bray Hammond is correct in stating, "The West's aversion for the federal Bank was like the nationalistic resentment in a 20th century underdeveloped economy which wants and needs imported capital but growls at the 'imperialism' of the country that is expected to provide it."[27] Because the merchants of Fort

[23] David H. Colerick to Tipton, September 20, 1832, *John Tipton Papers,* 2:711-12.

[24] *Ibid.,* 2:712.

[25] Samuel Hanna to Tipton, March 22, 1832, *ibid.,* 2:558.

[26] Whether the Jacksonian policy was motivated principally by the "hard-money, loco-foco" Democrats, by the agrarian debtor class, or by new entrepreneurs, the "Democrats by trade," the Fort Wayne merchant was inclined to reject it. With the first two groups, they disagreed in principle, and if the latter group concealed their real aims under an attack upon "privilege," they either failed to understand them or distrusted them. For the various interpretations of Jackson's bank policies, see Charles G. Sellers, "Andrew Jackson versus the Historians," in *Mississippi Valley Historical Review,* 44 (1958):615-34. In particular see Vernon L. Parrington, *Main Currents in American Thought (The Romantic Revolution in America, 1800-1860,* Vol. 2, New York, 1954); Arthur M. Schlesinger, Jr., *The Age of Jackson* (Boston, 1945); Bray Hammond, *Banks and Politics in America from the Revolution to the Civil War* (Princeton University Press, 1957).

[27] Hammond, *Banks and Politics in America,* 359.

Wayne understood this need for credit, they were less inclined to "growl." Over-all, therefore, their desire for government assistance in internal improvements as well as for a banking system that would be to their liking led to a process aptly described by Vernon L. Parrington: "The coonskin individualism that created Jacksonian democracy was gradually undermined by a middle class individualism that inclined to the Whiggery of Henry Clay. The former was a spontaneous expression of the frontier spirit, the latter a calculating expression of the maturing settlement. The one discovered its native habitat on the backwoods farm, the other in the county seat town."[28] Such a town was Fort Wayne, and it is not surprising that its voters supported Harrison in the elections in 1836 and 1840.

After Jackson had stifled the Federal Bank, the need for some reliable state bank was absolute. Just as the requirement for some action on the Wabash and Erie Canal had led Samuel Hanna to play a leading role in its inauguration, so now he worked for an improved banking system. As a member of the state Senate in 1833, he voted to postpone action on a hastily written bank charter. At the following session of the General Assembly, Hanna was appointed a member of the select committee on bank legislation which introduced a bill creating a State Bank. As the session progressed, the Senate bill was tabled in favor of one passed by the House after a conference committee worked out a compromise measure.[29]

[28] Parrington, *Main Currents in American Thought,* 132-33.

[29] *Laws of Indiana,* 1833-34, pp. 12-38; *Messages and Papers of Noah Noble,* 210n-11n. Hugh McCulloch wrote in 1888, "If the history of this Bank should be written, it would be both interesting and instructive." Despite the truth of this statement, there has been no definitive study on the State Bank of Indiana, only a monograph by William F. Harding, "The State Bank of Indiana," in *Journal of Political Economy,* 4(1895-96):1-38. Logan Esarey devoted considerable space to the Bank in his *State Banking in Indiana, 1814-1873* (Indiana University *Studies No. 15,* Bloomington, 1912), 247-78.

In some respects, the State Bank was similar to the Bank of the United States; in other respects it foreshadowed our present Federal Reserve System. Like the Bank of the United States it was given an exclusive charter for twenty years, but as McCulloch pointed out:

It was not, like the Bank of the United States, a bank *with* branches, but rather a bank *of* branches. It was a bank in this respect only: it had a president, a cashier, and a board of directors. . . . The president, who was *ex-officio* a member of the board, was elected by the legislature, as were also the five directors who represented the state. The other directors were elected by the branches, one director by each branch . . . each branch although independent in respect to its profits, was liable for the debts of every other branch. . . . This responsibility of each branch for the debts of the other branches created a general vigilance which was productive of excellent results.[30]

These features were likely designed to prevent a centralization of the Bank's authority in one region of the state as had existed on a national scale under the Bank of the United States. At the same time a rigid supervision was maintained by the branches acting jointly. The number of branches was limited to thirteen; the capital of each branch was to be $160,000, one half of which was to be furnished by the state. The means by which private investors could purchase shares of the Bank's stock was obviously designed with the landowners in mind. ". . . the charter provided that to every stockholder who should pay $18.75 on each fifty-dollar share for which he subscribed the state should at his request advance $31.25 as a loan so that the stock might be fully paid up. The loan was to be secured by bonds and mortgages on real estate at one half its appraised value. The stockholder was to be charged 6 per cent interest on the loan, and credited with whatever dividends might be declared on that part of the stock which was thus to be paid for by the state."[31]

[30] McCulloch *Men and Measures of Half a Century,* 117-18.
[31] *Ibid.,* 114-15.

In one respect this was the best manner of raising capital in a western state, where wealth consisted principally in the form of land. Still the profits resulting to the merchant-land-owner such as Hanna were great. For example, the returns of the Fort Wayne branch so far exceeded 6 per cent that the loan was paid seven years before the expiration of the charter.[32] The Fort Wayne branch was organized in 1835, the first branch chartered in northern Indiana. If this can be taken as an indication of the commercial importance of Fort Wayne, one must at the same time recognize that until then Fort Wayne had no bank. It is also an indication of the financial maturing of the town. Until then the established merchant had served as a primitive banker, advancing credit or allowing his name to be used for credit or, what was more rare, loaning what little money he had. In a sense, the change was but a step forward, as these older merchants now became the directors of the Fort Wayne branch of the State Bank. Of course this process was not novel, being characteristic of the capitalistic society since its foundations.

Since Samuel Hanna was a member of the state legislature at the time, he was excluded by law from becoming one of the original directors; however, he invested in the Fort Wayne branch, and his interests were undoubtedly looked after by Hugh Hanna, who was named along with Allen Hamilton and William Rockhill as directors to represent the state. At a meeting in November, ten directors were elected by the stockholders. These were Samuel Lewis, William G. Ewing, Francis Comparet, Joseph Morgan, Joseph Sinclear, Isaac Spencer, Jesse Vermilya, Asa Fairfield, David Burr, and Samuel Edsall. The next day Allen Hamilton was elected president of the Fort Wayne branch, and Hugh McCulloch was appointed as cashier and manager. McCulloch pointed out that he "had no practical knowledge of banking," but the directors felt he "was

[32] McCulloch, *Men and Measures of Half a Century,* 115.

better fitted for the place than anybody else whose services they could obtain. . . ."[33] McCulloch accepted the position with the understanding that he would be free later to return to his profession of law, but he never did resume his practice. Hamilton and the directors rarely interfered in the bank's affairs, for as McCulloch himself wrote, with a deserved pat on his own back, "The branch at Fort Wayne was not the best branch, but it was one of the best-managed branches."[34] Agreement with this belief has been general, both at that time and now.[35] In the years following 1837, when other banks throughout the nation collapsed and even the branches of the State Bank of Indiana were temporarily authorized to suspend specie payments, the Fort Wayne branch always paid in specie.[36] For this McCulloch won praise from the newspapers of northern Indiana most of which were violently opposed to banks at that time. Speaking of McCulloch, the Goshen *Democrat* commented that it was "gratifying to see men may be bankers, and not be scoundrels, even if only in one instance."[37] The editor of the Goshen *Northern Indianian* complained that at South Bend money was being used by the bank to buy eastern bonds, yet noted, "I have no doubt but some of these institutions are conducted by men of the most exalted sense of honor, — and such I believe to be the officers of the branch Bank at Fort Wayne.

[33] McCulloch, *Men and Measures of Half a Century,* 113; Griswold, *Pictorial History of Fort Wayne,* 1:326.

[34] McCulloch, *Men and Measures of Half a Century,* 115.

[35] "Men such as Samuel Merrill [President of the State Bank] . . . and Hugh McCulloch . . . were of a different caliber from those who were trusted with handling of the funds of the state. Not even the . . . derelictions of the fund commissioners could drag down the State Bank." R. Carlyle Buley, *The Old Northwest, Pioneer Period, 1815-1840* (2 vols. Indiana Historical Society, 1950), 2:285.

[36] Fort Wayne *Sentinel,* November 20, 1841.

[37] Reprint of article in Goshen *Democrat* in Fort Wayne *Sentinel,* January 8, 1842.

A more honorable and high-minded man than Judge Hugh McCulloch, the State cannot produce."[38]

The view of the Goshen editor becomes understandable especially when one remembers that the Fort Wayne branch seldom, if ever, invested in eastern securities as did some of the other banks. Therefore, without doubt the bank at Fort Wayne served to benefit not only the expanding commercial interests of the town itself but the surrounding agricultural area as well. Prior to 1837 a large percentage of its loans were made to men who were buying or improving lands. There were no great losses on these loans as a result of the crisis of 1837, but thereafter the loans "were confined mainly to bills of exchange based upon produce shipped or to be shipped to eastern or southern markets."[39] In this way the Fort Wayne bank furnished the means for sending surplus products of the area to market. Furthermore, as McCulloch mentions, ". . . by its judicious loans to farmers, it also enabled the farmers to increase their stock of cattle and hogs, which consumed their surplus of corn."[40]

In noting the above changes in the commercial life of Fort Wayne, we must not lose sight of the fur trade, the oldest of all trading enterprises and still occupying a position of importance. In fact conditions existing after 1837 led to a revival of the fur trade in the area of which Fort Wayne was the center. By 1835 important changes were occurring in the nature of the fur trade. Often the trappers were white rather than Indian. The latter were disappearing or becoming unreliable, while for the white settler the proceeds from trapping supplemented the income from farming. These furs were usually purchased from the white settlers by local storekeepers who paid for the skins with the necessities the settlers needed.

[38] Reprint of article in Goshen *Northern Indianian* in Fort Wayne *Sentinel*, May 1, 1841.

[39] McCulloch, *Men and Measures of Half a Century*, 116.

[40] *Ibid.*, 117.

W. G. Ewing complained in fact that the Fort Wayne merchants often paid more in goods for the furs than the Ewings paid in cash.[41] Then in the late 1830s "Dame Fashion" played her role. Just as she had decreed earlier that silk was to replace beaver in the making of hats, now she demanded mink, deer, and, above all, raccoon skins. Since the Maumee-Wabash region "produced enormous numbers of raccoons" it became "for a few years the center of interest of the fur business of America."[42]

Thus between 1838 and 1842 Fort Wayne became the base from which an extensive war for this fur trade was carried on. The Ewings who had extended their operations as far west as the Missouri River had for some time been preparing for battle with the American Fur Company, their great competitor. After the withdrawal of the Astors in 1834, the American Fur Company came under the presidency of Ramsay Crooks. Its chief agent, William Brewster, was located at Detroit, but men such as Comparet represented the company at Fort Wayne. On the other hand, the Ewings had established a number of firms in order to spread the risk of failure, to make sure of the self-interest of their various partners in the field, and to reach a wider area.[43] Their more important companies were Ewing, Edsall and Company at Fort Wayne, Ewing, Walker and Company at Logansport, Ewing, Aveline and Company at Fort Wayne, and the principal firm, W. G. and G. W. Ewing at Fort Wayne. The Ewings have been correctly described as "aggressive, unscrupulous but capable operators."[44] After a number of speculative adventures apart from the Indian trade had failed by late 1839, G. W. Ewing had written to his

[41] W. G. and G. W. Ewing to Captain John Fury, February 13, 1845, Ewing Papers.

[42] Frank Ross, "The Fur Trade of the Ohio Valley," in *Indiana Magazine of History,* 34 (1938):440.

[43] Anson, The Fur Traders in Northern Indiana, 160.

[44] Buley, *The Old Northwest,* 2:320.

brother, "Indian money . . . treaties . . . lands and lastly their skins must be our motto. No more building mills or dealing with white knaves I say."[45] During 1838, they won over to their company many of the American Fur Company's agents, and backed financially by Suydam and Sage in New York, they entered into a "war of extermination" with Crooks's firm.[46]

The war cost both sides heavily and a truce was arranged early in 1839. The Ewings renewed the war late in the year and the American Fur Company then made arrangements with Hugh McCulloch for financing their operations in the Fort Wayne area,[47] as the stakes here were high. Early in 1839 Brewster reported taking $40,000 worth of skins at Fort Wayne within the last few months.[48] The Ewings must have done equally as well in this area, for after one year of the war, they stated, "Our profits have been principally made on the superior raccoons skins of the Valleys of the Maumee & Wabash."[49]

The American Fur Company, as the larger firm, seemed to have the advantage, but the Ewings used almost any means. They wrote to the Secretary of War charging the American Fur Company with practicing fraud in the Indian payments and being owned by British interests.[50] G. W. Ewing, representing the Fort Wayne area in the Senate, introduced a bill which would have killed the American Fur Company through a heavy tax on all out-of-state companies operating in Indiana. Indiana citizens would have been prohibited even from trading with the American Fur Company anywhere outside of the

[45] G. W. Ewing, Peru, to W. G. Ewing, November 12, 1839, Ewing Papers.

[46] When Suydam and Sage failed in 1850, W. G. Ewing wasted no sympathy on the firm, noting only that it was fortunate that the Ewings did not suffer as a result. W. G. Ewing, Detroit, to G. W. Ewing, August 8, 1850, Ewing Papers.

[47] *Calendar of the American Fur Company's Papers. Part I:1831-1840* (American Historical Association, *Annual Report,* 1944, Vol. 2), 717, 720.

[48] *Ibid.,* 587.

[49] W. G. Ewing memo in Ewing Book, 1835-40, Eastern business, Ewing Papers.

[50] W. G. Ewing to John Bell, April 16, 1841, Ewing Papers.

state. This bill was defeated in the House. In general the people of Fort Wayne opposed Ewing's measure vigorously, it being reported "that if any Legislator voted for Ewing's bill, his hide will be on the fence and well stretched at that."[51] The political scene at Fort Wayne was dominated by the merchant-trader and personality differences played an important role. While the Ewings were on good terms with some of the older French fur traders,[52] they had angered at one time or another many of the other traders such as Hanna and Hamilton.[53] Of course, the main reason for the opposition to the Ewing bill was that the fur war had boosted the prices during a period of business stagnation after 1837 and so had helped the merchants and settlers considerably.

After the defeat of their bill, the Ewings suggested a merger with their competitor, but the offer was rejected.[54] During 1841 both firms used moderation, but in 1842 the war was renewed and ended only with the bankruptcy of the American Fur Company the following year. The Ewings were only partially responsible for this. An extremely mild winter, the closing of Chinese ports, and poor prices at the Leipzig fair, all contributed; nevertheless, bitter and delighted, W. G. Ewing wrote:

> The Great American Fur Company it seems has exploded! disappeared, overwhelmed with most miserable Bankruptcy!—they have met their just deserts;—they waged a Warfare against us, that cost us a loss of at least $60,000. But had we united with them

[51] Ross, "The Fur Trade of the Ohio Valley," in *Indiana Magazine of History,* 34:440. In reality the American Fur Company should not have protested too much about Ewing's bill inasmuch as John Jacob Astor's firm in 1816 had succeeded in having Congress prohibit Canadian fur traders from buying skins in the United States and earlier Astor had tried to gain a monopoly for his company from the state of New York.

[52] Joseph Holman to Tipton, February 21, 1829, *John Tipton Papers,* 2:145.

[53] Allen Hamilton to Tipton, January 19, 1837, *ibid.,* 3:347.

[54] *Calendar of the American Fur Company's Papers, Part I,* 814, 821, 838; Buley, *The Old Northwest,* 2:322.

in 1840 (when we were trying to buy our peace) we would have sustained double that loss, with a prostration of our Business.[55]

Although the Ewings were badly shaken, they continued to buy furs in 1843.[56] Thereafter, at Fort Wayne a permanent decline in the fur trade set in. As late as 1845, W. G. Ewing reported that the merchants of the town were still engaging heavily in the fur trade, but he also stated two weeks later that he was tired of "competition with Yankees" and ready to open trade in the Santa Fé country.[57] The Ewings continued to maintain their headquarters at Fort Wayne, but in reality the important trade had moved westward. Still the fur trade, which had played such a significant role in the early formation of the town, had helped to maintain it in the years between 1837 and 1843. It has been said of the fur-bearing animals, "They recede with the aborigines, before the tide of civilization."[58]

In addition to having the fur trade to fall back upon in time of depression, Fort Wayne was also fortunate in still having the Miami Indians within its vicinity. If the Miami had been moved west of the Mississippi prior to 1837 it would have been impossible for the hard-pressed settlers and merchants to benefit from the lucrative treaties of 1838 and 1840 which provided for the removal of the tribe. In the early part of the decade many of the white settlers in the vicinity, especially the farmers, were anxious to have the Miami removed, for although they lived at peace with their white neighbors, the fear of a possible uprising was always present. A collision between the Indians and the workmen on the canal was also a possibility for during the construction the Indians experienced less difficulty

[55] W. G. Ewing to John W. Edmonds, March 23, 1843, Ewing Papers.

[56] They purchased 210 packs at Fort Wayne and Logansport during this year. Anson, Fur Traders in Northern Indiana, 185.

[57] W. G. Ewing to John Fury, February 13, 1845 and W. G. Ewing to Colonel L. C. Owens, February 28, 1845, Ewing Papers.

[58] Ross, "The Fur Trade of the Ohio Valley," in *Indiana Magazine of History,* 34:442.

than usual in securing whiskey with their annuities.[59] The constant degeneration of the tribe by white influence led to periodic incidents.[60] On the other hand, during these years most of the Fort Wayne merchants would have agreed with W. G. Ewing, who wrote, "Yet their Removal from the State now I believe to be impracticable—would it not be well to suffer them to occupy back & unimportent situations for a while, as their increased annuity will be of material benefit in the first settleing of our country and there is yet room for all."[61]

Thus by 1836 while arrangements were being concluded to remove the Potawatomi from the state, little headway had been made to induce the Miami to agree to their removal. Apart from the attitude of many of the traders, one of the principal difficulties was the reluctance of the Miami chief, Richardville.[62] He lived in refinement near Fort Wayne and kept a trading store on Calhoun Street which was regularly visited by his tribe. Called the "Old Fox" by his white contemporaries, he was a man of "great natural shrewdness and sagacity." According to McCulloch, Richardville had no "equal

[59] James Chute to Absalom Peters, July 6, 1833, American Home Missionary Society Papers.

[60] For example, in 1830 the town was upset over the reaction of the Miami to a jury trial of a Miami brave for the murder of his Negro-Indian woman. The Miami considered her a slave, hence the warrier should be set free. W. G. Ewing to Tipton, April 12, 1830, *John Tipton Papers,* 2:265. Again in 1838 the murder of White Raccoon by another Indian resulted in tribal vengeance upon the murderer which the authorities were powerless to prevent. John W. Dawson, *Charcoal Sketches of Old Times in Fort Wayne.* Copied from Fort Wayne *Daily Sentinel,* March 8-May 20, 1872 (Fort Wayne Public Library, 1939), 20.

[61] W. G. Ewing to Tipton, February 3, 1830, *John Tipton Papers,* 2:245.

[62] There is some debate concerning Richardville's ancestors. Apparently he was more French than Indian. His father was Joseph Drouet de Richerville and his mother was Taucumwah. A very clever woman, she was termed "une Chieftess" by the French and was apparently half-French. See an article on Richardville by Bessie Roberts in the Fort Wayne *Journal-Gazette,* May 6, 1956, and a sketch in *John Tipton Papers,* 1:322n.

in diplomatic skill among the Government commissioners when treaties were to be made with his nation."[63] Tipton who often negotiated with him called him, "the ablest diplomat of whom I have any knowledge. If he had been born and educated in France, he would have been the equal of Talleyrand."[64] The Chief trusted few men except Allen Hamilton, his legal adviser, and the Catholic priest at Fort Wayne, Julian Benoit. Benefiting from the treaties and his store, Richardville had amassed a fortune in both land and silver and was reputedly the wealthiest Indian in the United States when he died in 1841. In specie alone he left $200,000.[65] Guided by avarice in his last years, he was determined to get the most from the government before agreeing to the removal of his tribe from Indiana.

After 1837 the pressure for the final extinction of Indian reservations and the tribe's removal from the area mounted. As one authority has pointed out, "the panic halted normal business opportunities, and also appeared to make the predominant squatter class of pioneers more impatient with the Indians' continued residence, so that from 1838 to 1840 there was an increased tempo of urgency for their removal."[66] The preemption laws passed by Congress in 1832 and 1834 worked against the Miami, since the squatters were anxious to obtain legal possession of the land which had been ceded.

In the fall of 1838 the Miami heard of the woeful plight of the Potawatomi and their "Trail of Death" to the West. While this must have frightened the Miami, it also revealed the determination of the whites to be rid of the Indians. On November 6, 1838, Richardville and the other chiefs agreed to cede most of their remaining lands and to accept a western reservation

[63] McCulloch, *Men and Measures of Half a Century*, 109.

[64] *Ibid.*

[65] Allen Hamilton's Account Book, in Fort Wayne—Allen County Historical Museum.

[66] Anson, The Fur Traders in Northern Indiana, 158.

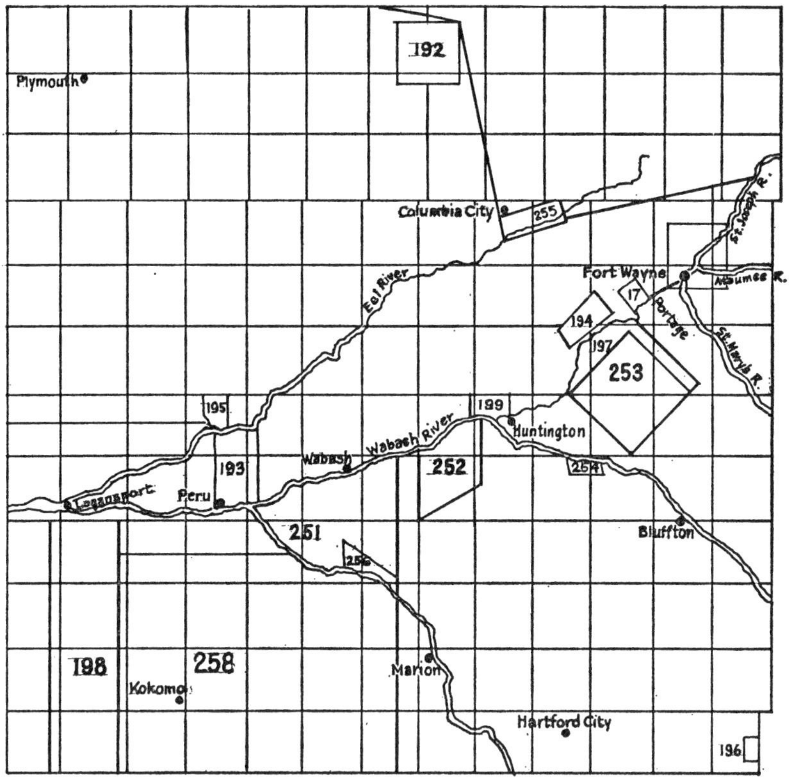

MIAMI INDIAN RESERVATIONS

Key to Map

R—Reserved C—Ceded

16-17 C Aug. 3, 1795

192-95 R to Miami, Oct. 23, 1826; C Oct. 23, 1834

196-98 R to Miami, Oct. 6, 1818; C Oct. 23, 1834

199 R to Miami, Oct. 23, 1826; patented to Richardville, Oct. 23, 1834

251-54 R to Miami, Oct. 6, 1818; C Nov. 6. 1838

255 R to Miami, Oct. 23, 1826; C Nov. 6, 1838

256 R to Miami, Nov. 6, 1838; patented to Meshingomesia, Nov. 28, 1840

258 R to Miami, Oct. 6, 1818; C Nov. 28, 1840

for the tribe. This treaty cost the government $335,680, of which $150,000 was set aside for payment of debts.[67] Two years later the Miami agreed to give up the residue of their last reserve, which was southwest of Fort Wayne, and to be removed to the country assigned them west of the Mississippi. The cost of this cession was $550,000, of which $300,000 was to be used for payment of debts contracted after the 1838 treaty.[68] The traders of the area benefited immensely as a result of these treaties. The claims against the Miami amounted to $103,765 in the treaty of 1838 alone. Among the 118 claimants were Ewing, Walker & Company of Logansport which was awarded $13,829 for goods sold to the Indians. Of the Fort Wayne traders, William G. Ewing & Company received $8,677; Comparet & Colerick, $7,451; Hamilton & Taber, $2,157, while others received smaller amounts for goods.[69]

Nathaniel West, the commissioner who investigated the claims, wrote in January, 1839:[70]

> The Miamies are fast falling away from their true character, imbibing more and more of the vices and none of the good traits of the white population. Indolence, extravagance, and a love of display pervade the whole nation; many of the young men wear clothing which cost at least $100; indeed, none but the finest goods will sell amongst them. They hunt but little, do no work, and the whole nation may be said to live from sources drawn from the store of the trader. They of course will obtain a credit as long as it is evident the remaining lands will be sufficient to pay the debts of the nation.

Eleven months later West wrote that the Miami were

[67] Kappler (ed.), *Indian Affairs, Laws and Treaties,* 2:384-88.

[68] *Ibid.,* 2:393-94.

[69] T. Hartley Crawford to Allen Hamilton, November 24, 1840, in Fort Wayne—Allen County Historical Museum. Claims under the 1834 treaty, which were not settled until 1838, amounted to $47,273. The reports of Nathaniel West, commissioner in charge of the investigation of claims under both the 1834 and 1838 treaties, are printed in U. S. *Senate Documents,* 25 Congress, 1 session, No. 302, and 26 Congress, 1 session, No. 164.

[70] U. S. *Senate Documents,* 25 Congress, 1 session, No. 302, p. 7.

fast sinking into those wretched habits originating from intoxication, and too great intercourse with the white people, as will, in a very few years, entirely destroy them, unless removed west of the Mississippi. I also regret to say that . . . the Miamies are fast diminishing in numbers. The chiefs inform that, since I was with them in 1838, more than sixty have died, and a very large proportion by violence.[71]

By the terms of the 1840 treaty the Miami were permitted to remain in Indiana for five more years, during which time government funds continued to be paid to Fort Wayne traders for such items as rations, agricultural implements, and clothing for the Miami youth who were sent to the Choctaw Academy in Kentucky. The annual annuity payments, special treaty obligations, and expenses of the subagency reached $100,000 during some years.[72]

The complete story of the final years of the Miami in Indiana and their forced removal in 1846 may be found in the correspondence of the Office of Indian Affairs in Washington. Only the highlights can be touched on here. Samuel Milroy of Delphi was appointed subagent for the Miami in April, 1839, replacing John T. Douglass; he was also to be superintendent of the Miami emigration when the time arrived.[73] Milroy had served his state in many capacities during his long residence which dated back to territorial days, but he was now almost sixty and it was soon discovered that he had too hasty a temper to organize the Indians for removal.

In June, 1841, the officials in Washington were happy to have Allen Hamilton take over the subagency. His experience in Indian affairs it was felt would be a valuable asset in ob-

[71] *Ibid.*, 26 Congress, 1 session, No. 164, p. 5.

[72] See, for example, T. Hartley Crawford to Samuel Milroy, August 13 and October 9, 1840, in Indian Office Letter Book, 29:126-27, 305, National Archives, Washington, D. C., microfilm in Indiana State Library.

[73] Joel R. Poinsett, Secretary of War, to Samuel Milroy, Delphi, April 17, 1839, and T. Hartley Crawford, commissioner of Indian Affairs, to Milroy, May 13, 1839, in Indian Office Letter Book, 26:244, 296-97.

taining the assent of the Indians to remove from the state.[74] One of his first duties was to aid the new commission appointed in 1841 to investigate the claims under the 1840 treaty. These claims were discovered to amount to $185,281 for the two years between the 1838 and 1840 treaties and $117,308 from the time the latter treaty was signed until it was ratified by the United States Senate with amendments.[75]

By 1844 the Indian office was beginning to bring pressure on the subagent to prepare the Indians for removal. "This is a measure that the President and Secretary of War have much at heart—and which cannot be permitted to go long unexecuted."[76] In May of that year the bid of Thomas Dowling, of Terre Haute, was accepted for removing the Miami and "subsisting" them for a year in their new home. The amount stipulated in the contract was apparently $53,000.[77] Realizing that the traders would continue to harass the Indians with claims, Hamilton was instructed in August, 1844, that the annuity for that year would be the last that would be paid in Indiana. At a council held that fall, the chiefs and headmen pleaded for more time to allow those who had personal property to dispose of it; a delay until May, 1845, was granted.[78]

Before that time arrived, Hamilton had resigned the office of subagent.[79] Perhaps he envisioned further delay on the part of the Indians which would bring additional pressure from Washington. Samuel Milroy was reappointed in March, 1845, but died almost immediately after assuming his duties. The appointment was then tendered to Joseph Sinclear of Fort

[74] Crawford to Allen Hamilton, June 23, 1841.

[75] Crawford to Hamilton, September 28, 1842.

[76] Crawford to Hamilton, April 23 and 24, 1844.

[77] Crawford to Thomas Dowling, Terre Haute, July 14, 1844; William Medill to Alexis Coquillard, June 12, 1847.

[78] William Wilkins, Secretary of War, to Hamilton, August 8, 1844; Crawford to Hamilton, October 28, 1844.

[79] Hamilton to Crawford, February 10, 1845, Indian Office, Letters Received.

Wayne, a former representative from Allen County in the General Assembly.[80] The Indians had again refused in May to assemble for the migration, one reason being that they were dissatisfied with the lands allotted to the tribe west of the Mississippi. But the real reason was probably the Indian traders who were influencing them to hold out. The Indian Office had ruled in 1842 that any further debts would have to be paid by the individuals who contracted them instead of by the tribe as a whole. There were repeated attempts to get this decision changed but the government held firm and refused all appeals. They did, however, consent to pay the 1845 annuity in Indiana, but the payment was marked by violence, murders, and bloodshed. Topeah or Francis Lafontaine who had been selected as principal chief after the death of Richardville in 1841 requested that his family be permitted to remain in Indiana but this was refused.[81]

In February, 1846, Sinclear received the additional appointment of superintendent of the migration which it was hoped would at last get started; he was to work under Dowling who still held the main contract. From the middle of April until October Sinclear devoted his full time trying to collect and organize the Indians for removal. On August 19 he reported that up to that time he had been unsuccessful; the Indians were persisting in their refusal to leave.[82] The receipt of this news in Washington brought forth a lengthy recital of the liberality of the government in dealing with the Miami ("their

[80] Crawford to Milroy, March 5, 1845; Crawford to Joseph Sinclear, June 5, 1845.

[81] Crawford to Sinclear, August 11, 1845; William Medill to George W. Ewing, November 3, 1845; Medill to Sinclear, January 13, 1846; Medill to Lafontaine and other chiefs, July 1, 1846. Metocinyah's band and Chief Richardville's family were permitted to remain in Indiana by the terms of the 1838 and 1840 treaties while a special act of Congress permitted the family of Frances Slocum to remain. U.S. *Statutes at Large,* 6:942.

[82] William Medill to Sinclear, February 19, March 17, August 19, 1846; Medill to Dowling, February 19, 1846.

annuities averaged $92 for every man, woman, and child in the tribe") in contrast to the bad faith which they were displaying. Still they recognized that the course taken by the tribesmen was not so much their own choice as that of claimants and other white persons who were able to control the chiefs. Sinclear was instructed to make one more appeal to them and if that failed he was to call one or two companies of Fort Wayne militia to force removal; it was hoped that the mere presence of the troops would bring a compliance of the Indians.[83] By October 1 the Indians had at last agreed to leave peaceably and a few days later all but about thirty were placed on boats and traveled by way of the Wabash and Erie Canal to Defiance where they were transferred to the Miami Extension Canal for the trip to Cincinnati which they reached on October 12. There they boarded river boats and continued to St. Louis where they arrived on October 21. Alexis Coquillard and Father Benoit accompanied them at least part of the way. The number of men, women, and children who made up the migrating party numbered approximately 325. The thirty who were allowed to remain to harvest the crops were to be sent on to join the main party the following year.[84]

Thomas H. Harvey, Indian agent at St. Louis, had been alerted as to the arrival of the Miami and warned that their creditors would probably attempt to obtain some of their annuities. "If this happens the Indians will be left without resources. . . . Their very existence may be involved. If the money goes into the hands of their creditors they will be left destitute and helpless." In spite of this warning and the delay in payment of the annuities until early March of 1847, and presumably after they had reached their final destination in

[83] Medill to Sinclear, September 7 and 11, 1846. The Fort Wayne militia was not used; instead, the United States Adjutant General ordered Federal troops to be sent from Cincinnati on September 11.

[84] Medill to Sinclear, October 16, 1846; Sinclear to Medill, September 29, October 1, 5, 6, 10, 12, 14, 21, 24, 1846, February 8, 1847.

eastern Kansas, the Indiana creditors who had followed them were on hand and took the largest share of the annuity payment. After spending the winter in the West Lafontaine and some of his band set out to return to Indiana but the Chief died at Lafayette on April 13, 1847, before reaching his former home. Those who had accompanied him continued on to Miami County where they were reported to be in destitute condition, wanderers in a land where they were no longer wanted.[85]

John Dawson of Fort Wayne who witnessed the departure of the Miami in the fall of 1846 wrote: "Well I remember the sober, saddened faces, the profusion of tears, as I saw them hug to their bosoms a litle handful of earth which they had gathered from the graves of their dead kindred . . . as the canal boat that bore them to the Ohio river loosed her moorings, many a bystander was moved to tears at the evidences of grief he saw before him."[86]

In all probability the average bystander at Fort Wayne that summer day looked upon the final departure of the Indians with mixed emotions. The Indian and fur trade had given the community its earliest economy. Even during the recent years the Fort Wayne citizen had used this trade to recover from financial embarrassments resulting from the speculation preceding 1837, but the Indian was no longer wanted by a maturing agricultural society nor by a town reaching its adolescence and depending more and more on the white farmer. In the same issue of the *Sentinel* which took note of the departure of the Miami from Fort Wayne, an article called attention to the fact that settlers were already flocking into the area of the Miami Reserve.[87]

[85] Medill to Thomas H. Harvey, St. Louis, November 3, 1846, May 5, 1847; Arthur L. Bodurtha (ed.), *History of Miami County Indiana* (2 vols. Chicago and New York, 1914), 1:32.

[86] Griswold, *Pictorial History of Fort Wayne,* 1:379.

[87] Fort Wayne *Sentinel,* October 10, 1846.

A fair-minded critic of this episode would write his observations in a later day.

> Long ago I formed the opinion that the tribes . . . were incapable of being civilized, by which I mean, incapable of living by manual labor upon land or in shops . . . they have been doomed to pass away with the game upon which they mainly subsisted. . . . Territory sufficient to support a thousand Indians by hunting and fishing, would furnish homes for hundreds of thousands of industrious white men. . . . As a race they will soon disappear, leaving no reliable record even of their own existence. While this is to be their fate, there is cause for national humiliation in the fact that their disappearance has been hastened by the vices, the cupidity, the injustice, the inhumanity of a people claiming to be Christians.[88]

Coupled with the changes occurring in industry and commerce during the period between 1832 and 1840 was the development of the land in and about Fort Wayne. Heavy land speculation coincided with the beginning of the canal's construction. Previous to March 12, 1832, the date when Colonel John Spencer succeeded Jonathan McCarty as receiver of public moneys at the government land office at Fort Wayne, there had been 1,143 entries and the total receipts amounted to about $100,000.[89] In the mid-thirties the sales increased enormously. Since this was a period of wild speculation throughout the greater part of the United States, one might expect that this increase in the sale of land at Fort Wayne was not above the average. However, the building of the canal motivated many to purchase in this vicinity particularly, so much so that in 1836, for example, the land office at Fort Wayne ranked third highest in the nation in the number of acres sold (1,294,357) and money received $1,620,617.34).[90] In Indiana during this year the Fort Wayne office sold over twice as much land as the next highest office, Vincennes. Although there was a definite decline in sales in 1837, the Fort Wayne office still reported

[88] McCulloch, *Men and Measures of Half a Century,* 102-3.

[89] Register of Receipts, Fort Wayne Land Office, 1823-1836.

[90] U. S. *House Executive Documents,* 25 Congress, 2 session, No. 23, pp. 11-14.

receipts for the first three quarters more than equaling the combined figures of the next two highest Indiana offices, Vincennes and Jeffersonville.[91]

The craze for land buying hit its peak during the years 1835, 1836, and 1837. Joseph H. McMaken who kept a public tavern at Fort Wayne during these years testified in 1844:

> that such was the continuous rush of the people from all parts of the whole confederated government to said place [Fort Wayne] with the view of entering the public lands, that his house, and such rooms and apartments as he could procure from his neighbors, were filled with his guests; and so numerous was the crowd, that he had to lodge large numbers of his guests on the hay in the stable; and that the throng was as great with the other taverns in said place, nay, every private house within the range of six miles around said place, that would, or could, be induced to keep travelers for money, was filled. That the country was then new—the accommodations limited—and the demand being great, made the prices high. That the vast crowds of land buyers and speculators seemed to fill the village and cover the wilderness in this section of the country. They made complaints about the slow manner in which business was done in the land office and even went so far as to charge that there was a combination between the tavern keepers and the officers of the land office, that they should be tardy in their business in said office, that the strangers might be detained at said place for the benefit of the tavern-keepers.[92]

This land speculation of the thirties undoubtedly contributed to the increasing value of the real estate in and about the town. The price of the lots laid out in the original plat had gone up considerably since 1823 when Barr and McCorkle paid $26.00 an acre for 109 acres. As early as 1828 Hamilton paid $200 to the original purchasers for one lot.[93] However, by

[91] *Ibid.*, 17. By this date much of the lands in the Vincennes, Jeffersonville, Crawfordsville, and Indianapolis land districts had been sold.

[92] *Letter to Col. John Spencer*, 35-36.

[93] Memo, December 1, 1828, Allen Hamilton Papers, Indiana State Library. The lots varied in size. The corner lot at Columbia and Calhoun streets, 60x140 feet, with buildings on it of little value, was sold at auction in 1842 for almost $6,000. Fort Wayne *Sentinel*, February 12, 1842.

1830 the price of lots had declined, and Henry Rudisill had advised Barr "to defer selling for a short time until we hear the fate of the Canal [bill] if it should pass lots will be brisk sale [*sic*]."[94] It was apparent to Rudisill, nevertheless, that the land was potentially valuable, as he felt that the assessment of the town's lots at 4 per cent would be very high under normal conditions.[95] Rudisill was correct, for the real increase in land values commenced with the beginning of canal construction and picked up steadily until the Panic of 1837. In October, 1832, W. G. Ewing sold three lots in the Ewing addition which was not yet even developed. One of these sold for $400, while the other two brought $250 each.[96] The following year he sold a half lot for $800.[97] Yet a few months later a comparable lot in Goshen, Indiana, brought the Ewings only $151.[98] By 1838 Allen County stood at the head of the tax list in the state from the standpoint of average valuation, $16 per acre. This was twice as high as most counties, four times as high as many and sixteen times as high as one of them. It is evident that the canal potentialities played a major role in these figures. As the state internal improvements program collapsed, at least temporarily after 1839, the evaluation of Allen County's land declined also. That year it dropped to an average of $8.00 per acre and in 1841 to $4.00.[99]

As indicated previously, land hunger had been one of the chief characteristics of the early traders in the Fort Wayne area. Samuel Hanna, Hamilton, Taber, and the Ewing brothers were among the largest purchasers of land in northern Indi-

[94] Henry Rudisill to John T. Barr, January 2, 1830, Rudisill Letterbook.

[95] *Ibid.*

[96] Memo in W. G. Ewing's hand, October 17-18, 1832, Ewing Papers.

[97] W. G. Ewing to G. W. Ewing, April 13, 1833, Ewing Papers.

[98] Memo, October 31, 1833, Ewing Papers.

[99] Fort Wayne *Sentinel,* January 8, 1841; State Auditor's reports in Indiana *Documentary Journal,* 1838-39, no. 12, p. 172; 1840-41, no. 3, p. 38; 1841-42, pt. 2, no. 4, p. 21. In 1837 the valuation was $26. *Ibid.,* 1837-38, no. 26.

ana.[100] All these men were Fort Wayne residents except G. W. Ewing who had moved by that date to Logansport. They had speculated for choice farm land, town sites, power sites, and of course the canal lands which became valuable as a result of its construction. In general the Fort Wayne merchant–landowner did not speculate excessively in farm sites; they could not wait until the frontiersman, who was usually poor, would be able to pay higher prices. Furthermore as the Indian trade declined, the Fort Wayne merchant needed white customers for his goods. Consequently, as it has been shown regarding the traders of northern Indiana, they "could not place capital in farm acreage, while mills, canals, boats and railroads offered greater possibilities."[101] This is not to deny that there was speculation in farm lands during the 1830s. The crowds of land buyers who descended upon the government office in the mid-thirties were not all settlers. We may conclude that many of these men were eastern speculators or acted for eastern interests in their buying. As late as 1842 M. S. Wines, representing Allen County in the state legislature, voted for a bill assessing one and one-fourth cents on each acre of land, without regard to improvements, for the purpose of constructing roads in northern Indiana. He pointed out that there were more acres of taxable land in Allen County than any other county, but three-fourths of this land was unoccupied and unimproved, and the owners of a good deal of it lived in other states.[102] Two years later W. G. Ewing suggested that an agency be established at Fort Wayne to handle the affairs of the many Easterners who held property in and about the town.[103] It is

[100] Anson, Fur Traders in Northern Indiana, 204; *John Tipton Papers,* 1:32.

[101] Anson, Fur Traders in Northern Indiana, 203.

[102] Marshall S. Wines to his Constituents, February 22, 1842, Fort Wayne *Sentinel,* February 26, 1842, reprinted in *Messages and Papers relating to the Administration of Samuel Bigger, Governor of Indiana, 1840-1843 (Indiana Historical Collections,* Vol. 44, Indianapolis, 1964), 436.

[103] T. K. Brackenridge to W. G. Ewing, February 3, 1844, Ewing Papers.

to be remembered that as early as 1829 Henry Rudisill had been sent to Fort Wayne to safeguard the interests of John Barr and promote the sale of his employer's land. The Baltimore firm of Barr and Campbell was engaged in many merchandising enterprises throughout the West but especially in Ohio and Pennsylvania. It is clear from Rudisill's letters that Barr had speculated in the Fort Wayne land not only to profit from the later sale of the real estate but also to develop the area for the sake of trade.[104] Probably the first objective was the primary one, but Barr should be considered as a merchant-financier-speculator rather than an out-and-out land speculator. Like the later railroad companies, his firm hoped to profit both from the selling of the land and selling of its services to the settlers.

The merchant-speculator from Fort Wayne did own land near the town which was valuable for farming and was used for such at least until other more profitable projects became worthwhile. For this reason merchants like Hamilton and Hanna entered into many working agreements with pioneer farmers respecting the temporary use of their land. In some instances the farmer would clear the land in return for which he would secure the timber and the right to harvest the first year's crop. Thereafter, he owed one third of the crop to the owner. Many contracts called for the merchant to furnish the basic tools—axe, spade, hoe, and plow in return for which the profits were divided equally between landowner and farmer.[105] In these instances there existed a type of pioneer

[104] Rudisill to Barr, January 2, 8, 16, February 20, March 6, 1830, Rudisill Letterbook.

[105] Agreement between David Gibb, farmer, and Allen Hamilton, landowner, September 30, 1835; and agreement between Comparet and Coquillard, landowners, and Mahlon Clark, farmer, March 17, 1827, Allen Hamilton Papers, Indiana State Library. There are many such contracts in the Hamilton, Ewing, and Samuel Hanna Papers, both in the Indiana State Library and in the Fort Wayne—Allen County Historical Museum.

sharecropping which put the land under cultivation and at the same time enabled the farmer to secure funds for a later land purchase of his own.

During the period of rapid expansion and, one might add, fearless speculation, four new additions were joined to the town of Fort Wayne. The first addition to the original plat of Barr and McCorkle was the "County Addition," consisting of seventy lots, which was made up from part of the site of the old fort and other government buildings. This tract came under the ownership of the county as a result of the act of Congress of May 31, 1830, authorizing the Allen County commissioners to enter at the minimum price as much of the forty-acre government reserve as did not come under the canal grant of 1827. It was recorded in August, 1833, its position being immediately east of and adjoining the original plat.[106] In 1835 Cyrus Taber purchased the remaining twenty acres of the old fort site and added a new area of forty lots to the town. It appears from a letter written by Tipton to Allen Hamilton and Cyrus Taber in 1836 that these men each had a third interest in Taber's addition.[107]

As land values around Fort Wayne started to skyrocket in 1835, and as the town seemed to be spreading south and east down the St. Mary's River in the direction of Hanna's lands instead of westward towards their land, the Ewing heirs agreed upon the immediate sale of part of their father's estate.[108] W. G. Ewing expressed the hope that William Rockhill would

[106] U. S. *Statutes at Large,* 6:448; Allen County Commissioners' Record, Vol. A, Allen County Courthouse.

[107] Tipton to Allen Hamilton and Cyrus Taber, January 6, 1836, *John Tipton Papers,* 3:201-2. For a description of the area covered, see Robertson (ed.), *History of the Maumee River Basin,* 2;94, and the map, page 110, in the present volume.

[108] W. G. Ewing to William Hood, August 31, 1835, Miscellaneous Papers, Fort Wayne—Allen County Historical Museum; Sophia Hood to W. G. Ewing, September 9, 1835, and G. W. Ewing to Charles and W. G. Ewing, September 17, 1835, Ewing Papers, Indiana State Library.

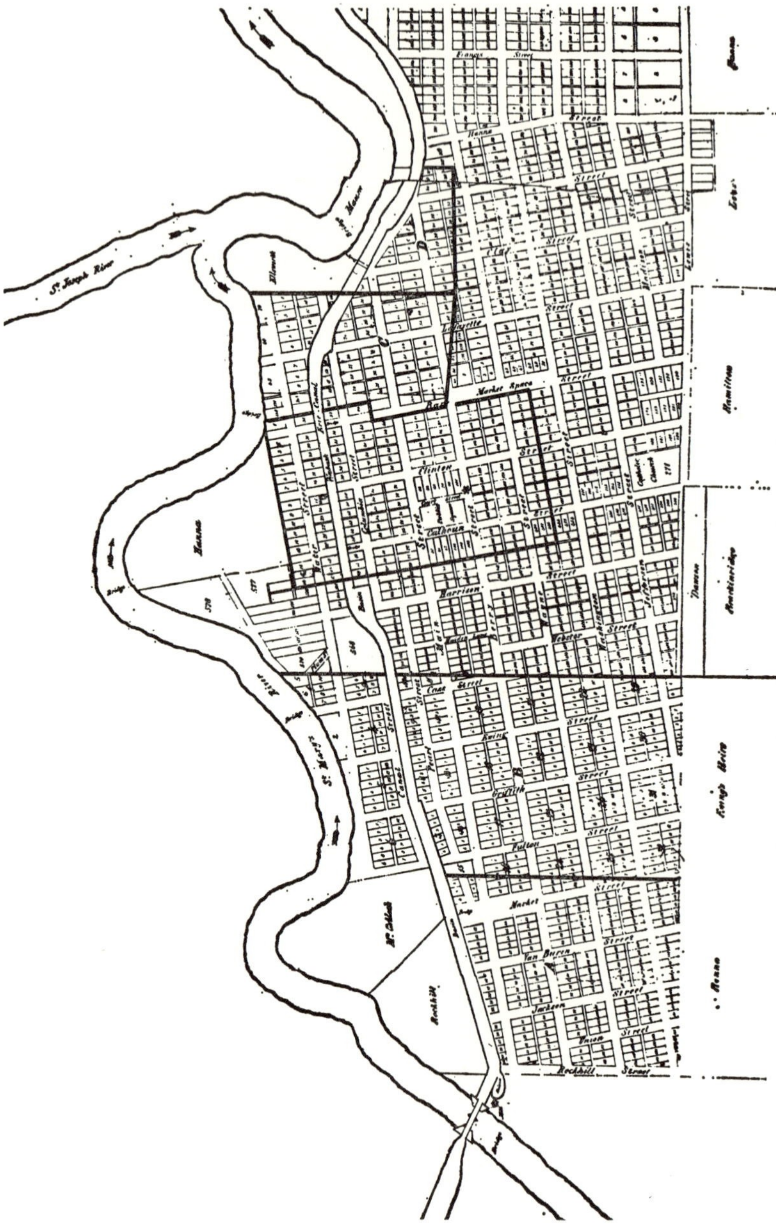

TOWN PLAT OF FORT WAYNE IN 1842

Key: A. Rockhill addition, 1839; B. Ewing addition, 1835; C. County addition, 1833; D. Taber addition, 1835; The balance is the Old Plat (1824) and Hanna's addition (1837)

then assist in bringing the town westward by laying off his land for sale. The Ewings decided to make no private sales but to auction off at least one half of the lots after they had been surveyed. G. W. Ewing thought that the completion of the first section of the canal and the excitement of the occasion would carry the sale successfully.[109] Consequently, in October, 1835, the Ewings advertised the sale of lots in their addition to Fort Wayne. These advertisements were carried in the Fort Wayne *Sentinel,* the Indianapolis *Indiana Journal,* the *Liberty Hall and Cincinnati Gazette,* the Detroit *Journal,* the Buffalo *Journal,* the Piqua *Inquirer,* and the *Miami of the Lakes,* as well as in three hundred handbills distributed throughout the tri-state area.[110] As planned the Ewing addition contained thirty-four blocks or fractional blocks of two hundred and seventy-eight lots. Through it, three streets—Cass, Ewing and Fulton—ran north and south, while Jefferson, Washington, Wayne, Berry, Main, and Pearl streets were continued west from the original plat. Lewis, the first street south of Jefferson, was also added to the town. To promote further the westward growth of the town, the Ewings entered into an agreement with William Rockhill and others to build a hotel in their section. Apparently, however, the Ewings were not satisfied with the final results of the sale. W. G. Ewing complained that the trustees had "bungled" by allowing a few private sales before the auction, and this served to "the advantage of Hanna."[111] Undoubtedly the Ewings profited from their real estate dealings in the Fort Wayne area, but not to the same extent that they did elsewhere. By 1840, they estimated the value of their

[109] G. W. Ewing to Charles and W. G. Ewing, September 17, 1835, Ewing Papers.

[110] Printed broadside advertising the sale of lots from the Alexander Ewing estate, and draft for advertisement in various newspapers, in Ewing Papers, Indiana State Library.

[111] W. G. Ewing to Alexander H. Ewing, Cincinnati, April 10, 1837, Ewing Papers.

Indiana land (approximately 15½ sections) to be $250,000, and by 1841, they held 1,388 acres of canal lands.[112] However, a decade later, embittered by the fact that the land values around Fort Wayne did not increase to the same extent as did those of St. Louis, W. G. Ewing acidly wrote, "How foolish of me to have stayed in that village of the Swamps. . . . The same exertions I have made there would have given us a million Dollars in St. Louis.[113] Shrewd masters of business, the Ewings evidently learned their early lessons well at Fort Wayne, for they were still to reap handsome profits from their real estate dealings in Chicago and St. Louis in the decade of the 1850s.[114]

Generally, Samuel Hanna did not use the Ewing tactics in land speculations. There is no evidence that he either bought or sold hurriedly.[115] However, in May, 1837, Hanna concluded that the time was ripe for the laying out of his first addition to Fort Wayne, containing 229 lots.[116] The greater part of this addition was made up from the 189.16 acres which he had purchased from the remaining interest of Barr's mortgaged estate. In laying out the new tract, Hanna offered to donate to the town sufficient lots on Barr Street to provide for the building of a city hall and a town market. He was undoubtedly looking forward to the day when the town would be incorporated as a city—a day in fact that was not too far distant—and hoped by this means to keep the center of the city within

[112] *John Tipton Papers,* 1:32. Also see Memorandum, 1842-44, of lands owned by the firm of W. G. and G. W. Ewing or in partnership with the Hamilton and Taber company, and the summary of real estate values made November 8, 1840, Ewing Papers.

[113] W. G. Ewing to G. W. Ewing, August 8, 1850, Ewing Papers.

[114] McCulloch, *Men and Measures of Half a Century,* 105-6.

[115] Samuel Hanna still held lots in South Bend, Indiana, as late as 1852, and in 1862 he held enough property in and about Fort Wayne to enable him to use it as collateral for $183,000 of railroad stock. Anson, Fur Traders in Northern Indiana, 205.

[116] See map on page 110.

his plat. The town market, which according to the provisions of the grant had to be constructed within a year, was erected rapidly. This structure was patterned after the Philadelphia market, although it was considerably smaller. Farmers were permitted to rent stalls for $5.00 a year, thus providing a merchandising outlet for their surplus products.[117] As a result of the Panic of 1837, many of the buyers of Hanna's land were unable to pay when the liabilities fell due. Hanna realized, however, that it was not in his interest nor that of the town to foreclose on these debtors, and although for a time he suffered some difficulty in making his own payments to the state and his eastern creditors, his policy eventually proved advantageous for all concerned.

Despite the economic situation following 1837, the area of Fort Wayne continued to expand in the last years of the decade, though often this expansion was more on paper than in wood or brick. In 1839, for example, William Rockhill laid out the final addition before the incorporation of the city the following year. The Rockhill addition contained 182 lots and extended westward beyond Broadway and the new Ewing section. As might be expected, the sale of the lots was relatively slow.

All the various additions to Fort Wayne made during the 1830s followed the customary gridiron plan, the lots being surveyed and laid out in a rectangular fashion. In this respect, Fort Wayne followed the typical pattern of the western cities. According to Richard C. Wade, the western communities

[117] Later this picturesque market was extended along Barr Street and after various improvements throughout the years gave way to modern change only in 1957. Throughout the one hundred and twenty years of its existence, it provided a source of income for the area farmers.

Barr mortgaged his entire 189.16 acres in May, 1833, to Stephen Gerard of Philadelphia. Before the mortgage was paid, Barr put up the mortgaged property as collateral to secure a loan from William Barr, who sold the tract the following year to John Ferguson. Ferguson paid off the mortgage held by Gerard and sold the entire tract in 1836 to Samuel Hanna.

borrowed the basic grid pattern from the original plat of Philadelphia.[118] This may very well be true, however, it must be remembered they were also following the familiar rectangular pattern established for surveying and selling of land according to the Ordinance of 1785. Finally the practical approach of the western mind would have devised in all probability such a pattern, for as Lewis Mumford has pointed out:

> Although the gridiron plan had the same relation to natural conditions and fundamental social needs as a paper constitution has to the living customs of a people, the simplicity of the gridiron plan won the heart of the pioneer. Its rectangular blocks formed parcels of land which he could sell by the front foot and gamble with as easily as if he were playing cards, and deeds of transfer could be drawn up hastily with the same formula for each plot; moreover, the least competent surveyor, without thought or knowledge, could project the growth of New Eden's streets . . . into an interminable future . . . the engineer was the willing servant of the land monopolist . . . he provided a frame for the architect—a frame in which we still struggle today—where site-value counted for everything, and sight-value was not even an afterthought.[119]

On March 6, 1838, John Dawson, a young man who was destined to follow a vigorous career of lawyer, newspaper editor, and politician,[120] approached Fort Wayne for the first time. Dawson came by way of the "New Piqua Road" (so called to distinguish it from the "Old Piqua Road" which was constructed by General Wayne and was better known as "Wayne Trace"). The new road "led out from Calhoun street directly south one mile, then in a southeasterly direction, and up the north side of the St. Mary's River." A few miles outside of Fort Wayne, Dawson passed a small settlement of German Catholics

[118] Richard C. Wade, "Urban Life in Western America, 1790-1830," in *American Historical Review,* 64 (1958-59):21.

[119] Lewis Mumford, *Sticks and Stones. A Study of American Architecture and Civilization* (New York, 1924), 85.

[120] Dawson, not yet eighteen years old, was to study law at Fort Wayne and Transylvania College in Kentucky. After returning to Fort Wayne in 1853 he became the owner and editor of the *Dawson Times* and in 1861 was appointed by Lincoln as governor of Utah.

and an occasional settler's cabin. His first glimpse of Fort Wayne was from an elevated part of the road, about 120 rods south of the present Pennsylvania Railroad depot, at which point he could see the spire of the old courthouse, and that of the old Catholic Church which stood where the Cathedral now is located. All other buildings were hidden from view.[121]

With the exception of two frame houses, only a few cabins could be seen south of Lewis Street. Hanna's addition, beginning at Lewis and running north to Wayne Street, had only one building in its western part and a half dozen more in its eastern section. This area had been cleared but high stumps still interrupted traffic along its unpretentious wagon roads. To the west, in Ewing's addition, "the few houses were in the thicket." The largest was the old home of Alexander Ewing. There was also an unfinished Methodist church. Rockhill's addition did not exist yet in 1838, but at the time was simply a cultivated field with Rockhill's home standing on the south bank of the canal.[122]

Actually, the major part of the town "was then almost entirely embraced in the space occupied by the Old Plot . . . laid off by Barr and McCorkle . . . , the 'County Addition' . . . and . . . Taber's Addition." Although there were a few stores west of Calhoun Street, most of the town's business took place on Columbia Street between Calhoun and Barr. Along these two blocks were the firms of Hamilton and Taber, Hanna and Barnett, Comparet and Colerick, F. D. Lasselle, J. B. Richardville, the Edsalls, Bourie, and the Ewings, as well as a number of smaller shops. Here also was located the branch of the State Bank, the Post Office, a number of hotels (including Washington Hall, the model hotel of northern Indiana), and a large brick building which served as a courthouse, clerk's office, and as a center for the printing office and various law

[121] Dawson, *Charcoal Sketches of Old Times in Fort Wayne,* 7-8.
[122] *Ibid.,* 7-8, 10-12.

offices.[123] At the canal basin on Columbia Street was a boat-yard.

From this boat-yard the common road ran down along the canal and across the old Fort-ground, between the old well and the only building of the Fort then standing. . . . A broken pole stood in the centre of the parade ground.[124]

Standing on the parade grounds of the "old Fort" on the morning after his arrival, Dawson looked eastward up the Maumee,

locked up in ice for three-fourths of a mile. . . . To the north . . . the junction of the St. Mary's and St. Joseph was seen . . . the whole margin of the river was cleared of brush and trees, and the bottom land under good cultivation . . . at seed time.

The Maumee was then crossed at a ford which entered the river from the town side, just above the present bridge [Lakeside Bridge]. . . . Large stones stood prominently in the river, and offered much obstruction to travel. . . . The ground in the bend of the river St. Mary's was very nearly clear of undergrowth, and presented the appearance of a cultivated field. . . . Passing now up the St. Mary's from the Fort, [one could see] the French part of the town, then of log buildings. . . . It was at this point on the St. Mary's where the road crossed, and just above the crossing was where all the boats [coming down the river in the spring flood] landed. . . . The main road north from the town led out along Calhoun street, and crossed the St. Mary's on a wooden toll bridge. . . .[125]

This road was then called the Mongoquinong road. From it other roads, notably the Goshen road to the northwest, branched out in various directions. Facing westward from the site of the "old Fort," Dawson saw the county addition to the town. Its soil was very fertile, and it included the eastern end of Columbia and Main streets, hence was considered as potentially valuable. To the west of this area, between Lafayette and Barr streets were a number of wooden buildings, including the old large Council House built for the Indian agency. "On

[123] Dawson, *Charcoal Sketches of Old Times in Fort Wayne,* 10-11.

[124] *Ibid.,* 11.

[125] *Ibid.,* 13-15.

the north, fronting on Columbia Street, from Lafayette to the corner of Barr, was a row of shanties, mostly inhabited by Irish canallers." Another poor area was to be found fronting on the corner of Berry and Calhoun. Across from these shanties was the courthouse square. The courthouse was "a large two-story brick, but was never finished. It was so insecure . . . that it was not occupied with safety for court purposes. . . . The County jail and jailor's house stood on the southwest corner of the square." The jail was as insecure as the courthouse.[126] Throughout the town there were finer structures such as the home of Dr. Lewis Thompson, but the real period of more substantial building was yet to come.

> Thus it will be seen that the space bounded on the north by Water [Superior] street, east by Lafayette street, south by Wayne street, west by Harrison street—16 squares—constituted Fort Wayne as a wooden town, buildings of an inferior sort, unpainted, generally one story high, some of logs, more of frame work, five [actually a few more] of brick, the streets bad, many lots destroyed by standing water. . . .[127]

Yet, in 1840, the taxable value of real and personal property in the town was $502,268.[128]

> The Canal *was* [italics added] then in operation, and behind the buildings which front on Columbia street was a space between them and the water which was called 'the Dock', and there all the boats landed and received and discharged freight and passengers, and to 'the Dock' people resorted for pleasure and business. The boat-horn announced the arrival and departure of the packets, and was a sweet sound to us who were so locked in by swamps and distances.[129]

[126] Dawson, *Charcoal Sketches of Old Times in Fort Wayne,* 16-18. One man imprisoned for debt was seen regularly at night outside the jail. Fort Wayne *Sentinel,* September 10, 1842.

[127] Dawson, *Charcoal Sketches of Old Times in Fort Wayne,* 10.

[128] H. S. Knapp, *History of the Maumee Valley, Commencing with Its Occupation by the French in 1680* (Toledo, Ohio, 1872), 380.

[129] Dawson, *Charcoal Sketches of Old Times in Fort Wayne,* 15.

If by 1840 its projected avenues still encompassed swamps and wilderness, Fort Wayne's citizens had already established the frame for its growth during the next three generations.

> If the older cities of the seaboard were limited in their attempts to become metropolises by the fact that their downtown sections were originally laid out for villages, the villages of the middle west labored under just the opposite handicap; they had frequently acquired the framework of a metropolis before they had passed out of the physical state of a village. . . . That a city had any other purpose than to attract trade, to increase land values, and to grow is something that, if it uneasily entered the mind of an occasional Whitman, never exercised any hold upon the mind of the majority of our countrymen. For them, the place where the great city stands *is* the place of stretched wharves and markets . . . that, and nothing else.[130]

[130] Mumford, *Sticks and Stones,* 87. After visiting various towns in Indiana, including Fort Wayne, in 1851, J. Richard Beste, an English traveler, wrote as follows concerning Hoosier towns: "The plan having been first laid out and the boundaries of the township being defined, buildings diverge from the core, and, here and there, they dot the line of the future streets, until they lose themselves in the forest . . . or the cultivated land. As the vacancies on each side of the streets are filled up, side pavements are made, trees are planted to overshadow them, the centre of the street is paved. . . . The plan of the rising town . . . [is] definitively settled." J. Richard Beste, *The Wabash: or Adventures of an English Gentleman's Family in the Interior of America* (2 vols. London, 1855), 1:264.

CHAPTER VI

POLITICAL GROWTH AND URBAN PROBLEMS OF A WESTERN TOWN

The cholera . . . fell like a bomb shell . . . and scattered death.

In the previous chapters we have seen how the increasing population of Fort Wayne mirrored itself in a corresponding economic and industrial development. It now must be shown how well Fort Wayne kept pace politically and socially with the above developments.

It was becoming apparent by the latter part of 1839 that the rapid growth of the town in the previous decade had created new conditions with which Fort Wayne's primitive form of municipal government was unable to cope. Since 1829 when the town was incorporated, a board of trustees, elected annually, had managed the affairs of the community. Most of the time the trustees were too busy to give much attention to their official duties. In fact they kept virtually no financial records, and the legality of many of their decisions was often questioned.[1] In the years 1838 and 1839, the trustees took no action to collect delinquent taxes and, therefore, permitted about one half of their revenue to escape them.[2] Apart from the market, erected immediately under the terms of Hanna's donation, the trustees had not acquired or constructed any public building. Public improvements had to be taken care of by a more

[1] Fort Wayne *Sentinel,* February 19, 1842.

[2] Records of the Common Council, April 7, 1840, p. 35. The records of the Council for the years 1840-49, together with the original City Charter, have been bound and preserved in the City Clerk's Office, City Hall, under the somewhat misleading title, "City Charter of Fort Wayne, City of Fort Wayne from February 22, 1840 to October 15, 1849."

responsible and more responsive governmental system. The streets were in need of repair, drainage had to be improved, and after the building of the canal, docks and wharves had to be maintained. The merchants also desired better municipal ordinances governing trade within the town.

Agitation for a change in government mounted until the attorney Franklin P. Randall was charged with the duty of preparing a charter for the incorporation of the City of Fort Wayne. This was approved by the state legislature on February 22, 1840, and was adopted by the citizens of Fort Wayne on March 2 by a vote of 116 to 53.[3] In almost every respect the charter was very carefully written, and containing forty-six sections was sufficiently detailed. It provided for the usual type of city government—a mayor to be elected triennially, and a Common Council composed of six aldermen to be elected annually. While the mayor served as president of the Common Council, he could vote only in the case of a tie vote in the Council. In addition to his administrative duties, the mayor also served as a justice of the peace and judicial officer who had "exclusive original jurisdiction in all cases for the violation of the ordinances of said city. . . ."[4] Unlike earlier charters for many western cities,[5] there were no property qualifications for holding office in Fort Wayne. There was not as yet complete democracy respecting the right to vote, however, since to be eligible to participate in municipal elections one had to be a municipal taxpayer. In addition, of course, the voter had to be

[3] The original charter as well as the "Certificate of the Charter Election" are to be found in "City Charter of Fort Wayne." The charter has been copied verbatim from the original manuscript and printed in the *Old Fort News,* 10: no. 3 (September, 1946). This was a special charter in that it applied to only one city in the state, Fort Wayne.

[4] "Charter of the City of Fort Wayne," in *Old Fort News,* 10:no. 3:6.

[5] For a discussion of property qualifications for officeholding in western cities before 1830, see Richard C. Wade, *The Urban Frontier. The Rise of Western Cities* (Harvard University Press, 1959), 74.

a citizen of the United States of the age of twenty-one years and a resident of Fort Wayne for at least six months prior to the election.

An indication of the importance of trade and agriculture to the city may be seen from the list of officials subject to appointment by the Common Council; "one recorder, one attorney, one or more assessors, one treasurer, one collector, one street commissioner, one high constable, one or more police constables, one clerk of the market, one or more measurers of grain, lumber, wood, coal and lime, a flour inspector, a gauger, a sealer of weights and measures, a weigher of hay, a scavinger, and a common crier or bell man."[6]

It has been stated concerning the towns of the Old Northwest that "The [state] legislatures, representing rural interests and generally suspicious of towns, responded [to the town's need for authority] with charters bestowing narrow grants of power which barely met current needs and failed to allow for expansion."[7] Respecting Fort Wayne's charter of 1840, this assertion is only partially correct. The powers granted under the charter to the municipal government were sufficient for the needs of the city at the time. If at a later date these powers proved insufficient for an expanding population, the failure seemed to be due more to a lack of foresight than anything else, since the Indiana legislature had approved all forty-five regulatory powers assigned to the Fort Wayne Common Council by the original draft of the charter.[8] Furthermore, the Council was given the power to "make, publish, ordain, amend and repeal all such ordinances, by-laws and police regulations not contrary to the laws of this State for the good government and order of the City and the trade and commerce thereof as

[6] "Charter of the City of Fort Wayne," in *Old Fort News,* 10:no. 3:5-6.

[7] Richard C. Wade, "Urban Life in Western America, 1790-1830," in *The American Historical Review,* 64 (1958-59):19.

[8] See Appendix.

may be necessary to carry into effect the powers given to said Council by this act. . . ."[9]

While it appears as if the regulatory powers of the city's government were adequate for their day, at the same time the local authorities of Fort Wayne were severely limited in their power to tax. Section 35 of the Charter provided that real and personal property within the city could not be assessed at more than one half of 1 per cent. According to Richard Wade, who made a general study of the question, such a restriction was common in these decades. He asserts that although restrictions on towns varied, "the rate never surpassed one per cent of real and personal property, and in one instance Ohio set a limit at a fifth that figure."[10] It should be noted that in the case of Fort Wayne at least the limitation upon the rate of taxation was in the original draft of the charter written by and agreed to by the city fathers; consequently, it cannot be argued that the Indiana legislature imposed such restrictions. Rather it would seem that the merchants who generally controlled municipal policy did not desire a higher tax rate. In 1840 the Common Council established a tax rate of 20 cents per $100 of assessed property.[11] Ten years later the rate had dropped to 15 cents.[12] Never during the decade did the city tax rate equal the one half of 1 per cent permitted. It should not be concluded from the above, however, that the average Fort Wayne citizen was opposed to civic improvements which required some public expenditure. When property owners along Calhoun Street petitioned for wooden sidewalk curbings due to "the lowness of a considerable portion of the ground through which Calhoun Street passes, south of the Wabash and Erie

[9] "Charter of the City of Fort Wayne," in *Old Fort News,* 10: No. 3:12.

[10] Wade, *The Urban Frontier,* 76.

[11] Records of the Common Council, August 11, 1840, p. 53.

[12] Council Ordinance, passed May 6, 1850, published in Fort Wayne *Times,* May 9, 1850. In addition to this city tax on real and personal property, there was a city poll tax of one dollar.

Canal," noting that "the unimproved condition of the same renders it almost impassable for man or beast," they were simply asking for an improvement the like of which was requested by every section of the town.[13] At first such requests could be met in a fashion by the Council, although it was limited in its taxing powers. However, as the population grew and commerce on the canal brought about clogged conditions on the city's relatively poor streets, and as greater demands were made for fire protection, the city officials in 1849 sought to increase revenue by taxing unimproved real estate within the city limits. They were advised by their attorney, Joseph K. Edgerton, that assessments for public improvements in such areas as were undeveloped were not permitted under a strict interpretation of Article 35 of the charter and that the state courts almost invariably followed a strict interpretation of city charters.[14] Edgerton then advised that the charter of 1840 be amended in such a way as to give the city government broader powers of taxation. The efforts to carry out Edgerton's proposals would lead, as we shall see, to a series of amendments in the 1850s.

Apart from petitions urging street improvements and the like, the average Fort Wayne voter paid little attention to his city government throughout the first decade of its existence. The accusation made today that most Americans are relatively unconcerned with local politics seems to hold true for the nineteenth century townsmen as well. In fact, it appears as if the early Fort Wayne officials seldom gave their duties the attention required. Since their salaries were nominal, they had to attend first of all to their private affairs. From the year the city was incorporated in 1840 until 1846 four mayors held office in Fort Wayne. Of these four, three resigned before the

[13] Records of the Common Council, June 18, 1842, pp. 109-10. See also the entries for May 10, 1842, pp. 102-3, and April 5, 1841, p. 71.

[14] Records of the Common Council, April 7, 1849, pp. 440-46.

expiration of their terms in office. George W. Wood, the first mayor, resigned during his second year in office in order to devote his full time to the editorship of his newspaper. Joseph Morgan was elected to fill the vacancy and did so until the next regular election in 1843. In that year the Fort Wayne voters elected Henry Lotz, a canal contractor, as their mayor. However, after sixteen months in office, Lotz found that he could not attend the regular meetings of the Common Council since he was frequently absent from the city, and tendered his resignation. Even before the receipt of the resignation the Common Council had declared the office vacant because of "the neglect and absence of the nominal incumbent."[15] At a special election John M. Wallace was named to complete the unexpired term. Wallace was re-elected in the spring of 1846, but resigned shortly thereafter, in all probability because the office conflicted with his position as state representative in which he had been serving since 1845.

The lesser municipal offices also changed hands frequently. For example, the high constable was dismissed in 1841 for nonperformance of duty.[16] Scarcely a year went by without a resignation from the Common Council, beginning with the first from which two members resigned. In 1844 the *Sentinel* lamented the fact that although the city elections were to be held in three days there were as yet no candidates for office; the newspaper called for a civic meeting that same evening.[17] This particular crisis was resolved by the hastily called assembly, but the general apathy was still apparent a year later when the *Sentinel* again complained that there was no interest in the forthcoming city elections.[18] In the latter part of the decade political interest in holding municipal positions increased, at

[15] Records of the Common Council, July 1, 1844, p. 233.
[16] Fort Wayne *Sentinel,* September 18, 1841.
[17] *Ibid.,* March 2, 1844.
[18] *Ibid.,* March 1, 1845.

least to the extent that elected officials resigned or were removed from office less frequently. For a period of twenty years following the election of Dr. Merchant W. Huxford in May, 1846, to replace John M. Wallace, none of the men elected as mayor of Fort Wayne resigned.[19] Apparently as the city grew municipal politics appeared more attractive.

While the earlier municipal officeholders were respected citizens—usually professional men—they were not the most prominent citizens of Fort Wayne such as Samuel Hanna, Allen Hamilton, or W. G. Ewing. As we have seen, these early traders had taken a very active part in the formation of the county and then had moved into the state legislative bodies in order to achieve their objectives—a program for internal improvements and an improved banking system. While by the latter part of the 1830s most of these merchants had come to favor Henry Clay's policy of a "protective tariff," they apparently were less concerned with this portion of the "American System" than they were with the other parts of his proposed program.[20] Also, judging from the scene at Fort Wayne, until approximately 1836 state politics was based largely upon personalities and particular issues and not upon party affiliation. By 1840, however, most of the merchant class of Fort Wayne had moved into the Whig party.

Of the early merchant-traders at Fort Wayne only W. G. Ewing ran for national office, and he was defeated in his bid

[19] The resignation of Mayor James L. Worden in 1866 was occasioned by his desire to devote full time to law. Worden had served as a member of the Indiana Supreme Court from 1858 to 1865 when he was elected mayor. He was re-elected to the court in 1871 serving until 1882 when he resigned to become judge of the Allen County Superior Court.

[20] For an insight as to how the tariff was viewed by merchants of northern Indiana, see Tipton's speech in the United States Senate in 1837, *John Tipton Papers,* 3:375-80. On the whole there are few references to the tariff in Fort Wayne newspapers of the period, and even less in the letters of the merchants; on the other hand, the issues of internal improvements and banking were discussed quite frequently and vehemently.

for Congress in 1847 by the Democratic candidate. It is rather hard to explain why men such as Samuel Hanna and Allen Hamilton did not attempt to run for Congress. Both had ability and drive. Apparently they were either too concerned with their business affairs or believed that they did not have sufficient support from the rural electorate.[21] Although Hamilton was a member of the state constitutional convention in 1850 and a state senator in 1859 and 1861, he generally preferred to hold county offices, being elected to almost every position that Allen County could offer. W. G. Ewing, on the other hand, seemed to prefer state office, while Samuel Hanna was active on both county and state levels, holding a number of county positions and being elected frequently to the Indiana General Assembly.

The above merchants were not the only individuals from Fort Wayne to participate in state and county politics during this period. Other men, such as Marshall S. Wines, the canal contractor and landowner, William Rockhill, farmer and owner of the extensive Rockhill addition, Lewis G. Thompson, physician, and the lawyers, David Colerick, Charles Ewing, and Franklin Randall, all held state or county offices frequently. In 1842 a grand jury investigating the affairs of Allen County reported that "the situation of our County is truly distressing."[22]

Although in existence since 1824 and one of the wealthiest counties in the state, there was still not a courthouse or a jail worthy of the name. "What are termed county buildings . . . are a mass of worthless trash, unsafe and unfit [as a] depository

[21] Allen Hamilton also suffered the disadvantage of being an Irishman, although he was Protestant. See G. W. Ewing to Tipton, February 27, 1829, *John Tipton Papers,* 2:148. While Hanna never ran for Federal office, his commercial and land investments in northern Indiana made him a center of Whig influence. He was an important figure at state conventions and participated in the selection of party slates.

[22] Allen County Circuit Court, Civil Order Book, D :133, in Courthouse, Fort Wayne.

of the public records."[23] The courthouse, started in 1831 and finally completed in 1835 at a cost of some $3,000, was reported to be entirely unfit for public functions.[24] By 1842 the only place to hold court was a church and permission was soon to be refused by the congregation. As for the county jail, it "only served as an asylum for the felon, exhausted from hot pursuit, until he availed himself of a little repose and then made sure his escape."[25] Induced in part by the report of the grand jury but even more so by the fact that Fort Wayne was awakening to a sense of civic pride with the completion of the canal, the county commissioners authorized the construction of a new courthouse in 1842.[26] Although this building eventually proved unsatisfactory, its construction indicated a new interest in county affairs.

This political awakening of the early 1840s is shown also by the formal organization of the Democratic party in Allen County in 1842. Up until then the Democrats of the county had no formal organization; usually the more active members of the party, such as Henry Rudisill, Thomas Tigar, M. S. Wines, and William Rockhill, quietly named the party's candidates. In 1842, however, the farmers of the county demanded a greater voice in party decisions. Hence, at a meeting held at Peter Kiser's store, Judge James W. Borden was commissioned to draw up a plan of party organization. His plan, which was patterned after that of Berks County, Pennsylvania, was then accepted.[27]

[23] Fort Wayne *Sentinel*, September 10, 1842.

[24] Allen County Commissioners' Record, A:163, 165, 167, 182, 279; B:92, in Courthouse, Fort Wayne. During the January term, 1841, the court had to adjourn to the county clerk's office. *Ibid.*, B:92.

[25] Fort Wayne *Sentinel*, September 3, 1842.

[26] Allen County Commissioners' Record, B:207.

[27] Louis S. C. Schroeder, "History of the Democratic Party of Allen County," in *History of the Indiana Democracy, 1816-1916*, edited by John B. Stoll (Indianapolis, 1917), 523.

In the same manner the proceedings of the City Council became more orderly and more effective. The first Common Council seemed in fact little better than the town trustees insofar as it failed to keep any accurate financial records;[28] beginning in 1841 more accurate records were kept. The receipts of $1,697.85 were not only sufficient for the year's expenses but also enabled the Council to pay off the previous indebtedness of the town as far as this could be determined.[29] While the expenditures increased to $1,079.35 in the following year,[30] this amounted to less than $1.00 per person, as Fort Wayne had a population of approximately 1,500. Beyond the repair of streets and the draining of water the municipal services were extremely limited.

Since Fort Wayne was principally a commercial town, the local Council paid particular attention to mercantile requirements. One of the first decisions of the Common Council was to approve the building of a bridge across Columbia Street at the culvert.[31] In action taken the same day the Council also set aside funds for the improvement of streets and alleys. Other early ordinances regulated and licensed taverns, groceries, and coffeehouses, and required auctioneers, hawkers, and peddlers to obtain a city license.[32] Another law required "foreign merchants" to pay the treasury of Fort Wayne fifty cents on every hundred dollars valuation of their stocks in trade.[33] Special attention was paid to the improvement and regulation of the market, where by law all retail trade in meat and perishable

[28] Fort Wayne *Sentinel,* February 19, 1842.

[29] *Ibid.*

[30] *Ibid.,* February 18, 1843.

[31] Proceedings of the Common Council, April 5, 1841, Fort Wayne *Sentinel,* May 1, 1841.

[32] *Ibid.,* Revised Ordinances of the City of Fort Wayne, Fort Wayne *Sentinel,* August 13, 1842.

[33] Revised Ordinances of the City of Fort Wayne, *ibid.,* August 13, 1842; Records of the Common Council, March 3, 1842.

food had to be conducted.[34] In addition, in order to protect the public, the Council required the inspection of food, weights, and measures by appointed officials. Forestalling and regrating were also prohibited.[35] Professor Buley has stated, "One way of following the development of western towns from a cluster of houses . . . through the village-town stage, and . . . into a city, is by way of the town's ordinances."[36] This is evident if one follows those ordinances dealing with the physical welfare of Fort Wayne. Fire protection was first organized in 1833, when the trustees of the town responded to a petition of the citizens by authorizing the organization of a volunteer company equipped with hooks and ladders.[37] Six years later the trustees arranged for the erection of a firehouse.[38] After the incorporation of the city, volunteer companies still provided the manpower, but government participation and regulation increased. Fire wardens were appointed in 1842 and granted the right of inspection and the right to demand that corrective action be taken by property owners.[39] Additional ordinances legislated against other kinds of fire hazards and public money was used to purchase more equipment.[40] In 1841 the first fire company to be furnished with an engine and hose, the "Anthony Waynes," was organized. Four years later a new firehouse was constructed on city property, and shortly thereafter a second fire company, the "Hermans," composed of German immigrants, was created. From

[34] Revised Ordinances of the City of Fort Wayne, Fort Wayne *Sentinel,* August 13, 1842.

[35] *Ibid.*

[36] Buley, *The Old Northwest,* 1:236.

[37] The town furnished the hooks and ladders, but each citizen had to furnish his own fire bucket. Records of the Town Trustees, February 23, 1833, in Fort Wayne City Hall.

[38] *Ibid.,* November 3, 1839.

[39] Revised Ordinances of the City of Fort Wayne, Fort Wayne *Sentinel,* August 13, 1842.

[40] *Ibid.*; Records of the Common Council, May 2, 1842, p. 106.

that time on progress was steady although it was not until 1855 that a fire department was officially created as part of the municipal corporation. At that time a fire chief and two assistants were named to supervise the volunteer companies.[41] Throughout the 1830s and 1840s these volunteer organizations prevented any general conflagration in the city, although there were occasions when such a disaster was threatened.[42]

As in most western towns prior to 1860, the development of an adequate police force was much slower. In 1834 the town trustees established by ordinance "a watch . . . to consist of at least four judicious men . . . to guard the town from the ravages of fire and to prevent disorderly conduct within said corporation. . . ."[43] The watchmen were empowered to stop anyone found on the streets after 10:00 P.M., and in the event the individual had no reasonable excuse to place him in the "lockup." One wonders how effective this proved when the jail was so inadequate that its "walls have never had any terrors for the offender. . . ."[44]

Law enforcement for the most part was in the hands of the county sheriff and his deputies, the town marshal, and a few constables. With but minor improvements this remained the situation until 1863, when the first regularly organized police force was created. Several factors help to explain this slow development of police protection. Although statistics are totally lacking, certain evidence indicates there were very few major crimes of violence committed by white settlers within the vicinity of the town until after 1850. The Fort Wayne newspapers during this period seldom carried any accounts of local crime, even though they delighted in printing such

[41] *Charter, Amendments, and Ordinances of the City of Fort Wayne* (Fort Wayne, 1855), 27-29.

[42] Fort Wayne *Sentinel,* April 24, 1841; Fort Wayne *Times,* June 6, 1848.

[43] Griswold, *Pictorial History of Fort Wayne,* 1:317.

[44] Grand Jury Presentment, August Term, 1842, Fort Wayne *Sentinel,* September 10, 1842.

stories from other regions. It may be admitted that John Spencer, the receiver of government money at the land office, felt a guard was necessary for the specie being sent East since "the country was inhabited generally by a rude, and to some extent lawless people. . . ."[45] Still these shipments were never molested and there can be reasonable doubt that a single guard alone prevented this. Hugh McCulloch reported that money shipments to the Fort Wayne Branch Bank were never endangered and that he personally made the journey to Indianapolis for fifteen years "without the slightest fear of being robbed . . . and it was well known that I had money with me, and a good deal of it. . . ."[46] There was also a general feeling that a citizen of the town must to a great extent look after the protection of his own property. Finally, respectable citizens did not usually risk life, limb, or reputation by appearing on the streets late at night.

Of major concern to the municipal authorities was the prevention of plague. One of the earliest ordinances of Fort Wayne, passed in 1831, required all persons afflicted with smallpox to remain one quarter of a mile outside the town limits.[47] This was simply a duplication of similar town ordinances throughout the West, but coming when it did in 1831 may have served to emphasize the belief that Fort Wayne was prone to epidemics.[48] More positive action to prevent disease was the decision of the town trustees in 1836 "to drain the cellars and remove the nuisance of dead matter."[49] After the incorporation of the city the expense that occurred most frequently was that for the draining of water and filling of low places. Like most western canal and river towns, Fort Wayne's problem was rarely a lack of water but a lack of good water. The city

[45] *Letter of Col. John Spencer,* 8.
[46] McCulloch, *Men and Measures of Half a Century,* 122.
[47] Records of the Town Trustees, May 8, 1831.
[48] See above, page 38.
[49] Records of the Town Trustees, July 13, 1836.

authorities required wells to be kept clean and stagnant water to be drained from private lots.[50] Enforcement was difficult, and at best conditions were far from perfect. More efficiently enforced was the ordinance restricting the construction of new slaughterhouses within the city. Yet hogs were permitted to run "at large in the City of Fort Wayne" provided they were marked and had the mark recorded by the City Recorder.[51] In a sense this freedom for hogs was beneficial for the health of the people, since Fort Wayne at this time would undoubtedly have made the same impression on Mrs. Trollope as did Cincinnati where the English lady did not know whether to be indignant or pleased with the hogs which roamed its streets devouring the scattered garbage.[52] In Fort Wayne, improvement in both respects must have been made, however, for by 1855 the city ordinances prohibited swine from running on the streets. By this date, dead animals also had to be removed at the expense of the owner.[53]

Of greater significance for the preservation of health was the organization of the Fort Wayne Board of Health in 1843. The first man to head the board was Dr. Lewis Beecher, a New Yorker. He was a cousin of Lyman Beecher and apparently was possessed with a greater sense of humor than some other members of the family. When in 1845 Fort Wayne was visited with a minor outbreak of smallpox, the *Sentinel* went to great lengths to explain that the exaggerated reports were not true, that in reality there had been only three cases and one death. Obviously the objective of the article was to assure outsiders

[50] Revised Ordinances of the City of Fort Wayne, Fort Wayne *Sentinel,* August 13, 1842.

[51] *Ibid.*

[52] Frances Trollope, *Domestic Manners of the Americans,* edited by Donald Smalley (New York, 1949), 39.

[53] *Charter, Amendments, and Ordinances of the City of Fort Wayne* (1855), 25, 45-46.

that it was safe to transact their business in Fort Wayne.[54] Added to the very serious statement of the *Sentinel,* however, was a "Report from the Board of Health" signed by Dr. Beecher. This forecast the rapid disappearance of Fort Wayne as a city with a death rate of 161 people a *day,* while there had been only 120 births in the city within the last *year.* Beecher added that the dead were so numerous they could not be buried and that "the atmosphere is so impregnated at this time with *infection,* many are able to see it like a dense fog hanging over our city. . . ."[55]

No one joked, however, about the outbreak of cholera which occurred in 1849 and returned in 1852 and 1854. Actually the epidemic which hit the city repeatedly during these years was but part of the international outbreak of this dreaded disease. As the cholera approached along the canal line each year the people of Fort Wayne watched with apprehension.[56] Efforts were made to clear the streets of water and to remove filth, but with little avail. In 1849 early reports of the cholera's appearance in the West induced such preparations.[57]

> And yet it came as if nothing had happened. Citizens talked of cutting the canal, or drawing off the boats. But the cholera did not come by water. It fell like a bomb shell upon the S. E. part of town, and scattered death . . . itself quite capriciously into other parts of town & then disappeared. Sixty or Seventy deaths were attributed to this Scourge. The principle [*sic*] scope of its operation was among Germans. . . . Since the disease left—the city has forgotten altogether that there was ever such a thing—and business roars loud.[58]

[54] Fort Wayne *Sentinel,* January 4, 1845. Naturally such reports could seriously injure the economic life of the community. Just how seriously can be seen only by reading the newspapers of the day, e.g., see the Fort Wayne *Sentinel,* June 29, 1850.

[55] Fort Wayne *Sentinel,* January 4, 1845.

[56] *Ibid.,* July 7, 1849; Fort Wayne *Times,* July 4, 18, 1850.

[57] Records of the Common Council, April 12, 1849, pp. 447-48.

[58] Charles Beecher to Milton Badger, October 31, 1849, American Home Missionary Society Papers.

Each year in which the plague struck the city officials established temporary hospitals outside the city limits where the sick were cared for by paid attendants or by volunteer nurses such as the Sisters of Providence who had recently established an academy at Fort Wayne.[59] One physician has estimated that in Fort Wayne and vicinity there were about six hundred deaths from cholera during these three years.[60] This seems rather high considering that in 1849 there were at the most seventy deaths. Still by 1854 the loss of a good number of its inhabitants during such a brief period was a severe shock to the small community in every respect.

Perennially present but taken almost for granted was the ague. This malarial type of fever existed throughout the West, but was especially prevalent in regions around Fort Wayne where the low areas along the rivers and canal provided excellent breeding places for mosquitoes. Indeed, so interesting was Fort Wayne in this respect that the city was given particular mention in Dr. Daniel Drake's *Principal Diseases of the Valley of North America.*

> Where the town of Fort Wayne now stands . . . is a post-tertiary plain, at the junction and on the right or eastern side of the two rivers which form the Maumee. The plain rises above high-water mark; but is overspread with basin-like depressions, in which foul matters and rain-water accumulate, to be acted upon by the summer sun. At the depth of twenty or thirty-feet, hard well-water, of an excellent quality, is obtained. Between the town and the river there is a slip of low ground, which, although subject to inundation in spring, formerly became dry in summer, but is now kept wet by the leakage of the Wabash and Erie canal. . . . On the opposite side of the St. Mary, and of the Maumee River, there are rich alluvial grounds, under cultivation. About two miles west of the town, a grassy marsh or wet prairie begins, and stretches off, indefinitely,

[59] Records of the Common Council, August 22, 1849, p. 464. The city paid the medical expenses of anyone unable to pay. The Council also acknowledged the heroism of the nuns.

[60] Benjamin S. Woodworth, "The Medical Profession," in *Valley of the Upper Maumee River,* 2:332.

to the south-west. Its width is from a few hundred yards to a mile and a half . . . at the distance of a few miles to the east of Fort Wayne, [there lies] a wooded swamp—the western edge of the "Black Swamp," . . . known here as the "Maumee Swamp." . . . As to Fort Wayne, from the time it was settled as a military post, down to the present day, it has been infested with intermittents and remittents. . . . Of the prevalence of these fevers a judgment can be formed, from the fact, stated by Doctor Sturgis, that about 400 ounces of sulphate of quinine are annually consumed by the people of Fort Wayne and the surrounding country.[61]

Against all the various diseases the doctors of Fort Wayne struggled for the most part valiantly but almost as often ineffectually. With medical knowledge limited throughout the United States during this period, it is difficult to say whether the doctors at Fort Wayne were equal to the national average or not. Dr. Benjamin S. Woodworth, a mid-nineteenth century physician, who knew some of the earlier doctors practicing at Fort Wayne, has written of them, "some . . . were quite clever, but most have not left an enduring name."[62] Of the earlier physicians, Lewis G. Thompson was considered the best by many. Hugh McCulloch wrote of him, "so accurate was his intuition in locating diseases, that he was rarely at fault in treating them. I admired Dr. Thompson for his medical skill and for his many noble and manly qualities, but more than all for the conscientiousness and humanity which compelled him to treat with equal carefulness and attention those who were able to pay for his services and those who were not."[63]

Some of the earlier physicians did not confine themselves exclusively to medicine. Dr. Thompson was quite active in politics as a Whig. Dr. Lewis Beecher spent most of his time as a druggist. Dr. Charles Schmitz edited the first German news-

[61] Daniel Drake, *A Systematic Treatise, Historical, Etiological, and Practical, on the Principal Diseases of the Interior Valley of North America* . . . (Cincinnati, 1850), 361.

[62] Woodworth, "The Medical Profession," in *Valley of the Upper Maumee River,* 2:334.

[63] Hugh McCulloch, *Men and Measures of Half a Century,* 107.

paper, *Der Deutsche Beobachter von Indiana,* published in Fort Wayne and energetically served the cause of the Democratic party.[64] Another early German doctor, Bernard Sevenick, ran a brewery "where he dispensed beer in profusion."[65]

All of the resident Fort Wayne doctors advertised occasionally in the local paper. These advertisements were moderate in tone, especially when compared to the claims made for the many patent medicines. A typical doctor's advertisement was as follows:

> DOCTORS THOMPSON & STURGIS respectfully inform the citizens of Fort Wayne and vicinity, that they will continue the practice of MEDICINE & SURGERY in all their various branches.[66]

Occasionally, however, a particular doctor would praise his own skill, especially when inaugurating his practice. Such would seem to be the case of Dr. William H. Brooks, who,

> RESPECTFULLY tenders his services to the citizens of Fort Wayne and surrounding country. . . . Dr. B. is a graduate of the Medical School at Lexington, Ky., and of the Medical College of Ohio. . . . His familiarity with the *Reformed System of Practice* render his treatment . . . eminently successful.[67]

It must be remembered that prior to 1885 the state of Indiana did not require physicians to have a license; undoubtedly there were many men unworthy of the title. Yet the early Fort Wayne physicians in general did serve the community well. Naturally the doctors of the town treated not only the people of Fort Wayne but also the sick of a large area surrounding the city, and in doing so they often traveled long distances under difficult conditions in a region just emerging from a wilderness; in emergencies they frequently arrived too late.

[64] Fort Wayne *Sentinel,* July 1, 1843. Dr. Schmitz was most instrumental in advocating vaccination as the preventative against smallpox.

[65] Woodworth, "The Medical Profession," in *Valley of the Upper Maumee River,* 2:334.

[66] Fort Wayne *Sentinel,* April 10, 1841.

[67] *Ibid.,* August 21, 1841.

In any case, the Fort Wayne doctors were the principal means of assistance for the sick within a radius up to fifty miles. If the pioneer "bravely faced the doctor," it is only right to add that the doctor "boldly faced the wilderness."[68]

Just as the city authorities tried increasingly to protect the physical well-being of the inhabitants of the town, so they attempted to safeguard the morals of the citizenry. As a fur-trading and military post dating back to the French occupation of the site, Fort Wayne was noted for its free social life.[69] The Indian trade and payments had attracted during the course of the 1820s a number of undesirable whites who had contributed to the debauchery of the Indians. By the time Henry Rudisill arrived in 1830 many of this type had moved on. In general he found the people warm and hospitable, but he noted that there was still a good deal of riotous living and heavy drinking. Speaking of the best known tavern-hotel in the town, Rudisill said, "I am very anxious to get out of the House we at Present occupy Henderson keeps a Rough House it is a real Brothel or grog shop."[70] Although Rudisill was a temperate man he was not inclined to Puritanism and had lived a number of years in the West before coming to Fort Wayne. The Reverend James Chute who came to Fort Wayne a year after Rudisill and who was more Puritan in spirit was convinced that Fort Wayne needed "the influence of some pious laymen."[71] As the construction of the canal began he noted, "The influence of a canal, especially in its incipiant [*sic*] stages, is decidedly adverse to morality and reli-

[68] Madge E. Pickard and R. Carlyle Buley, *The Midwest Pioneer, His Ills, Cures and Doctors* (Crawfordsville, 1945), quotation taken from the dedication.

[69] Poinsatte, A History of Fort Wayne, from 1716 to 1829, pp. 35-37.

[70] Henry Rudisill to John Barr, January 16, 1830, Rudisill Letterbook. Zenas Henderson was an early Indian trader who, as the trade declined, built a tavern at the corner of Calhoun and Columbia.

[71] James Chute to Absalom Peters, December 17, 1832, American Home Missionary Society Papers.

gion."[72] Thereafter his letters revert constantly to this theme. "Tho' canals and rail roads are valuable in a political point of view, yet the construction of them doubtless has a most injurious effect upon the interests of virtue & religion."[73] However even Chute admitted that there had been some improvement in morality since his arrival.[74] Already in 1833 we find "The Christian Temperance Ball . . . Tuesday, December 24, [is] to be given at the house of Zenas Henderson."[75] Obviously the period of change had set in. By 1842 the *Sentinel* carried a series of letters in which the anonymous writer spoke of the liberal, carefree life of the settlers who came before the construction of the canal began, then noted, "this spirit is still lingering among us, but is rapidly passing away. The 'Yankee and Yorker' are in our midst."[76]

Indeed the ordinances of the same year show characteristics of the Yankee "blue laws." One could be fined

> For playing at any of the different games of ball; rolling a hoop; flying a kite; throwing of stones, brickbats, . . . tilting of sticks, levers or bars of iron; running, hopping, or jumping; or any other wanton exercise or practice that is calculated to collect a crowd of people, obstruct the street, frighten horses, or otherwise incommode passers-by, in any street, lane or alley of said city. . . .
>
> For swimming or bathing in the canal within the limits of the city, or in the Maumee or St. Mary's river adjoining the same, at any time during day light, without being covered with a sufficient bathing dress. . . .
>
> For any licensed retailer of spirituous liquors to sell or give away the same on Sunday, except to actual travelers. . . .
> For profane cursing or swearing. . . .[77]

[72] Chute to Peters, July 6, 1833.

[73] Chute to Peters, January 27, 1834.

[74] Chute to Peters, March 20, 1833.

[75] Invitation sent by the managers of the Christian Temperance Ball to Henry Cooper and Lady, in Fort Wayne—Allen County Historical Museum.

[76] Fort Wayne *Sentinel*, April 23, 1842.

[77] Revised Ordinances of the City of Fort Wayne in Fort Wayne *Sentinel*, August 13, 1842.

All "gaming" for money was prohibited—billiards, roulette, Spanish needle, shufflleboard, Faro, and even bowling.[78] By the 1850s, "Sabbath breaking" was illegal.

> Every person of the age of fourteen years or upwards, who shall be found on the first day of the week . . . rioting, hunting, fishing, quarrelling, or at common labor, works of charity and necessity only excepted, within the limits of said city, shall be fined in any sum not exceeding ten dollars. . . .[79]

Yet it must be noted that some of these ordinances were honored more in the breach than in the observance. Gambling was too popular in the city to be suppressed entirely by an ordinance and complaints were forthcoming from indignant citizens. One wrote, "That we have as many law-abiding and moral inhabitants as any town. . . . To this class do I appeal to cleanse the small sewer of its filth. . . ."[80] As our anonymous writer of 1842 pointed out, the citizens did as they pleased provided they did not violate moral obligations or the law. They dressed and lived as they saw fit. They went to church or they stayed home.[81] We may conclude that in Fort Wayne during this period there was not a narrow or concentrated public opinion despite the customary nineteenth century "blue laws." This was due to a combination of several factors. The original French ambience had blended with a liberal western code. Added to this was the influx of Irish and German immigrants during the 1830s and 1840s. James Chute recognized this when he wrote, "the cause of virtue" suffered because "a large proportion of these emigrants are Irish & Dutch Catholics. . . ."[82] In his opinion, "The influx of Irish and

[78] *Ibid.*

[79] *Charter, Amendments, and Ordinances of the City of Fort Wayne,* 26-27.

[80] Fort Wayne *Sentinel,* April 15, 1843. Another letter published in 1852 complained that the city officials themselves often gambled in "the rum-holes." Fort Wayne *Times,* February 26, 1852.

[81] "Letters from Indiana, II," Fort Wayne *Sentinel,* April 23, 1842.

[82] James Chute to Absalom Peters, January 27, 1834, American Home Missionary Society Papers.

Dutch has added nothing to the *moral power* of our community."[83] The Germans especially in the 1840s served to counteract a growing tendency towards a more rigid society. Finally the fact that Fort Wayne was a canal port prevented the authorities from enforcing codes which would be considered too strict. For example, liquor was never refused, even on Sunday, to travelers.

Compared with the problems of a modern city those of a small western town in the middle of the nineteenth century seem today to have been very small. Nevertheless, we must remember that these were the foundations for later municipal development. If these foundations seem inadequate to historians writing of the latter part of the century when America was becoming rapidly urbanized, they must not forget that the people of western towns like Fort Wayne did establish the framework of their local government and did co-operate to some extent for the protection of life and property as well as for the general well-being and morality of the community.

[83] Chute to Peters, July 8, 1835.

CHAPTER VII

URBAN RELIGION IN THE WEST

Politics, elections, vetoes, and all that sort of thing have given way to religion.

Of major importance in the social and cultural development of Fort Wayne was the formal organization of the various churches which began in the early 1830s. Four religious groups —the Presbyterians, the Catholics, the Lutherans, and the Methodists—were to establish organized congregations by 1840. Since the early days of French settlement the site of Fort Wayne had been visited by Catholic missionaries.[1] These visits were very infrequent, but, as it has been pointed out, "the French around Vincennes, at Fort Wayne, and near the old St. Joseph Mission were the connecting link with the old Church [in Indiana]. . . . Catholicism had never died in the hearts of the simple habitants, even though lack of priests had prevented the full observance of Catholic services for such long intervals."[2] Thus in the early 1830s when Stephen Badin, one of the great missionary priests of the Old Northwest,[3] first began to organize the Catholics of the Fort Wayne area,

[1] There is definite evidence that the site of Fort Wayne was visited occasionally by French priests both during and after the French occupation. See Thomas T. McAvoy, *The Catholic Church in Indiana 1789-1834* (Columbia University Press, 1940), 61, 150-51; Poinsatte, A History of Fort Wayne, from 1716 to 1829, pp. 17, 35.

[2] McAvoy, *The Catholic Church in Indiana 1789-1834,* 205-6.

[3] Stephen Theodore Badin was born in Orleans, France, on July 17, 1763, and studied with the Sulpicians in his native city. Having fled from Revolutionary France while still a seminarian, he came to the United States in 1792 and the following year became the first priest to be ordained in the United States. Regarding his many activities in Indiana and the West, see McAvoy, *The Catholic Church in Indiana 1789-1834,* and Schauinger, *Stephen T. Badin.*

he had a nucleus with which to start. The early baptismal records at the Cathedral of Fort Wayne, containing as they do many French names, are a clear indication that "the French were the foundation of the later church organization."[4] After the beginning of canal construction, however, Irish and German Catholics soon outnumbered the earlier French.

It was almost two years before the construction of the canal commenced when Father Badin first visited Fort Wayne in June, 1830.[5] During the next few years, this energetic experienced missioner began the work of permanently organizing the Catholic element in and around the town. In July, 1831, Badin made arrangements for the purchase of what is now the southwest quarter of the present Cathedral square. The property was obtained from John Barr in the name of the trustees of the Catholic Church of Fort Wayne.[6] Francis Comparet appears to have been the most active Catholic layman among these French settlers. He was the principal lay adviser of all the priests who came to Fort Wayne,[7] and until a church was constructed Mass was celebrated at his home. Comparet aroused the zeal of Badin with an estimate of one hundred Catholic families in the immediate Fort Wayne area.[8] Badin apparently made Fort Wayne his headquarters during a good part of 1833-34. Hugh McCulloch who was extremely ill dur-

[4] McAvoy, *The Catholic Church in Indiana 1789-1834,* p. 177.

[5] Schauinger, *Stephen T. Badin,* 250n; H. J. Alerding, *The Diocese of Fort Wayne* (Fort Wayne, 1907), 201.

[6] Article of agreement between John T. Barr and John B. Bruno, John B. Bequette, and Francis Comparet, Trustees of the Catholic Church, July 18, 1831, Chancery Office, Diocese of Fort Wayne-South Bend. Henry Rudisill signed as Barr's agent. The land was purchased on contract.

[7] See the letters of Badin to John B. Purcell, September 23, 1834, Simon Bruté to Frederick Resé, March 4, 1835, and Simon Bruté to J. Claude Francois, June 13, 1839, in University of Notre Dame Archives.

[8] Badin to J. B. Purcell, February 15, 1834, in *ibid.* A year earlier Father Ghislain Boheme had informed Bishop Purcell that there were two hundred Catholics at Fort Wayne. Boheme to Frederick Resé, May 26, 1833, in *ibid.*

ing this time speaks of being visited by Father Badin two or three times a week for several months. Of the French priest McCulloch wrote, "He spoke the English language fluently, and I recollect vividly how charmed I was by the tones of his voice, and how he seemed to strengthen me in my contest for life by his description of the fortitude he had witnessed of those of his own order under the cruelties to which they had been subjected [during the French Revolution]."[9]

Although Father Badin had the French population as a nucleus upon which to build, he experienced a great deal of difficulty in carrying forward his projects at Fort Wayne. The title for the lot on which the church was to be built was tied up by the legalities which followed Barr's mortgaging and subsequent disposal of his land in Fort Wayne.[10] In the meantime, Badin had also contracted for a "glebeland" about three miles from Fort Wayne.[11] In order to make the payments on these contracts and to build a church Badin depended to a great extent upon the labor and financial support of the canal workers.[12] However, construction of a chapel was delayed as many of these men moved beyond easy access to the town. In March, 1834, James Chute reported to his superiors that the Catholics in Fort Wayne had raised about $600 "towards a meeting house" and would probably build in the summer

[9] McCulloch, *Men and Measures of Half a Century*, 112.

[10] By the time the trustees paid off the contract for the property in 1833, John Barr had mortgaged all of his land in Fort Wayne. When subsequently Samuel Hanna obtained title to the land, he apparently failed to make out a deed for the property to the trustees. In 1842 the trustees conveyed the land contract to Bishop Celestine de la Hailandière of Vincennes. Two years later the Allen Circuit Court awarded legal title to Bishop Hailandière. These documents are to be found in the Chancery Office, Fort Wayne-South Bend Diocese.

[11] Badin to Purcell, September 23, 1834, University of Notre Dame Archives. This property eventually became the site of a later church and academy, Sacred Heart.

[12] John F. Lang, "The Catholic Church in Allen County," in *Valley of the Upper Maumee River*, 2:412.

as the Germans and Irish were coming "in great numbers."[13] It appears, however, that the work did not begin until after September, for in that month Badin, somewhat discouraged, wrote to his superior, "No time should be lost in forwarding the erection of chapels along the line, the Catholic hands move to another section, and the prospect of such erections diminishes or vanishes — This has been evidenced in Fort Wayne: the timber alone has been procured."[14] In his report on what proved to be his last visit for many years to Fort Wayne, the old priest went on to complain about the character of his parishioners, saying "they rather confirm Protest[ant] prejudices that are available to any conversion." In a note of hope, he added, "Our resource must lie in the education of youth. The introduction of Germans & German-French will offer also consolation to a resident pastor."[15]

After Badin's departure in the fall of 1834, the Catholics in Fort Wayne were left without the services of a priest for seven months and during this interval Fort Wayne came under the jurisdiction of the new diocese of Vincennes. Francis Comparet wrote to the newly created Bishop of Vincennes, Simon Bruté, to appeal for a priest, on the grounds that there were six to seven hundred Catholics at Fort Wayne and be-

[13] James Chute to Absalom Peters, March 17, 1834, American Home Missionary Society Papers.

[14] Badin to Purcell, September 23, 1834, University of Notre Dame Archives.

[15] Badin to Purcell, September 23, 1834. Badin paid his last visit to Fort Wayne in 1849. He must have found satisfaction as he viewed the results of his earlier endeavors. Even then the 80-year-old priest did not rest. He was discovered one day high up in the belfry with a hatchet knocking away the latticework. To the pastor's protests, Badin cried down, "Don't you want your bell heard and if you do why crib up the sound with these painted boards." Schauinger, *Stephen T. Badin,* 281.

tween fifteen hundred to two thousand along the canal line.[16] To meet the latter situation Badin had called for "two priests riding constantly along a line of 80 miles" extending from Fort Wayne.[17] Bishop Bruté, however, found it impossible to achieve this immediately. The best that could be done was to send priests periodically to Fort Wayne. In May and June, 1835, for example, Father Simon Lalumiere stopped at Fort Wayne on his tour of the eastern half of the diocese. Here he found 150 Catholic families and a church, 60x30 feet, completed.[18] Just when this Catholic chapel, the first church built in Fort Wayne, was completed is a matter of some conjecture. It must have been erected between the time of Badin's departure and the latter part of 1835. It is possible that there were two Catholic churches built in 1835, one being St. Mary's on the site of the present Cathedral square, and the other St. Joseph's located in Wayne Township.[19] In any case, we find only St. Mary's Church mentioned in *The Metropolitan Catholic Almanac, and Laity's Directory for . . . 1838,* St. Joseph's apparently

[16] Bruté to Resé, March 4, 1835, University of Notre Dame Archives. Comparet's figures were probably very close to being correct, since the population of Wayne Township in 1835, approximately 1,800, must have been at least one third Catholic. The letters of James Chute and Susan McCulloch (Presbyterian) indicate this.

[17] Badin to Purcell, September 23, 1834, University of Notre Dame Archives.

[18] Letter of Bruté to the Leopoldine Society written in the summer of 1835, quoted in Alerding, *The Diocese of Fort Wayne,* 26. See also the letter of Bruté, August 21, 1835, in Godecker, *Simon Bruté de Rémur,* 249.

[19] The writer of a scholarly article in *Our Sunday Visitor* (October 30, 1960, pp. 8B-11B) has amassed a good deal of evidence to indicate that such was the case. That the Catholics were building a church in July, 1835, is verified by a letter of James Chute to Absalom Peters, July 8, 1835, American Home Missionary Society Papers. It is possible, however, that this church was the same one referred to by Bishop Bruté in his letter to the Leopoldine Society, and in fact it was not quite finished when Lalumiere reported to his bishop.

having ceased to exist during the previous year.[20] The first church of Fort Wayne must have been a simple structure for when Father Ruff was sent there in 1835 it was expected that he would find "nothing of altar furnishings, linens, vestments, etc."[21] Still Bishop Bruté noted, "I was happy to send them the Rev. M. Ruff from Metz, in France, recently ordained and speaking the three languages, French, English and German. Of the latter there are a good many living there and in the environments."[22] The last statement was confirmed the following year when the bishop appointed Father Louis Mueller, a German priest, as Fort Wayne's first resident pastor. Mueller remained at Fort Wayne until April 16, 1840, and sometime during his last two years at that place he started the construction of a new church, St. Augustine's, to replace St. Mary's. In doing so it appears that he ran deeply in debt, and because of his personality he encountered opposition from his parishioners, principally the Irish and French.[23] Therefore it remained for his successor, Father Julian Benoit, to complete the frame structure as well as pay off the indebtedness.

Born in Septmoncel, a mountain village in the Jura range of France, Julian Benoit was educated in French seminaries and was teaching as a deacon at Lyons when he answered the call of Bishop Bruté to come to Indiana. After being

[20] The Catholic directories for 1836 and 1837 refer to two churches in Fort Wayne. See James Myres (ed.), *The United States Catholic Almanac: or Laity's Directory for . . . 1836,* 74; James Myres (ed.), *The Metropolitan Catholic Almanac and Laity's Directory for . . . 1837,* 121.

[21] Bruté to John Timon, May 28, 1835, University of Notre Dame Archives.

[22] Bruté to the Leopoldine Society, quoted in Alerding, *The Diocese of Fort Wayne,* 26. Bruté had been searching for a German and English speaking priest. See Bruté to Resé, January 8, 1835, University of Notre Dame Archives.

[23] Bruté to J. Claude Francois, June 13, 1839, University of Notre Dame Archives. While not suspended by the bishop, Mueller was required to move outside the city and limit himself largely to the care of the Germans, while Francois performed Mueller's duties in Fort Wayne as best he could from his post at Logansport.

ordained by Bruté, Benoit spent three years in southern Indiana and Illinois before coming to Fort Wayne in 1840. Although shortly before coming to Fort Wayne he expressed a desire to return forever to France, Benoit was to spend the remaining forty-five years of his life, apart from periodic trips to France and New Orleans, in his adopted city.[24] During these decades he became the chief architect who built upon the foundation of Catholicism laid in Fort Wayne by Badin and the other early missionaries. In his early years at Fort Wayne Benoit ministered not only to an area extending in a thirty-mile radius from the town, but he also cared for the canal workers, and became the confidant and adviser of the Miami in their last years in the area and during their departure from Indiana.[25] As previously mentioned, Benoit's first undertaking was the completion of St. Augustine's Church (particularly the interior) and the payment of the debt left by Mueller which amounted to $4,367. To help raise the necessary funds for this and for the purchase of the remaining portion of the present Cathedral square, Benoit returned to France in 1841. Before his death he returned twice more to France and journeyed twice to New Orleans to seek contributions for his work in Fort Wayne. By this means and through judicious real estate investments in the city, Benoit was able to contribute extensively to the erection not only of the Cathedral in 1860 but to most of the buildings constructed on the square by 1885.[26] In addition to his financial abilities, Benoit was responsible for bringing the Sisters of Providence and the Holy Cross Brothers

[24] Father Benoit's last sermon to his congregation was delivered upon his return from his third trip to Europe. "He spoke with emotion and in a trembling voice told his beloved hearers how glad he was to again see their familiar faces and be at his old home—a home and people he loved so dearly." Fort Wayne *Daily Sentinel,* January 27, 1885.

[25] Griswold, *Pictorial History of Fort Wayne,* 1:356.

[26] The Diocese of Fort Wayne was created in 1857. Alerding, *The Diocese of Fort Wayne,* 20.

to Fort Wayne for the education of the youth of the city. When Benoit died in 1885 the *Sentinel* acknowledged that Fort Wayne had "lost one of its founders, as well as one of its greatest and grandest citizens. When this city had not inviting prospects Father Benoit was the nucleus about which the pioneers and substantial people gathered. He encouraged every one to build up the city and led the work himself by erecting the most magnificent church edifice in the west."[27]

Shortly after his arrival in 1840 it became apparent that Benoit needed an assistant, especially to care for the German-speaking Catholics. Consequently, Joseph deMutzig Hamion, a young priest of German-French origin, was sent to Fort Wayne in September. After Hamion's death in 1842, Benoit brought Father Joseph Rudolph from Europe to minister to the increasing number of Germans. This arrangement continued until 1848 when the German Catholics at Fort Wayne organized their own parish, St. Mary's.

Contemporary with the organization of the Catholic church in Fort Wayne was the establishment of the First Presbyterian Church of Fort Wayne in 1831. Actually various Protestant missionaries had on occasion visited the site since 1804,[28] and during the 1820s two Presbyterian ministers paid visits to Fort Wayne. The first of these, the Reverend John Ross, who came five times between 1822 and 1826, found Fort Wayne extremely "unpromising."[29]

It is not surprising that he found it so coming as he did when Fort Wayne was the center for the Indian trade and annuity payments and the scene of the debauchery which accompanied the payments. Despite Ross's viewpoint there was

[27] Fort Wayne *Daily Sentinel,* January 27, 1885.

[28] The first recorded visit of Protestant missionaries was in 1804 when the Quakers sent two men to instruct the Miami in agricultural methods. See Poinsatte, A History of Fort Wayne, from 1716 to 1829, p. 80.

[29] *First Presbyterian Church in Fort Wayne* (Allen County—Fort Wayne Historical Society, 1959), 6.

sufficient interest in Presbyterianism at Fort Wayne to lead to an appeal for a resident minister. The appeal was directed to the corresponding secretary of the American Home Missionary Society and was signed on December 10, 1828, by Allen Hamilton on behalf of the Fort Wayne citizens.[30] In his letter Hamilton pointed out that although Fort Wayne and its immediate vicinity had a population of "about 500 souls," there had been no resident minister since the town had been laid out. Hamilton added that while he had no religious preference he believed the Presbyterian ministers were "of a better character" and that others in Fort Wayne also favored Presbyterianism. The petitioners were civic as well as religious minded, and in their appeal they called attention to the fact that if a canal should be built farmers might still hesitate to settle near Fort Wayne if they were to be deprived of religious services.[31]

The Society was unable to send a resident minister, but did direct the Reverend Charles E. Furman to Fort Wayne, possibly for the purpose of investigating the needs of the town. Furman came late in 1829 and stayed for six months. Perhaps because he came after the Indian agency had been removed from Fort Wayne, Furman considered the town an excellent place to establish a church. "The people are hospitable, and have more intelligence and liberality of feeling than any similar town I have found in the country. I never knew for the same number of inhabitants in any place, so many attendants upon the preaching of the gospel."[32] Apparently Furman's recommendation was sufficient, for the American Home Missionary Society sent the Reverend James Chute from Columbus, Ohio, to serve as Fort Wayne's resident minister. Chute arrived in

[30] Allen Hamilton to Absalom Peters, New York, December 10, 1828, American Home Missionary Society Papers.

[31] Hamilton to Peters, December 10, 1828.

[32] Jesse L. Williams, *Historical Sketch of the First Presbyterian Church, Fort Wayne, Indiana* (Fort Wayne, 1881), 15.

June, 1831, and on July 1, seven persons, "members of the Presbyterian Church from different sections of the country, in regular standing, met for the purpose of being regularly organized into a Presbyterian Church."[33] The following day five additional members were received. Although there were only twelve individuals admitted officially to membership, forty-four citizens of the town and its vicinity agreed to contribute annually to Chute's salary.[34] Considering the high cost of living at Fort Wayne Chute found his salary of $250 a year insufficient, but decided to stay because of the potential opportunities for spiritual work and in the hope that the proposed canal would lower the cost of living.[35] During his four years at Fort Wayne Chute labored diligently. He established a Sunday School and a Bible Society and was especially active in promoting the cause of temperance. Most of the time he faced discouragement as the anticipated religious revival failed to materialize.[36] In 1834 he wrote, "There are a few liberal warm hearted Christians who try to support the gospel, but a large majority are either of other denominations or came from the outposts of Ohio and have been born and educated without the influence of the gospel."[37] As we have noted previously, Chute was especially discouraged by the influx of Irish and Germans. Still he expressed the "desire to live and labor in this part of the Lord's vineyard" in the hope that there would be a "different population emigrating from the east, when our canal is opened to the Lake. . . ."[38] At the same time Chute announced that he had started to raise funds for the

[33] Charles J. Worden, *Historical Sketches concerning the First Presbyterian Church, Fort Wayne, Indiana* (Fort Wayne, 1945), 6-7.

[34] *Ibid.*, 7-8.

[35] Chute to Peters, September 20, 1831, American Home Missionary Society Papers.

[36] Chute to Peters, December 12 and December 17, 1831, January 27, 1834.

[37] Chute to Peters, January 18, 1834.

[38] *Ibid.*

construction of a church, but these plans had to be put aside when he died rather suddenly in December, 1835. For over a year the Presbyterians were left without a resident pastor, although the Lutheran minister, Jesse Hoover, preached regularly to them.[39]

If nineteenth century Protestantism in general is to be noted for its tendency towards disunity or division, the frontier conditions in such a small town as Fort Wayne at first tended to create an atmosphere in which a certain degree of unity was essential. Until the late 1830s almost all the Protestants of Fort Wayne joined together in worshipping with the Presbyterian congregation. Even while Chute was alive other Protestant ministers preached to the combined congregation at times during his absence. Another factor which bound the various bodies together during the early years was the joint need to use whatever facilities were available for their services. During the first six years of their existence the congregation of the First Presbyterian Church held services wherever possible, and it was natural for others to join them. To a certain extent eastern church agencies recognized these conditions and on occasion were ready to give some financial support to ministers of other denominations, especially when it could be argued that a particular minister might help save the souls of immigrants from Catholicism. Such was the case when the American Home Missionary Society heard with favor the appeal to support Jesse Hoover even after the arrival of a new Presbyterian minister in Fort Wayne in 1837.[40]

One may note, however, a gradual change in this spirit of co-operation at Fort Wayne after 1837. In that year the Presbyterians secured once again a resident minister, the Reverend

[39] S. R. Ball, William Corbin, A. Rankin, Smalwood Noel to Samuel Lowry, January, 1837 [1838], American Home Missionary Society Papers. Until Hoover came to Fort Wayne Daniel Jones, a Presbyterian minister, served for a short time.

[40] *Ibid.*

Alexander T. Rankin, as well as a definite place of worship. This first Protestant church was located on Berry Street between Lafayette and Barr. It was a simple, one-room, frame structure, surmounted by a steeple which housed the bell. Alexander Rankin, who came from Ohio, served the Fort Wayne First Presbyterian Church as stated "supply" until September, 1843, and was undoubtedly the most controversial and controversy-provoking Protestant minister of the period. His brother, John Rankin, was also a Presbyterian minister and one of the best known abolitionists of the West, being the author of *Letters on Slavery* and director of the famous underground railroad station at Ripley, Ohio.[41] Alexander Rankin was likewise a warm abolitionist and, as Jesse Hoover the Lutheran minister feared, this in itself was sufficient to provoke controversy in Fort Wayne,[42] whose citizens were not inclined towards the abolitionist doctrines, especially before 1850. On at least two occasions Rankin was denounced in the press for his abolitionist tendencies.[43] In addition, Rankin was a "teetotaller" who belonged to the Cold Water Society. It was also noted that he "looks on the Masons with a suspicious eye."[44] Finally, his efforts at times to interfere in the social life of the town were deeply resented. A certain P. H. Mills openly warned Rankin that he "should let both fiddling and dancing alone, and mind his own business. . . ."[45]

[41] Louis Filler, *The Crusade Against Slavery 1830-1860* (Harper Torchbook Edition, New York, 1963), 18. The Rankins were originally from Tennessee. Filler holds that John Rankin was the "most important" of the abolitionists before Garrison and calls the *Letters on Slavery* "a landmark in American abolitionism." Dumond also accords Rankin a high position in the abolitionist movement. See Dwight Lowell Dumond, *Antislavery. The Crusade for Freedom in America* (University of Michigan Press, 1961), 134-36.

[42] Jesse Hoover to Susan Man, November 10, 1837, McCulloch Papers.

[43] Fort Wayne *Sentinel,* August 19, November 25, 1843.

[44] *Ibid.,* May 14, 1842.

[45] *Ibid.,* November 18, 1843.

It is not surprising, therefore, that this strong personality left a marked impression upon the townspeople. After hearing Rankin's first sermon the young Hugh McCulloch was delighted with him, although he acknowledged that the minister was not very well educated.[46] A few months later, McCulloch wrote, "our settled preacher . . . is a great favorite of mine and decidedly the best preacher I have heard in the West."[47] Judging from Rankin's own letters he did not have a very good formal education, but in his own estimation the qualities needed for a minister to succeed in the West were to be intelligent and above all to be a good speaker.[48] Hugh McCulloch, who at this time was inclined to Unitarianism, was in all probability at first impressed by Rankin's rationalism. A few years after Rankin's arrival a rather impartial critic noted Rankin's fine appearance and spoke of him as "bold and energetic," yet added that Rankin was

> not . . . destined ever to be very popular as a preacher, or eminently successful in winning souls to Christ. . . . Nature intended him for a lawyer, and his reputation would have been higher, had he not done violence to her intentions. His mind is strictly a legal one. Keen, clear, discriminating. He can refute and split hairs, and draw distinctions in a manner that would have given him a high rank among special pleaders. In debate he is always ready, ingenious and forcible; but as a preacher he seems to lack feeling, sympathy, heart. He labors under the great mistake of supposing that sinners are to be convicted of sin, and brought to embrace the terms of the gospel, by *argument!* Every thing is to be effected by the cogency of his logic. . . . Mr. R., it might be said, is eloquent in denunciation. There is no tenderness in his discourses. The love of the Saviour, the compassion and kindness of the Father, are subjects which he rarely touches. But in holding up before his hearers the terrors of the law—in describing the vengeance of the

[46] Hugh McCulloch to Susan Man, September 19, 1837, McCulloch Papers.

[47] McCulloch to Susan Man, November 26, 1837, McCulloch Papers.

[48] Alexander Rankin to Milton Badger, January 22, 1839, American Home Missionary Society Papers. For these reasons Rankin advised against Calvin Stowe being sent to Fort Wayne by the Society, commenting that the people would say Stowe "is a good man, but not intended to be a preacher."

Almighty, and the sufferings of the damned, he is powerfully eloquent. . . . In touching upon them, his language becomes more than usually vigorous, his gestures more than usually energetic. His eye flashes, his lips are compressed, and I cannot at such times, for the life of me, escape the impression, that he would like to be the instrument by which the vials of divine wrath should be poured upon the heads of the unconverted.

Mr. R. is a bold and independent thinker. . . . Contending himself for the largest exercise of public opinion, he does not appear willing to extend to others the same right that he claims for himself. . . . Himself a man who is not to be driven, by fear or favor, from the advocacy of what he considers truth and justice, he is nevertheless, intolerant and uncharitable. Had he been a Protestant in the days of Queen Mary, he would have been a martyr; had he been a Catholic in Spain, during the existence of the inquisition, he would doubtless have been an inquisitor. . . . Still, I think you will like him. He is courteous and unassuming in his manners—easy and affable in his intercourse with his fellow men.[49]

It was only natural that the above letter when published in the *Sentinel,* "produced an excitement in our young city."[50] Two weeks later the writer observed that the majority of the citizens agreed with his opinion of Rankin, and that even the minister himself was rather flattered as he preferred to be noted for his "intellect" rather than for "piety and Christian devotion."[51] Although the *Sentinel's* correspondent admitted that some of Rankin's close friends defended him against the charge of intolerance, the writer noted, "Intolerance is different in different ages. If the heart of Mr. R. is filled with . . . love for his dissentient brethren, — then have those who have

[49] "Letters from Indiana, III," Fort Wayne *Sentinel,* April 30, 1842. It is rather hazardous to attempt to guess who wrote these revealing but anonymous letters. It is possible that it was Hugh McCulloch since the writer was from New England and was well educated, well read, and deeply interested in religious topics. The writer had lived in Fort Wayne for about ten years as had McCulloch. If the writer was McCulloch, then he had changed his viewpoint somewhat about Rankin. This is quite possible since five years had elapsed since Rankin came, and McCulloch was always inclined to be rather a freethinker in regard to religion.

[50] "Letters from Indiana, IV," Fort Wayne *Sentinel,* May 14, 1842.

[51] *Ibid.*

heard him speak of these brethren, and particularly . . . those who have heard his able lectures upon catholicism, received the most improper impressions."[52]

Rankin's influence was undoubtedly felt throughout the small community. This was especially true because by the late 1830s most of the prominent citizens of Fort Wayne belonged to the First Presbyterian Church—Samuel and Hugh Hanna, Allen Hamilton, Doctors Thompson and Sturgis, Mrs. McCulloch, William Rockhill, Jesse Williams, and Marshall S. Wines.[53] Often others such as the Ewings who were not officially members of the church, joined the congregation. On occasion the church wielded its authority over its members with as much vigor as did the early Puritan bodies; in 1841 an elder, John McIntosh, was tried and convicted by his church for being intoxicated on election day.[54]

Despite the frequent criticism directed against the pastor, the Presbyterian church made decided progress during Rankin's ministry. In 1843 the Synod of Northern Indiana (Old School) was organized with Fort Wayne as its center. In the same year the First Presbyterian Church of Fort Wayne was incorporated by a special act of the Indiana General Assembly.[55] One of the first decisions reached by the trustees was to make arrangements for paying Rankin his annual salary of $400 which had been consistently in arrears during the depression

[52] *Ibid.*

[53] The writer of the "Indiana Letters" stated that the more wealthy of Fort Wayne were generally to be found in the First Presbyterian Church. Fort Wayne *Sentinel,* April 30, 1842.

[54] Worden, *Historical Sketches concerning the First Presbyterian Church,* 30-33. Although McIntosh pleaded "not guilty" apparently it was not his first offense. After his conviction McIntosh replied, "Gentlemen . . . I have left my son at a grocery and I must get him and go home. If it is an offense to go to a grocery you will have another charge against me as I am going directly to one."

[55] *First Presbyterian Church in Fort Wayne* (Allen County—Fort Wayne Historical Society), 16.

years.[56] After six years at Fort Wayne Rankin left in September, 1843. The reasons for his departure are not clear. On his part he must have wearied in the constant struggle for his salary and of the controversies in which he was engaged during his last years. Added to this was his seeming failure to achieve any revival in Fort Wayne.[57] It is also possible that the congregation had grown weary of what Charles Beecher called Rankin's "stiff dose of Calvinistic Logic as dry as brickdust & hard as the nether mill-stone."[58] Rankin did not leave the area entirely, for he remained as a missionary in northern Indiana, associating himself with the "Old School" Presbyterians.[59]

By the time Rankin left the church's membership had increased from the original 12 members to 139. The result of this was twofold: first, it was recognized that the old place of worship was too small, and plans were set in motion to build a new one on the southeast corner of Clinton and Berry streets. Samuel Hanna, as head of the board of trustees and the building committee, successfully raised the necessary funds through the sale of pews to the highest bidders. While the

[56] Rankin to Milton Badger, September 3, 1840, American Home Missionary Society Papers.

[57] Rankin to Badger, February 29, March 31, 1840. Concerning the controversies, see below, pp. 174-77.

[58] Charles Beecher to Badger, February 5, 1846, American Home Missionary Society Papers.

[59] Beecher to Badger, September 16, 1844. The American Home Missionary Society was dominated by the "New School" Presbyterians. It appears as if they withdrew their financial support from Rankin after September, 1840. The division between the "Old School" and "New School" Presbyterians is too complicated to deal with in this study. In a general sense, the "Old School" represented the more conservative, Calvinistic view. Fearing the more "liberal" New England theology, they opposed the Plan of Union of 1801 which encouraged close co-operation between the Congregationalists and Presbyterians especially in the missions fields. The "New School" represented the more "liberal" faction, which mitigated Calvinism and stressed salvation for the many through revivalistic methods. In the "New School" one was more likely to find the radical minded reformers, although Rankin as an abolitionist also belonged with this reform element.

church was in use by 1847, the final structure seating 320 people was not ready before 1852. Built in a colonial style, the church cost $13,500.[60]

Secondly, the relatively large congregation as well as the prominence of many of its members invited a struggle for control of the church after Rankin's departure. The issue was directly related to the nation-wide conflict between the "Old School" and "New School" factions of Presbyterians. This war, carried on with great acrimony especially in the West during this period, was brought to Fort Wayne when Henry Ward Beecher, then pastor of the "New School" Presbyterian Church in Indianapolis, hurried to Fort Wayne in order to secure the pulpit for his younger brother, Charles, and the "New School" element. The Fort Wayne elders who favored the "Old School" had anticipated such action, however, and had called Dr. William C. Anderson, a professor of English at Hanover College, to fill the vacancy left by Rankin. Although in the past the Fort Wayne church had received assistance from the American Home Missionary Society, until now it had not been required to decide officially for either "School." Both "Schools" were particularly desirous of winning Fort Wayne since it was the headquarters for the Synod of Northern Indiana. Charles Beecher observed, "The old school know the value of northern Indiana . . . it will soon be the garden spot of the state & its beautiful prairie Counties full of eastern people. . . . They have thrown in their ablest leader in the state, Mr. Anderson, pliable, affable, travelled-sagacious-crafty-eminently skillful."[61]

Anderson arrived just in time to preach on Sunday, April 14, 1844, and thus saved the day for the "Old School" by winning the call for the pastorate. Henry Ward Beecher hurried into the city the following Saturday after a hard trip by horse-

[60] *First Presbyterian Church in Fort Wayne* (Allen County—Fort Wayne Historical Society), 26-27.

[61] Beecher to Badger, September 16, 1844.

back from Indianapolis. Arriving spattered with mud at the home of Jesse L. Williams, Beecher announced to Mrs. Williams, "I have just come to divide your church!"[62] He then hastened to a meeting of some of the church members, where, according to McCulloch, having attended to the business at hand, he delivered an impromptu address, "in language so beautiful and appropriate, in a voice so tender and affectionate, that all present were spellbound, and when he closed there was not a dry eye except his own in the room."[63] In McCulloch's view this particular sermon was one of the most effective that Henry Ward Beecher ever delivered. For two weeks Beecher threw himself into the fray, preaching in the old courthouse or wherever possible, but despite his eloquence he did not win a majority of the congregation. A sufficient number, however, was won over to the "New School" doctrines to enable Beecher to organize the Second Presbyterian Church of Fort Wayne. Financial assistance was obtained for Charles Beecher from the American Home Missionary Society, the directors of which felt that even though he was young they must have a church at Fort Wayne.[64] Dr. Lyman Beecher came to Fort Wayne from Cincinnati early in November to officiate at the ordination and installation of his son Charles as the pastor of the new congregation. The elder Beecher, then close to seventy, had ridden throughout the night in order to be present at the ceremonies.[65] With Henry Ward Beecher also in attendance Lyman Beecher delivered the principal sermon at the "all-Beecher" services the following day.

[62] Fort Wayne *Journal-Gazette,* May 15, 1878.

[63] McCulloch, *Men and Measures of Half a Century,* 142.

[64] Nathan Farrand and Josiah Conklin to the Executive Committee of the American Home Missionary Society, June 17, 1844, American Home Missionary Society Papers.

[65] McCulloch, *Men and Measures of Half a Century,* 148-49. Upon his arrival Lyman Beecher asked for some whiskey to "rub himself down with," as he said. The whiskey was sent to his room and soon after he joined the family "apparently as fresh as if he had been resting for hours."

Charles Beecher served as pastor of the "New School" Presbyterians for seven years. Judging from his letters the young Beecher had a good mind and was sincerely dedicated to his work. To a certain extent he appears overly introspective, and his zeal for the "New School" led him to be very suspicious of the other religions, Protestant and Catholic, especially the latter. Concerning the "Old School" Presbyterians he felt that they had "entrapped and bound hand & foot a decided New School majority" within the First Presbyterian Church.[66] When they failed to complete the construction of their new church as early as expected, he wrote, "I cannot but regard it as God's significant work here."[67] Beecher got along better with Anderson's successor, the Reverend Hugh S. Dickson, but warned the Society that the people in the East do not understand the opposition that the "New School" faces from the "Old School" in the West.[68] Besides his struggle with the "Old School," Beecher claimed he met the opposition of the Episcopalians "who feel that they would be larger if it were not for the n. s.," of the Methodists "who feel we are 'stealing their thunder' — and of the Baptists who are dead."[69] As for the Catholics, he said, "I wish I had a *Converted Roman Catholic Colporteur*. I will venture to say there is not a richer field for such a man to work in all the U. S. than this same Allen Co.—Papists papists everywhere & their priest, Benoit is sharp as a brier & a perfect Jesuit."[70]

Although Charles Beecher never succeeded in promoting a true revival in Fort Wayne and on one occasion he referred to the town as "a Babylon as bad as N. York," he came to respect many of the townspeople. Above all he was attracted to Hugh McCulloch. Beecher admitted that his own theological views

[66] Beecher to Badger, September 16, 1844.
[67] Beecher to Badger, May 5, 1848.
[68] Beecher to Badger, August 3, 1846.
[69] Beecher to Badger, September 16, 1844.
[70] Beecher to Badger, October 2, 1845.

were "rather original" as were those of McCulloch. Although they disagreed often, McCulloch had a great influence on Charles Beecher.[71] Beecher's strong abolitionist views and his independence in politics brought him at times into difficulties with his congregation. In 1844, for example, he refused to vote, although all but one person in his church voted Whig.[72] Still when he left in 1850 due to the ill health of his family and his own exhaustion, his congregation was unanimous in wishing him to stay, and he actually counted on returning. By this time the Westminster Presbyterian Church (as the Second Presbytrian Church was then called) had a membership of approximately one hundred families. However, the First Presbyterian Church remained the larger body and retained the favor of the more prominent citizenry. It is quite likely that its more conservative views in respect to the Negro and temperance contributed to its continued status.

Although Methodist preachers were in the Fort Wayne area as early as their Presbyterian counterparts, at first they did not advance quite as rapidly nor are their records as complete. In 1824 James Holman, a Methodist preacher from Boston, cleared a farm just outside Fort Wayne and held regular services in his log cabin until 1830. It appears that in that year the Fort Wayne Mission was placed under the direction of the Ohio Conference. Part of the Maumee Mission, the town

[71] After leaving Fort Wayne Charles Beecher wrote to Mrs. McCulloch concerning her husband, "I cannot prepare a sermon without him rising to my mind. I cannot read a speech of Kossuth, nor a paper on European affairs, but that I see him before me. It is true we did not agree in politics, nor altogether in religion, but I would give more for his differences than for most men's agreements. . . . Tell him that for a year or more I followed his advice . . . to stop studying and *see the world*. . . . I am once more returned to my studies with new zest." Charles Beecher to Susan Man McCulloch, January 21, 1852, McCulloch Papers.

[72] Beecher to Badger, December 16, 1844, American Home Missionary Society Papers.

was served by Reverend Nehemiah B. Griffith.[73] Three years later Fort Wayne was transferred into the Indiana Conference, and the Fort Wayne Mission became part of the Fort Wayne circuit which was under the direction of the Reverend James S. Harrison. Under his leadership the Methodists of Fort Wayne made plans for the erection of a church and Samuel Edsall, one of the leading laymen, secured the donation of a lot from the Ewings on condition that a church be built thereon.[74] The congregation was unable to pay for the completion of the structure, however, and the lot reverted to the Ewings on condition that the latter donate $100 to the building of a new church.[75] Until this church was built in 1840 the Methodists used the Presbyterian schoolhouse on the corner of Harrison and Berry streets for their meetings, and with the erection of this building the Fort Wayne circuit became the Fort Wayne station with a resident pastor, the Reverend Francis A. Conwell. In 1841 the Methodists attempted to organize a mission for the Germans at Fort Wayne, but the project failed. However, by 1847 they had gained sufficient strength among the native American element to make plans not only to open a college for women but to organize a second congregation, the Wayne Street Methodist Church.[76]

It may be assumed that a contributing factor to the Methodists' failure in organizing the Protestant Germans was the strong position of the Lutheran church in the Fort Wayne area by this time. Moreover, the Lutheran body at Fort

[73] William W. Sweet, *Circuit Rider Days in Indiana* (Indianapolis, 1916), 45; Robertson (ed.), *History of the Maumee River Basin,* 2:438.

[74] W. G. Ewing to William Hood, April 15, 1834, Miscellaneous Papers, Fort Wayne—Allen County Historical Museum.

[75] Note signed by Ewing to pay $100 for building a new Methodist church provided the present unfinished church is removed in three months, July 18, 1840, Ewing Papers, Indiana State Library.

[76] Griswold, *Pictorial History of Fort Wayne,* 1:389, 404-5; Beecher to Badger, July 19, 1847, American Home Missionary Society Papers.

Wayne became one of the principal bulwarks supporting the conservative forces of "Old Lutheranism."

The formation of the Lutheran church in Fort Wayne owed much to the efforts of Henry Rudisill. As we have noted previously, Rudisill was motivated by both economic and religious reasons in promoting the settlement of Germans in and around Fort Wayne. He not only corresponded with John Barr in this connection, but he also wrote to the Emigrantenkommission and to the Missionsgesellschaft in Philadelphia and Baltimore asking them to send Lutheran immigrants to Fort Wayne.[77] Having attracted a number of German Lutherans to the area, Rudisill wrote to a Lutheran periodical in the East in 1836 requesting a minister for the Fort Wayne area.[78] When in July, 1836, the Reverend Jesse Hoover, a Lutheran missionary from Virginia, came to Fort Wayne in response to Rudisill's request, he found a body of Lutherans awaiting his organizational efforts. On October 14, 1837, twenty-three families assembled in the courthouse to adopt the discipline of the Evangelical Lutheran Church and to organize the First Evangelical Lutheran Church of Fort Wayne.[79] Fortunately Hoover spoke both English and German; therefore, he was able to serve both groups within his congregation as well as the Presbyterian congregation in the interim between the death of Chute and the arrival of Rankin. He also supplemented his income by teaching.[80] After Rankin's assumption of duties at the Presbyterian church, an appeal for financial assistance was made to the American Home Missionary Society by the various Protestant ministers on behalf of Hoover, since his German

[77] H. G. Sauer and J. W. Miller, *Geschichte der Deutschen Ev.-Luth. St. Pauls-Gemeinde zu Fort Wayne, Ind., vom Jahre 1837 bis zum Jahre 1912* (St. Louis, 1912), 10.

[78] *Ibid.*

[79] *Ibid.*, 8.

[80] S. R. Ball, William Corbin, A. Rankin, Smalwood Noel to Samuel Lowry, January, 1837 [1838], American Home Missionary Society Papers.

congregation could not afford to pay a sufficient salary,[81] but before the appeal could be acted upon Hoover died at the age of twenty-eight. In his two years at Fort Wayne he had succeeded in organizing the Lutherans not only in the town but to a certain extent also in the surrounding counties, especially Adams County.

Only for a short time was the congregation without a pastor; in the fall of 1838 the Reverend Friedrich C. D. Wyneken arrived, who, it has been rightly stated, "may well be compared with the eighteenth century patriarch of the Lutheran church in America, Henry M. Mühlenberg."[82] Indeed Wyneken was the real organizer of the Lutheran church west of the Appalachians. As the tribulations of France had furnished the Catholics of Fort Wayne with the services of a Badin, so now the conflicts within the Germanies sent this scholarly Lutheran minister. Educated at Göttingen and Halle, Wyneken had a firm theological foundation which was decidely confessional in outlook.[83] Arriving in Baltimore in the summer of 1838 he witnessed Lutherans of the city attending a Methodist prayer meeting, and being alarmed by this tendency and the consequent lessening of Lutheran doctrine, he determined to re-establish the orthodox confessional church in the United States. He wisely selected the West as his field and was commissioned as a missionary by the Pennsylvania Synod to serve the states of Ohio, Indiana, and Michigan. Having read in the Lutheran church bulletin about the death of Hoover and the subsequent appeal of the Fort Wayne congregation for a new pastor, Wyneken immediately set out for Fort Wayne. He began preaching and baptizing as soon as he arrived. At his own request he was dismissed as a missionary by the Pennsyl-

[81] S. R. Ball *et al.*, to Samuel Lowry, January, 1837 [1838].

[82] Carl Mauelshagen, *American Lutheranism Surrenders to Forces of Conservatism* (University of Georgia Press, 1936), 66.

[83] *Ibid.*, 67.

vania Synod in order to accept a permanent pastorate at Fort Wayne.[84] In doing so Wyneken lost the financial support of the parent organization, but he gained greater independence for promoting his orthodox viewpoint in the West. It is clear that he had no intention of giving up his missionary endeavors in the tri-state area. With Fort Wayne as his base he carried the Lutheran doctrines to German communities throughout the region, making trips that at times lasted up to six weeks. Wyneken found the situation on the frontier truly distressing; while some German Lutherans in the backwoods received him warmly, they refused to go out of their way to help organize a congregation or even to invite others to hear him preach. Some were completely indifferent and discourteous. As he described conditions in his small book, *Die Not der deutschen Lutheraner in Nordamerika,* these people, who often had not even heard a German sermon for periods up to twelve years, were well on their way to agnosticism.[85] Eventually Wyneken's fervor as well as his understanding of the problems of the frontier and his willingness to enter into the life of the people enabled him to win most of them back to the faith of Lutheranism. At Fort Wayne his ability to speak English and the Low German dialect enabled him to keep contact with the older communicants as well as to gain the confidence of the newly arrived German peasants. When in the city he taught four days a week at his school for German immigrants and thus saved many of these children from illiteracy. Since Wyneken was unmarried he lived at the home of Henry Rudisill or wherever one of his parishioners would board him. His low salary in addition to his many acts of charity did not permit him to dress often as a minister, thus he appeared usually in

[84] Sauer, *Geschichte der St. Pauls Gemeinde,* 14.

[85] For a description in Wyneken's words, see *ibid.,* 15-17.

the leather pants of the frontiersman or as a simple farmer in bluejeans.[86]

Under Wyneken the congregation of St. Paul's erected their first church in 1839 on the lot where the present church is located. In April of that year Wyneken established definite rules and doctrines for his congregation to follow. Not only were his parishioners required to lead a life of piety but no one was to be admitted into membership unless he accepted the doctrines of orthodox Lutheranism, and only registered members of the parish were permitted to receive communion.[87] It is evident that Wyneken intended to preserve Lutheranism in Fort Wayne from what he considered the corrupting influences of interdenominationalism and "Americanization."

Wyneken's influence was to be carried far beyond the confines of the Fort Wayne area, however. He was responsible to a great extent for the organization of the Lutheran missionary program in the West when the General Synod accepted his proposals for the establishment of definite missionary posts and his policy of methodical extension of their efforts. More than this, his letters from America, which were published in Germany between 1838 and 1842, did more to awaken the German Lutherans to the spiritual needs of their American brethren than any other message or effort.[88] In October, 1841, he returned to Germany where he stayed for two years seeking support for his endeavors in America. His trip also deepened his confessional outlook, and he returned to America more than ever determined to check the Methodist influence in the General Synod and prevent the union of Lutheran and Reformed churches in the United States.[89] During his absence his own

[86] Sauer, *Geschichte der St. Pauls Gemeinde,* 19-21. Wyneken called this time of poverty "die schonsten seines Lebens." *Ibid.,* 20.

[87] *Ibid.,* 19-20, 21-23. This document is also very interesting inasmuch as it shows the relationship between the Lutheran pastor and his congregation.

[88] Mauelshagen, *American Lutheranism,* 70-71.

[89] Sauer, *Geschichte der St. Pauls Gemeinde,* 26-28.

congregation had almost divided over these issues, the English speaking group being more inclined to the Methodist practices. Enforcing the doctrines of "Old Lutheranism" in his own parish, Wyneken called for a gathering of the Western Synod to meet in Fort Wayne in October, 1844. By this time he was already in close communication with C.F.W. Walther, founder of the Missouri Synod, in St. Louis. In the course of the assembly Wyneken was attacked by some of his own parishioners, but in a brilliant two hour address, first in German, then in English, he defended the doctrines of "Old Lutheranism," and united the great majority of both his congregation and the assembly behind him.

In 1845 Wyneken accepted a call from the Lutherans of Baltimore, and although he deeply regretted leaving Fort Wayne, he provided for the continuance of his policies by securing the pastorate for Dr. Wilhelm Sihler. Sihler, the son of a Prussian army officer, was born in 1801, and traveled extensively in Germany and the Baltic area as a youth before and after his studies for the ministry.[90] His convictions concerning "Old Lutheranism" were very similar to those of Wyneken, if anything Sihler was even more militant. Convinced that the Lutheran church was the only true church, Sihler had a ". . . real hatred for the Catholic church and a contempt for church union which he believed to be the work of the devil."[91] He became acquainted with the problems of the Lutherans in America through the writings of Wyneken.[92] Sihler had the opportunity to meet Wyneken when the latter came to Germany and thereupon decided to immigrate to America in order to assist Wyneken in his work. With the aid

[90] Concerning the life of Wilhelm Sihler before he came to the United States, see W. Sihler, *Lebenslauf von W. Sihler bis zu seiner Ankunft in New York* (St. Louis, Mo., 1879).

[91] Mauelshagen, *American Lutheranism,* 76.

[92] Sauer, *Geschichte der St. Pauls Gemeinde,* 27; Sihler, *Lebenslauf von W. Sihler,* 144.

of the Dresden Missionary Society sponsored by Wilhelm Lohe, Sihler came to the United States in 1843.

Sihler was to remain as pastor of St. Paul's church in Fort Wayne until his death in 1885. During these forty years he built upon the foundations of Wyneken making Fort Wayne into a center from which "Old Lutheranism" convictions were to be planted and kept alive in the West. Sihler broke with the Ohio Synod in 1845 because of its American tendencies and because of its use of English in the seminaries. He and two other ministers sent by Lohe to Ohio journeyed to St. Louis to begin negotiations with C. F. W. Walther for the organization of a new synod based on the principles of "Old Lutheranism." In July, 1846, a preliminary meeting of all the western pastors was held at Fort Wayne, out of which came the agreement on the basic doctrines and which led to the formation of the "Evangelical Lutheran Synod of Missouri, Ohio and other States" at Chicago in 1847.

In the previous year Sihler, with the aid of the Lohe association, began a seminary at Fort Wayne. He had already instructed two men for the ministry, but now with the assistance of another professor, Sihler made the seminary the stronghold of "Old Lutheranism" from which for years to come men were sent out ". . . imbued with the pietistic spirit of a Lohe and a militant and confessional attitude of a Sihler to build a bulwark in the West against the tide of religious liberalism."[93] In the first nine years of its existence ninety-seven students had been admitted to the seminary, seventy-two of whom either entered the ministry or became parochial school teachers.[94]

[93] Mauelshagen, *American Lutheranism,* 80-82.

[94] By 1850 Wilhelm Lohe had sent forty men from Germany to complete their missionary training at Fort Wayne. After that date the number of Lohe representatives declined, but other German agencies offset the loss. See *ibid.,* 73, 162. In 1861 the seminary was transferred to St. Louis, and in its place Concordia College was established.

From the beginning St. Paul's congregation in Fort Wayne was intimately linked with the seminary. In part the rapid growth of the congregation under Sihler was due to the fact that some German parents wished to bring their children to a city where they could secure an education that was both religious and of a high academic standard. Sihler himself was noted more for his teaching ability than as a preacher, according to the testimony of H. G. Sauer, Sihler's assistant and ultimate successor.[95] Sihler's accomplishments were not achieved without some loss, however; in 1846 the English speaking members of the congregation under the leadership of Henry Rudisill withdrew from St. Paul's in order to form the Trinity English Lutheran Church. This withdrawal was occasioned more by linguistic difficulties than by doctrinal differences since the new congregation accepted the Augsburg Confession and in general the doctrinal beliefs of "Old Lutheranism." Still national differences were important in the struggle that took place within the Lutheran church in the United States at this time. One senses this in the words of Sauer:

> It had to be a special providence of God that Wyneken was sent to Fort Wayne as successor of Hoover. If, instead of Wyneken, another man of Pennsylvania had taken up Hoover's work, not only would the German spirit have been lost . . . but also the pure Lutheran faith would not have come to Fort Wayne, especially since the records of the formation of this congregation [St. Paul's] and the records of the baptisms, confirmations, weddings and funerals had been written into the Church ledger by Hoover in English! . . . If Sihler would not have come to Fort Wayne, the seminary which was founded at the instigation of the Missouri Synod would not have been established at Fort Wayne. In short, all the blessings which have come over the Lutheran Church of this country from Fort Wayne would have been lost. Therefore, in the history of the Lutheran Church of America, the Evangelical Lutheran Church of St. Paul's in Fort Wayne will remain an especially great memorial of the mercy of God for all times.[96]

[95] Sauer, *Geschichte der St. Pauls Gemeinde,* 31.

[96] *Ibid.,* 18-19 (author's translation).

It must be remembered, however, that not all the German Protestants of Fort Wayne were Lutheran. A smaller but significant number were members of the Calvinistic Reformed Church. In the minds of the Presbyterians these Germans were in danger of being absorbed into the Lutheran congregation or, worse yet, into the Catholic church. For this reason Charles Beecher in 1845 urged the American Home Missionary Society to give financial support to John Bayer, the minister of the Reformed German congregation.[97] According to Bayer the "Old School" Presbyterians also desired to incorporate his congregation into the First Presbyterian Church and in fact the Reverend Dickson of the latter church had deliberately fomented difficulties among the Germans.[98] Despite these problems St. John's Reformed Church managed to survive as a separate entity and gradually increased its membership in the late 1840s. The success of Wyneken and Sihler in preventing any union between the Lutheran church and other Protestant groups undoubtedly encouraged (one might even say "required") the German Reformed Church to maintain its own identity.

Generally speaking, apart from the Presbyterians, Methodists, and Lutherans, other Protestant religions made little headway in Fort Wayne until the mid-1840s. It is true that the Baptists had organized by 1837; however, progress was made difficult by their inability to secure the services of a regular pastor until 1841. In that year the Reverend William Gildersleeve became pastor, and under his direction the congregation erected a modest building on a lot donated by Samuel Hanna. Still the financial position of the congregation was

[97] Beecher to Badger, August 1, 1845, American Home Missionary Society Papers. The request was granted. In another long letter Beecher dwelt on the problems which faced anyone who ministered to the spiritual needs of the Germans. The letter is interesting not only for Beecher's comments on the Germans, but also because it reveals Beecher's own prejudices. See Beecher to Badger, July 3, 1846, in *ibid.*

[98] John Bayer to Badger, April 23 and May 15, 1846.

never strong, and until 1853 they relied at times on the assistance of the American Baptist Home Missionary Society.[99]

In 1842 our anonymous writer to the *Sentinel* noted that as yet the Episcopalians had not achieved any success in Fort Wayne. He believed that the city was "not yet old enough for a society of this kind. . . . [There were] not people enough in this county, who are constitutionally fitted to be Episcopalians, to support a preacher of this denomination."[100] Apparently there was a good deal of truth in the above statement. In 1839 an organization was effected under seemingly favorable circumstances with persons such as Allen Hamilton, Samuel Stophlet, Merchant W. Huxford, Samuel Hanna, Dr. Lewis Beecher, and Philip G. Jones attending. By 1843, however, almost all of these had transferred their allegiance to the First Presbyterian Church, in part perhaps because of the difficulty in finding qualified Episcopalian ministers, but also because these people felt more akin to the latter church. Consequently, it was necessary to begin anew in 1844 when a new congregation of seventeen members was organized by the Reverend Benjamin Halstead under the title of Trinity Church. By 1848 when Halstead resigned a small church had been built. During the next decade the Episcopalians established a firm foundation in the city.

The only other Protestant denominations which achieved some degree of organization in the 1840s were the Universalists and the previously mentioned German Reformed Church. The Universalist Church in Fort Wayne was established principally through the efforts of Dr. Lewis G. Thompson. In 1843 Dr. Thompson invited Erasmus Manford, editor of *Manford's Magazine,* to speak in Fort Wayne. Manford gave a series of

[99] Graham N. Berry, "Baptist Churches," in Robertson (ed.), *History of the Maumee River Basin,* 2:460-63. From 1820 to 1822 a Baptist minister, Isaac McCoy, maintained a mission school for the Indians at Fort Wayne. After his departure the small Baptist congregation disbanded.

[100] "Letters from Indiana, III," Fort Wayne *Sentinel,* April 30, 1842.

lectures in the city in that year. He and other Universalist ministers continued to visit Fort Wayne periodically.

By 1848 there was a sufficient number of people of the Jewish faith living in Fort Wayne to enable them to organize "The Society for Visiting the Sick and Burying the Dead." Almost all of the original eleven members came from Germany. Their charter read as follows:

> We who like so many other immigrants from Europe have come to these shores in order to find a refuge against European oppression:
>
> We, who have gone away from our native homes, kinfolk, and everything that was precious and sacred to our youth, realize, when any calamity visits us, that we have left all assistance behind, and feel deprived of the consolation of our religion:
>
> We, the undersigned citizens of Indiana, organize the Society for Visiting the Sick and Burying the Dead.[101]

Within a short time the society under the formal title, Achduth Veshalom Synagogue of B'nai Israel was attended by Rabbi Solomon, who visited Fort Wayne at stated intervals. While the Jews were considered as being different, the general attitude towards them as merchants was one of friendliness. In referring to the Jewish merchants of Fort Wayne the newspapers occasionally carried such comments as, "We often hear about 'beating the Jews,' but it's hard to do."[102]

Assessing the religious groups in Fort Wayne, we may conclude that by 1845 the more important congregations were the Presbyterians, the Catholics, the Lutherans and, to a somewhat lesser extent, the Methodists. While there had been a tendency among the Protestants to unite in their services, this practice had virtually ceased by the mid-forties. In general the foreign immigrants settling in Fort Wayne remained faithful to their religions—the Irish to Catholicism and the

[101] Fort Wayne *News-Sentinel,* July 5, 1958; Griswold, *Pictorial History of Fort Wayne,* 1:403.

[102] Fort Wayne *Times,* September 27, 1849.

Germans to either Catholicism, "Old Lutheranism," or the Reformed Church. In fact, the tendency may be seen towards ethnically oriented congregations. There are some notable differences between the religious development of this small urban community and the more rural sections of the West. Speaking of the West, Professor Wade has noted regarding religion, "Progress in the cities was steadier and more substantial—though less spectacular—than in the back country . . . the growth owed nothing to the sporadic revivals which burned across the countryside. . . . These movements were essentially rural."[103] This was quite obvious at Fort Wayne, where ministers such as Chute, Rankin, and Charles Beecher all complained that they could not initiate a true revival. The *Sentinel* noted in 1841 that religious revivals were quite rare in Fort Wayne and the vicinity.[104] It was not until that year that Fort Wayne had its first camp meeting. The First Presbyterian Church was correctly credited as having increased its numbers "without having been enlarged by those religious excitements, which, in other places have brought so many servants of Satan into the christian fold."[105] Mrs. Jesse Williams, who was required to live in southern Indiana for a short time, wrote to her friend Mrs. Wines in Fort Wayne that she did not care for the prayer meetings in that region of the state "as shouting and hollering is not in accordance with my feelings."[106]

Certainly the sects often considered as belonging to the frontier in a special manner, such as the Mormons and the

[103] Wade, "Urban Life in Western America, 1790-1830," in *American Historical Review*, 64:28.

[104] Fort Wayne *Sentinel*, August 28, 1841.

[105] "Letters from Indiana, III," Fort Wayne *Sentinel*, April 30, 1842.

[106] Mrs. Jesse Williams to Mrs. M. S. Wines, February 19, 1845, in Miscellaneous Papers, Fort Wayne—Allen County Historical Museum.

Millerites, gained little if any popularity in Fort Wayne.[107] This was true despite the fact that it was reported as early as 1842 by one Fort Wayne citizen that Mormonism was quite likely to succeed in many sections of the West.[108] There were, of course, religious disciples such as John Chapman, better known as "Johnny Appleseed," who labored in the neighborhood of the city.

This horticultural evangelist first appeared in Fort Wayne no later than 1830. He died on a farm a short distance outside the city and is buried nearby. In a rather lengthy obituary, the *Sentinel* noted, "The deceased was well known through this region by his eccentricity and the strange garb he usually wore. He followed the occupation of a nurseryman and has been a regular visitor here upwards of twenty years. . . . He was a follower of Swedenborg, and devoutly believed that the more he endured in this world the less he would have to suffer and the greater would be his happiness hereafter. . . . He always carried with him some work on the doctrines of Swedenborg. He was perfectly familiar with his writings and would readily converse and argue on his tenets, using much shrewdness and penetration. . . . His death was quite sudden. He was seen on our streets a day or so previously."[109]

If the people of Fort Wayne seldom experienced the spiritual effects of camp meetings, it is no indication that they were apathetic towards religion. During the early 1840s the town was stirred often by religious controversy. The more bitter and prolonged controversies usually were of the Protestant vs. Catholic nature. Yet, as the writer of the "Indiana Letters" stated, there were times when the Protestants "prefer . . . making inroads upon the ranks of each other, to carrying the war into the dominions of the Devil."[110] These battles within the ranks of Protestantism seriously disturbed Charles Beecher, who wrote "cold Rome quietly pursues her farsighted policy—

[107] See articles in the Fort Wayne *Sentinel,* February 11, April 1, May 21, 1843, October 4, 1845.

[108] "Letters from Indiana, VII," Fort Wayne *Sentinel,* July 30, 1842.

[109] Fort Wayne *Sentinel,* March 22, 1845.

[110] "Letters from Indiana, VII," Fort Wayne *Sentinel,* July 30, 1842.

Neglecting our childish broils. . . ."[111] Still it was the Beecher attempt to gain control of the First Presbyterian Church which provoked a good many of these battles and at the same time created a great deal of religious interest in Fort Wayne. There were other interProtestant debates which stimulated the people of the city, such as that between Universalist Erasmus Manford and an Episcopalian minister in 1843.[112] In the same year a nondenominational minister from England, a "Mr. W. W. Stevens," clashed with Rankin,[113] the struggle continuing for over a year.[114] The two figures had distinctive personalities and not only disagreed on theology but on slavery, alcohol, and Freemasonry as well, the English preacher being in favor of all three.[115]

Alexander Rankin was again the central Protestant figure in a polemic with Father Benoit and another priest, Father Michael Edgar Shawe. The struggle must be seen in the light of the "Protestant Crusade" which was then being carried on throughout the nation. Incidents that had occurred in nearby communities, such as the resignation and supposed imprisonment of Bishop Frederick Resé of Detroit and the trial of an Evansville priest for a purported attack upon a woman while in the confessional, had aroused a great deal of interest in Fort Wayne.[116] Rankin was well known for his opposition to Catholicism. On the other hand, Benoit was not one to shrink when his church was attacked. Therefore the situation was such that when Father Shawe, known as a Catholic apologist, came to Fort Wayne to deliver a series of lectures, the stage was set for battle. Shawe had appeared in Fort Wayne before

[111] Beecher to Badger, March 28, 1845, American Home Missionary Society Papers.

[112] Robertson (ed.), *History of the Maumee River Basin,* 2:490.

[113] Fort Wayne *Sentinel,* January 14, 1843.

[114] *Ibid.,* February 3, 1844.

[115] "Letters from Indiana, IV," Fort Wayne *Sentinel,* May 14, 1842.

[116] Fort Wayne *Sentinel,* August 21, 1841, and June 4, 1842.

and apparently was quite popular as a speaker. The *Sentinel* reported that St. Augustine's was crowded every evening for a week and that Shawe had made a good impression upon the people with his courteous language. The editor believed that such lectures would serve to dispel prejudice; he also denied that Shawe had come to provoke controversy as was the current rumor.[117]

This belief, however, was prevalent and was apparently instigated by or at least fully accepted by Rankin. It also appears as if many of the people of Fort Wayne were anxious even before Shawe's arrival to arrange a debate between Rankin and the Catholic priest.[118] The result was a series of informal challenges, claims, counterclaims, and in the end, some harsh letters between Benoit and Rankin. After a week of Shawe's lectures, Rankin wrote an open letter to Shawe and Benoit asking the former to debate certain questions. At the same time Rankin told the citizens he would debate if challenged.[119] Shawe and Benoit both wished to avoid a debate because, as Benoit wrote:

> 1. It is not generally productive of good, but the contrary; it seldom subserves the cause of truth, never that of charity. 2. The office of the christian ministry is to announce the truths of religion, not to dispute about them. 3. The very idea of discussion supposes the matter to be discussed a matter of doubt or of opinion, but as we catholics, have no doubt whatsoever of the verity of our tenets we have no motive for debating them.[120]

Benoit added, however, that Shawe would accept *if* formally challenged lest refusal indicate weakness in the Catholic position.

Rankin claimed that he had challenged Shawe in a personal interview. This Benoit, speaking for Shawe, denied, saying

[117] *Ibid.*, August 20, 1842.

[118] Letter of Benoit to the Fort Wayne *Sentinel,* September 17, 1842.

[119] Correspondence of Rankin and Benoit published in the Fort Wayne *Sentinel,* August 27, 1842.

[120] Fort Wayne *Sentinel,* August 20, 1842.

that in the presence of Dr. Thompson, Shawe had stated to Rankin that he (Shawe) "will not suffer himself for a moment to be considered as a polemical gladiator. . . ."[121] Unsuccessful in securing the debate, Rankin still delivered during the following week a series of lectures intended to disprove Catholic doctrine. By now the religious excitement in the small city was intense. "Politics, elections, vetoes, and all that sort of thing, have given way to religion," the *Sentinel* reported.[122] The editor felt that in his lectures Rankin had sustained his character as a controversialist, but then commented, "His lectures we believe have been highly satisfactory to his Protestant hearers, but we are much inclined to doubt whether they have been listened to with as much pleasure and profit, and appeared as convincing to those who differ with him, as Mr. Shawe's were to those of a different crowd from the one [the faith] he advocated."[123]

Benoit and Rankin continued the controversy through letters to the *Sentinel* for over a month. Benoit insisted that he had no uncharitable feeling toward Rankin but was prevailed upon to answer the minister by men not of the Catholic faith.[124] In the final exchange Rankin referred to Benoit as "a blackguard. . . . A man so low and vulgar as he has shown himself to be, and so far destitute of all sense of decency and courtesy, is undeserving of notice." As for Shawe, Rankin considered him "as stamped with the brand of cowardice."[125] Although Benoit replied but briefly to this "last *highly polite and courteous* communication" of Rankin,[126] the priest must have enjoyed adding a postscript a few months later when Fort

[121] Correspondence of Rankin and Benoit, Fort Wayne *Sentinel,* August 27, 1842.

[122] *Ibid.*

[123] *Ibid.,* August 27, 1842.

[124] *Ibid.,* September 17, 1842.

[125] *Ibid.,* September 24, 1842.

[126] *Ibid.,* October 8, 1842.

Wayne received the news that Father Weinzoepflein, the Evansville priest, had been vindicated regarding the alleged attack on a woman. Benoit wrote:

> This is another striking example of the fairness and charity of protestant bigotry with respect to their christian brethren—the catholics. . . . We have been Maria-Monkised, Slokumised, Brownleeised, Brackenridgeised and Campbellised. . . . Have we been stopped on our onward way? Do not our ranks fill up in a wonderful manner?[127]

After pointing out that when the first bishop in the United States was consecrated in 1790 there were only a few thousand scattered Catholics living throughout the country and there were now fifteen bishops and six hundred priests, Benoit concluded "the time is not far when we will have a reckoning of millions."[128] Such a prediction was enough to provoke an apoplexy from Rankin.

As was usual during this period of American history, this religious controversy between Catholic and Protestant clergymen did not produce any clear-cut decision. However, it is apparent that Shawe had been listened to with attention by the people of Fort Wayne, and he was well received by some Protestants when he returned a year later. In the opinion of one, "if he does not make converts, he has removed many strong prejudices. . . ."[129] Certainly anti-Catholic feeling existed in Fort Wayne during these years,[130] but it was never as strong as it was in some other areas of the state or certain sections of the nation. The writer of the "Indiana Letters" stated that before coming to Fort Wayne he, like most New Eng-

[127] *Ibid.,* January 21, 1843.

[128] *Ibid.*

[129] *Ibid.,* September 30, 1843.

[130] In 1845 Captain McLane resigned as commander of the Wayne Guards because of repeated attacks on his religion. However the members of the Guard championed McLane and requested his return. See *Ibid.,* March 1, 1845.

landers, feared the Catholic church as an enemy of liberty, but afterward he no longer felt the same. He believed that rather than a religion corrupting the state, the state, if unlimited, would corrupt religion to its own ends.

Whatever the Catholic religion may have been in other countries—whatever it may be in those countries even now, on this side of the Atlantic it must assimulate itself to our peculiar institutions. . . . In my opinion, there is more reason to apprehend that the Catholics may be deprived of their just rights in the United States, than that our people will ever be brought under the control of the Roman See.[131]

The writer closed by noting that while the Catholics were making a strong effort in the West, their increase in numbers did not come from conversions of Protestants but from immigration, and that at Fort Wayne the Presbyterians and Methodists were holding their own.[132] In all, these letters represented a very keen analysis of the religious process which was unfolding in the West. It is not surprising that they were written by an urbanite from a town in which the immigrant played a significant but not an overwhelming role. Again it reveals the possibility that townspeople were more likely to adjust to the new climate. Certainly not all was "sweetness and light," but there could be understanding in decades remembered at times for their spirit of intolerance.

[131] "Letters from Indiana, VII," Fort Wayne *Sentinel,* July 30, 1842.
[132] *Ibid.*

CHAPTER VIII

TOWN AND COUNTRY: THE MATURING OF SOCIAL AND CULTURAL PATTERNS

Wealth has here (as it must everywhere) its influence and its power, but it is not with us a certain passport to respect and favor.

Perhaps in our day it is difficult to understand the important role of religion in the cultural aspects of community life in a town the size of Fort Wayne during the second quarter of the nineteenth century. Any detailed study of the period, however, will reveal the direct relation between the organization of the different religious denominations and the advancements in education and various social reform movements. The Presbyterians and the Methodists were the most active in the latter respect. One of the most important reform movements of the age, the Temperance Crusade, had a rather early beginning at Fort Wayne, considering the town's prior reputation as a military post and Indian agency. When the Reverend James Chute arrived in 1831, he found two temperance societies already organized at Fort Wayne, "one for people of all classes, & one young men's temperance society."[1] Shocked by the conditions in Fort Wayne, Chute spent most of his time, apart from preaching, in promoting the cause of temperance. In the spring of 1832, for example, he held weekly meetings of his newly organized Temperance Society to persuade the most influential men of the town to join.[2] In addition, he was constantly distributing tracts on the subject and laboring to prevent the issuing of whiskey to the canal workers. Although

[1] James Chute to Absalom Peters, December 12, 1831, American Home Missionary Society Papers.

[2] Chute to Peters, March 12, 1832.

Chute's efforts aroused a good deal of opposition, at times from some of Fort Wayne's leading citizens, the cause of temperance was advanced. In September, 1832, he was told by "a respectable physician . . . that two years ago a gallon of whiskey was drunk to one pint now." By this time the Society numbered 112 members.[3] Although Chute was discouraged in his efforts by the influx of Irish and German laborers, "the scum of Europe and New York,"[4] still the temperance movement was well launched by the time Alexander Rankin came to Fort Wayne in 1837. Characteristically, Rankin championed the cause with extreme vigor. His efforts were seconded by a member of his congregation, John Dawson, who was equally ardent in his views. With Rankin's encouragement, the Society met regularly at the Presbyterian church. However, the Methodist chapel was also used frequently by the Society after 1841. By 1842, with the support of these two congregations, the Temperance Society had a membership of some three hundred.[5] Since the 1830s the Society had promoted such events as the "Temperance Balls" held on Christmas and other holidays. It must not be assumed, however, that membership in the Society made the individual completely immune to the allurement of alcohol, especially on election days. In 1836 Susan Man wrote:

> all the bank directors were high on election day and we had a fine description of the scene from Mr. McCulloch as he was the only sober one in the bank. Judge Hanna and his oldest son were both carried home drunk with champagne. Mr. Hamilton and most of the other directors are very much mortified and wish it to be kept still for they are members of the temperance society . . . nearly all the little boys got drunk at the Harrison dinner after the example of their parents.[6]

[3] Chute to Peters, September 12, 1832. In a later letter Chute wrote, "From what I have seen, it is believed that no part of the west has been more addicted to intemperance than this region." Chute to Peters, December 17, 1832.

[4] Chute to Peters, January 27, 1834.

[5] Fort Wayne *Sentinel,* March 27, 1841, February 19, 26, 1842.

[6] Susan Man to Mrs. Frederick Halsey, November 27, 1836, Susan Man McCulloch Papers, Lilly Library, Indiana University.

Of course many of the townspeople, especially the immigrants, were not in accord with the methods employed by the advocates of temperance. One of the opponents, Peter Kiser, called upon the temperance leaders "to be temperate in all things and not denounce their fellow man so intemperately."[7] The opposition also benefited by the division in the temperance movement, which had occurred in Fort Wayne, as elsewhere, by the late 1830s.[8] The issue was whether the Society should demand total abstinence or only temperance in the use of alcohol and whether moral persuasion or legal persuasion should be employed. The "Fathers of Temperance and Friends of Literature," supposedly a secret society, was organized to teach sobriety but also had an interesting feature, a weekly confession to one another of sins of intemperance.[9] Because the "Fathers of Temperance" did not advocate total abstinence they were condemned by others as a group of "drunken loafers."[10] After 1844 the group advocating "total abstinence" centered around the person of Charles Beecher, and through his efforts the "New School" Presbytery of Fort Wayne adopted the following resolution: "Dram-drinking, dram-selling, dram giving . . . or the furnishing of materials for the manufacture of the same, are crimes which require church discipline."[11] After thus declaring drinking a moral crime punishable by the church, the "New School" Presbyterians of Fort Wayne then called for "total abolition through State action."[12] In Fort Wayne itself action was taken by the Common Council to prevent the erection of a distillery within

[7] Fort Wayne *Sentinel,* April 3, 1841.

[8] Alexander Rankin to Milton Badger, April 7, 1839, American Home Missionary Society Papers.

[9] Fort Wayne *Sentinel,* July 24, 1847. Some of the members must have been known by name, for as the *Sentinel* stated, "some of our best citizens have become members." Fort Wayne *Sentinel,* August 7, 1847.

[10] *Ibid.,* August 28, 1847.

[11] Letter of Charles Beecher published in *ibid.,* May 22, 1847.

[12] Fort Wayne *Times,* October 11, 1849.

the corporation limits.[13] In part this legal action was motivated by a desire to keep the city free from the odor accompanying a distillery's operations. At the same time, however, the would-be distiller was warned even before the Council acted that he would "never be permitted to erect and maintain that nuisance in the midst of this community."[14] While for some time the Council had prohibited the sale of alcoholic beverages on Sunday, in 1850 a new ordinance prohibited the sale of liquor in quantities of less than a quart.[15] As far as local authority went, however, this was the high point of the prohibition movement. Although in 1853 and again in 1855 state prohibition laws were enacted, the legislator from the Fort Wayne district voted against these statutes.[16] There are two reasons for the local failure of the prohibition movement at Fort Wayne. First, the German population, which was becoming a sizeable political factor by the 1840s, was opposed to it. Secondly, some citizens came to oppose it for, in their view, the prohibition efforts were too closely linked with the other reform movement for which they had little liking, the abolition of slavery.

There was some validity behind this viewpoint; however, it is an oversimplification to say that in Fort Wayne the two reform movements were equally championed by the same personalities. While John Dawson, one of the foremost temperance leaders in Fort Wayne, eventually became one of the first members of the Republican party and as editor of the Fort Wayne *Times* was to support the campaign of Lincoln, until

[13] Fort Wayne *Times,* December 6, 1849.

[14] *Ibid.,* November 29, 1849.

[15] Common Council Ordinance" passed May 6, 1850, printed in the Fort Wayne *Times,* May 9, 1850. One of the first ordinances passed by the Council prohibited the sale of alcoholic beverages to intoxicated persons, minors, and Indians.

[16] Fort Wayne *Times,* February 15, 1855. Concerning the legislation, see Charles Canup, "Temperance Movements and Legislation in Indiana," in *Indiana Magazine of History,* 16 (1920).

the mid-1850s he was more ardent as a prohibitionist and a nativist than he was as an abolitionist.[17] The other temperance leaders, Alexander Rankin and Charles Beecher, were both abolitionists. In the eyes of the people of Fort Wayne the link appeared as quite obvious since the members of both the Beecher and Rankin families had ties with the reform movements. Another relationship, at first, seems quite clear—both movements had an affinity with Presbyterianism. However, there was a difference between the two Presbyterian congregations in Fort Wayne. Alexander Rankin did not have the full support of the members of the First Presbyterian Church in Fort Wayne, that is the more conservative group. This lack of support was especially evident in regard to his views on slavery. This may have been due in part to the fact that Rankin was serving at a time when the new abolition movement of men such as William Lloyd Garrison, Theodore Weld, and John Rankin was being initiated. At any rate, under Charles Beecher the "New School" Presbyterians in Fort Wayne went much farther than their brethren. At the same meeting in which drinking was declared a crime subject to church discipline, the members of the "New School" Presbytery also resolved, "That slavery is a great sin, opposed to the word of God, and contrary to the rights of man. That slavery in the church should be a subject of discipline. . . ."[18] Even these resolutions were not enough for Beecher who proposed one more in a public statement to the press. "Resolved, that the disfranchise-

[17] A good number of Fort Wayne's early Republican leaders were abolitionist minded. Dawson was one of the first to enter the party after strongly opposing the Kansas-Nebraska Act. Although he was somewhat of a political weathervane, Dawson was known to be ardent in his views on temperance, slavery and, as he saw them, all moral issues. In fact his death resulted ultimately from a beating administered by Mormons who resented his attempt to stamp out polygamy while he was serving as Governor of Utah during Lincoln's first administration. In 1864 he opposed the re-election of Lincoln.

[18] Fort Wayne *Sentinel,* May 22, 1847.

ment of free people of color as practised in the state of Indiana, is a Crime analogous to that of slavery."[19] Indeed Beecher's racial views were far more advanced than many of his fellow abolitionists, not to mention the average citizen of Fort Wayne. He publicly criticized the National Society of the Sons of Temperance for stating that they were relieved to learn that a colored group of temperance advocates organized in Lafayette, Indiana, did not belong to their society. After asking why colored people should be excluded from the organization, Beecher concluded, "tho' I can conceive of reasons enough, I can conceive of not a single *good* one."[20] When the editor of the *Family Visitor* replied that the reason for excluding Negroes from the Sons of Temperance was to maintain "peace and harmony," Charles Beecher responded with a lengthy appeal for civil and social rights for the colored people and this time demanded to know if his fellow ministers, "including H. W. Beecher of Brooklyn, New York," were aware that the Sons of Temperance seemed to be interested "only in *white* drunkards."[21]

While it is apparent that these were the singular opinions of Charles Beecher, the abolition movement did have support from some of the other Protestant clergy of Fort Wayne. Among the Methodists the best known was Samuel Brenton from Kentucky who opposed slavery in principle and because it was injurious to the small farmer. Brenton served as president of the Methodist Female College in Fort Wayne and was instrumental in promoting coeducation. In 1851 he was elected as a Whig and Free Soil candidate from Indiana's Tenth Congressional District.[22] In 1854 he was re-elected as a Free

[19] Fort Wayne *Sentinel,* May 22, 1847.
[20] Fort Wayne *Times,* October 4, 1849.
[21] *Ibid.,* November 8, 1849.
[22] Riker and Thornbrough (comp.), *Indiana Election Returns,* 126. The election

Soil candidate, and shortly thereafter joined the newly created Republican party. In 1856 he was re-elected as a Republican, thus being the first Republican Congressman from Fort Wayne's Congressional district.[23]

If men such as Samuel Brenton, Alexander Rankin, and Charles Beecher must be classified as abolitionists, even if of varying shades of opinion, just where did the average Fort Wayne citizen stand in respect to the antislavery movement? Did he differ from his rural neighbor of northern Indiana? An early account written by a Quaker, Frederick Hoover, relates how a group of fugitive slaves guided by Quakers were permitted to pass through Fort Wayne in 1829 on their way to Detroit, provided they "would not turn to the right hand or to the left hand and if they took anything from thence they would give pieces of silver."[24] By agreement with "the chief men" of the town, food was purchased also.[25] This sense of official neutrality coupled with an underlying sympathy for the slave generally prevailed throughout the decade of the 1830s. As the great majority of the new settlers came from the northern states or from foreign countries they had no contact with slavery and little sympathy for it. Hugh McCulloch

returns in Allen County were divided almost equally between Brenton (1,112) and his Democratic opponent (1,100). In the presidential elections of 1852, 1856, and 1860, the county went Democratic. *The Whig Almanac and United States Register for 1853,* p. 60; *Tribune Almanac for 1861,* p. 62.

[23] Brenton died in 1857, and Charles Case an abolitionist of the most orthodox school was elected to take his place. Case was a Fort Wayne lawyer who in the early 1850s also edited the *Standard,* a weekly newspaper dedicated to the causes of "Abolition, Free Schools, and Prohibition." For the career of Case, see Fort Wayne *Journal-Gazette,* February 27, 1873.

[24] Frederick Hoover MS, facsimile reproduction in Griswold, *Pictorial History of Fort Wayne,* 1:291.

[25] While a map in William M. Cockrum, *History of the Underground Railroad* (Oakland City, Ind., 1915), 8, shows Fort Wayne as a station on the route from Cincinnati to Detroit, there is no other documentation to support such a belief. If Fort Wayne was a station it must have been a minor one.

probably spoke for most of his fellow townsmen when he said, "We feel that this [slavery] is a blot upon our national banner. Would to God that we were able to wash it out!"[26] Nevertheless, although he was to become a close friend of Charles Beecher, McCulloch was equally convinced that "slavery is never to be abolished in America, by exciting the slave to rebellion, or by heaping bitter and unqualified reproach upon his master."[27] Judging from their lack of participation in any of the antislavery movements, we may conclude that the merchants of Fort Wayne generally agreed with McCulloch. Men like Samuel Hanna or Allen Hamilton were more interested in internal improvements, land values, or the banking system than the question of slavery.

While during the 1830s the people of Fort Wayne could ignore the question of slavery if they chose to do so, during the next decade they were increasingly faced with the problem of the free colored people who settled in the city. According to John Dawson, there was only one Negro living in Fort Wayne in 1838.[28] Yet in 1850 Fort Wayne had 81 free colored people out of a population of 4,282, while the whole of Allen County in the same year had only 102 free colored people out of a population of 16,919.[29] It is apparent that the free Negroes preferred the city where greater opportunities were available for labor. When, in 1850, the state constitutional convention was faced with the proposal to exclude Negroes from residing

[26] Speech of Hugh McCulloch delivered July 4, 1835, printed in the Indianapolis *Indiana Journal,* September 18, 1835.

[27] *Ibid.*

[28] Dawson, *Charcoal Sketches of Old Times in Fort Wayne,* 20. Dawson, who was so interested in abolition, was likely to have remembered such a fact clearly. Moreover, the Federal census for 1840 indicated that there were only 18 free colored people living in Allen County. See *Compendium of the Sixth Census* (1840), 80-81. Since the population of the town may be estimated at 1,500 compared to the 5,942 living in the county, it is difficult to imagine that there could have been more than nine Negroes living in Fort Wayne by 1840.

[29] *Compendium of the Seventh Census* (1850), 757.

in Indiana, Allen Hamilton, the Whig delegate from the Fort Wayne district, chose to write an open letter to his constituents asking for instructions on how to vote.[30] This was the only issue which Hamilton referred directly to the voters. Not only did this indicate the importance of the decision in Hamilton's mind but it also seems to indicate that either Hamilton himself had no firm convictions on the matter or that he was uncertain as to the will of the majority—possibly both. The most interesting reply was a letter supposedly written by a Fort Wayne "mechanic" which appeared in the Whig paper, the *Times.* In the first place, the writer agreed with the editor of the *Sentinel* that no hastily called meeting should try to decide such a momentous issue. It is quite likely that the writer of the letter feared the result of such a meeting for it is soon apparent where he stands. He argued that if the exclusion clause was adopted slaveholders would find it more difficult to free their Negroes, especially since they wanted the freedmen to leave the slave states. Also, he asked, what would be done with the escaped Negroes fleeing into Indiana? He admitted that similar legal action by nearby free states might "subject us to a greater Negro population than we desire," but, he concluded, "Indiana, it is to be hoped will not subject herself to be the object of future reproach. If this provision is adopted then the Constitution must be rejected. Whatever reforms we may by experience have found necessary, let us adopt—but spare us! spare us now! and spare posterity! the mortifying

[30] Fort Wayne *Sentinel,* December 7, 1850. Neither Hamilton nor James Borden, the Democratic representative from Allen County at the convention, spoke in the debates on this issue although Borden especially entered many other debates. Strangely enough both men broke with their parties on a proposed resolution putting the convention on record as favoring the Congressional Compromise of 1850. Hamilton was the only Whig who favored the resolution. While he thought the Fugitive Slave Act unjust, his major concern was the preservation of the Union. See *Report of the Debates and Proceedings of the Convention for the Revision of the Constitution of the State of Indiana, 1850* (2 vols. Indianapolis, 1851), 1:909-10; 2:1017-19.

legacy, that so inhuman a provision as the one proposed was ever incorporated in the *Constitution of Indiana.*"[31]

The viewpoint of this writer (whether or not a mechanic) need not be taken as characteristic of the laboring man in Fort Wayne. The Fort Wayne *Sentinel,* which as the Democratic paper claimed to speak for labor, frequently expressed opposition to the abolitionist movement and on one occasion stated, "the mechanics and laboring men are 'dead set' against the abolitionists."[32] Moreover, the paper delighted in showing the relationship between some of the abolitionists and the nativist opposition against the immigrant.[33] As for the German element in Fort Wayne, there is no evidence that they were in accord with the abolitionists. There is no record of any of their clergy speaking out vigorously against slavery, and as Democrats, they generally opposed abolitionists who were more often than not associated with certain elements of the declining Whig party. Moreover, as mentioned before, abolitionism was tainted with the temperance movement as well. Above all, the Germans in Fort Wayne were devoted to the Union, and it is quite possible that they looked upon the abolition movement as leading to the division of the nation. On the other hand, this sense of patriotism and devotion to the Union, which we shall see as a marked characteristic of the German population of Fort Wayne, would later make of the Germans ardent defenders of the nation during the Civil War.

Thus, the merchant, the laboring man, and the immigrant at Fort Wayne generally looked upon the abolitionist as fanatical. If any group within the city tended towards abolitionism,

[31] Fort Wayne *Times,* December 12, 1850. The editor of the *Times* opposed the exclusion clause for similar reasons, yet he took exception to a sermon of Henry Ward Beecher which was printed in the *Times.* In the sermon Beecher called the proposed Constitution "sinful" and one that should be disobeyed. *Ibid.,* March 6, 13, 1851.

[32] Fort Wayne *Sentinel,* July 26, 1845.

[33] *Ibid.,* March 15, 1845.

it was the professional class of men—some of the Protestant ministers, such as Rankin, Charles Beecher, and Brenton, lawyers and newspaper editors, such as John Dawson and Charles Case, and the physician, Dr. Lewis Thompson.[34] We cannot conclude, however, that by 1850, apart from a few, the people of Fort Wayne were largely indifferent to slavery itself. Rather it would seem that the average citizen opposed slavery in theory, but had little real concern for the Negro as an individual apart from the question of slavery. This theoretical opposition could take the form of voting against G. W. Ewing in 1847 because his fur company owned slaves in Missouri,[35] and yet agree to prohibit the Negro from migrating to Indiana four years later. In the 1851 state-wide referendum on whether Negroes should be excluded from entering Indiana, Allen County supported the proposed clause in the constitution by an overwhelming vote, 1775 in favor to 261 opposed.[36] This seeming contradiction between opposition to slavery and opposition to the Negro did not appear to bother the townsmen of the Old Northwest any more than such incongruities as calling for greater civil rights in the South while refusing membership in private clubs appears to trouble the conscience of the present generation of northerners.

While the Presbyterians and Methodists were the most active of the various religious bodies in such questions as temperance and the antislavery movements, all four of the major faiths in Fort Wayne promoted the cause of education. Until 1853 there were no public schools in the city, only private and

[34] Thompson was a Whig, but shortly before he died the *Sentinel* accused him of being more of an abolitionist than a Whig. Fort Wayne *Sentinel,* July 19, 1845.

[35] Fort Wayne *Sentinel,* July 24, 1847.

[36] Riker and Thornbrough (comp.), *Indiana Election Returns,* 388. There are no statistics available for Wayne Township, however, the size of the majority would indicate that the people of Fort Wayne could not have differed considerably from the viewpoint of their rural neighbors.

parochial ones. The first school established at Fort Wayne was in fact that of the Baptist missionary, Isaac McCoy. Beginning in 1820 the Reverend and Mrs. McCoy taught for two years a heterogeneous group of forty-two pupils in the old council house, including English-speaking Americans, French-speaking children of the original settlers, and Indians.[37] In 1825 through a liberal grant of property by the original proprietors, Barr and McCorkle, the county erected Fort Wayne's first school building, called the "County Seminary." This one-story brick structure was located on Calhoun Street behind the county jail and adjacent to an old graveyard. Theoretically, according to the Indiana Constitution, the school was to be supported by public funds raised through levies assessed against citizens who were exempted from militia duty and through fines for any breach of the penal law. The spirit of this provision in the state constitution was in keeping with the Ordinance of 1787, yet invariably throughout the state the fines were seldom collected. In Allen County some effort was made by the commissioners of the Seminary Fund; still, in 1841, an inquest revealed the seminary funds were in a deplorable condition. Out of fines totalling $3,392.70, only $1,630.15½ was still collectible, owing to the statute of limitations.[38] By September, 1842, only $217.81 had been collected.[39] Therefore, the students who attended the County Seminary paid their own tuition while the county simply maintained the building with whatever funds were occasionally collected. The price of tuition, as in all private schools, was determined

[37] Isaac McCoy's pupils nearly drove the Indian agent, John Hays, to complete distraction since the latter had to share the government building with the teacher and his "scholars." In addition to this a good deal of government property was destroyed. Robertson, "John Hays and the Fort Wayne Indian Agency," in *Indiana Magazine of History*, 39:226.

[38] Fort Wayne *Sentinel*, April 24, 1841.

[39] *Ibid.*, September 10, 1842.

according to the subjects studied.[40] The early teachers usually had to follow another vocation in addition to teaching in order to secure a livelihood. Their ability varied, but on the whole they appear to have been far more qualified than the type of teacher often represented on the frontier. It is true that the first teacher at the County Seminary, John P. Hedges, an Indian trader, had little to recommend him for the position except a certain popularity with his fellow townsmen. He also served as county sheriff and apparently found no difficulty in watching both jail and schoolhouse because of the proximity of the two buildings.

For about six years, beginning in 1825, Henry Cooper, a young lawyer from Maryland who later became one of Indiana's most prominent attorneys, also conducted a private school in the debtor's room of the county jail. By 1832, however, Jesse Aughinbaugh, who had assumed the position as teacher at the County Seminary, was the only teacher in the town. He gave almost all of his time to teaching since he also instructed the Catholic children in their religion.[41] The fact that Aughinbaugh, a Catholic, was Fort Wayne's only teacher disturbed James Chute, the Presbyterian minister, who called for a Protestant replacement.[42] Consequently, after Aughinbaugh resigned, Smalwood Noel, an elder in the First Presbyterian Church became the teacher at the County Seminary. In the meantime, Susan Man had learned of the need of Protestant teachers in the West.[43] She was the daughter of a Presbyterian minister and had attended the Hartford Female

[40] *Ibid.*, December 26, 1846; Statement of George Brackenridge in Lura Woodworth, Carolyn Fairbank, and Martha Hanna (comps.), *Reminiscences of Old Fort Wayne* (Fort Wayne Public Library, 1953), [25].

[41] Ghislain Boheme to Bishop Purcell, May 26, 1833, University of Notre Dame Archives.

[42] James Chute to Absalom Peters, December 17, 1832, American Home Missionary Society Papers.

[43] Susan Man to Mrs. Frederick Halsey, April 1, 1836, McCulloch Papers.

Seminary in Connecticut. Apparently she learned of Fort Wayne's situation through her friend, Alida Hubbell, whose brother was employed in Fort Wayne. The two young ladies were accompanied to Fort Wayne by Samuel Hanna and established their school in the courthouse in the spring of 1836. Jesse Hoover, the Lutheran minister, also taught in Fort Wayne during that year. In the fall of 1836, he joined Susan Man and Alida Hubbell in teaching in the new Presbyterian church. Susan Man's salary for the year was $250.[44] The classes, altogether numbering some one hundred students, met five times a week for a ten-month period. After the marriage of Susan Man to Hugh McCulloch and the death of Jesse Hoover, Alexander McJunkin took charge of Hoover's English-speaking students late in 1837. While the two young ladies were remembered for their gentle ways,[45] such was not the case of McJunkin, who was described by one of his pupils as "a fine scholar, a strong, judicious instructor and a stern, rigidly strict disciplinarian . . . [who] most forcibly impressed his ideas and teachings upon the minds of his scholars and not infrequently with equal force upon their bodies."[46]

In 1837 the English nondenominational minister W. W. Stevens and his wife opened the "Fort Wayne Select Classical and Commercial Academy."[47] Other private schools also appeared in the late 1830s, but most of them were associated with a particular religious denomination. The death of Jesse Hoover was but a temporary setback for Lutheran education in Fort Wayne, for with the arrival of Wyneken the Lutherans renewed their efforts to provide schooling for their children. Classes were conducted in German by the pastor four times weekly in the small school which he established. By the time

[44] Susan Man to Mrs. Frederick Halsey, August 18, 1836, McCulloch Papers.

[45] "Reminiscences of A. C. Comparet," in *Old Fort News,* 18:no. 4-19:no. 5:5.

[46] Griswold, *Pictorial History of Fort Wayne,* 1:341.

[47] Fort Wayne *Sentinel,* September 25, 1841.

Sihler became pastor of St. Paul's Church in 1845, the Lutheran parochial school was a well established and respected institution in Fort Wayne. In the previous chapter we noted the founding of the important Lutheran Theological Seminary at Fort Wayne in 1846, this being in conjunction with Lohe's efforts to promote conservative Lutheranism in the United States. The graduates of this seminary were soon furnishing St. Paul's Church with teachers for the youth of the congregation.

Although it was very significant in its own right, the Lutheran Theological Seminary was not the only institution of advanced learning established in Fort Wayne during this period. In addition, the city was to witness the creation of three secondary academies and one more college. All of these institutions were affiliated with the principal religious denominations of Fort Wayne—Lutheran, Catholic, Methodist, and Presbyterian. Although the Catholic children of Fort Wayne had some religious instruction from the resident priests and from Jesse Aughinbaugh during the 1830s, there was no Catholic school established until midway in the following decade. No later than 1844 Father Benoit secured the services of William B. Walter from Maryland as an instructor for the young boys of the area.[48] Later Joseph Graff served as an assistant to Walter. In 1852 this school, St. Augustine's Institution, came under the supervision of the Holy Cross Brothers from the University of Notre Dame. The Brothers taught both primary and secondary levels until after the Civil War when the Sisters of Providence took charge of the lower grades. This order of nuns from St. Mary-of-the-Woods, Indiana, had been sent by Mother Theodore Guerin to Fort Wayne in 1846 at the request of Benoit, who two years previously had expressed a desire to provide educational opportunities for the young

[48] Fort Wayne *The People's Press,* September 17, 1844. In this issue the paper informed its readers that St. Augustine's Institution under W. B. Walter "resumed its annual session on Tuesday last."

women of the community. From the outset St. Augustine's Academy for girls enjoyed success. The school was well furnished through Benoit's financial assistance, and the first year found sixty pupils enrolled, fifteen of whom were from outside the city.[49]

In 1844 the Presbyterians established the Fort Wayne Female Seminary under the direction of Lydia Sykes. However, after two years, because of the illness of the headmistress, the seminary was abandoned until 1852 when a new Presbyterian academy was opened under the direction of George A. Irvin, a graduate of Hanover College.[50]

A major step in Fort Wayne's educational efforts was taken in 1846 when the Northern Indiana Methodist Conference agreed to proposals by Fort Wayne citizens to establish the Fort Wayne Female College at an estimated cost of $20,000.[51] The college was to be located on West Wayne Street on land donated by William Rockhill. In addition to this gift, the citizens of the city initially subscribed $13,000 towards its construction. When completed in 1849, the college, a four-story brick building, had room for three hundred students.[52] Classes began in 1847 with a curriculum which included grammar, arithmetic, geography, Latin, Greek, French, Spanish, music, drawing, logic, algebra, chemistry, literary criticism, and history.[53] Tuition was $22.50 a year. Beginning in September, 1850, men were admitted to the college, but it was promised that "this will not interfere with the rights of Females."[54] For

[49] Katherine Burton, *Faith is the Substance. The Life of Mother Theodore Guerin* (St. Louis, 1959), 194; Fort Wayne *News-Sentinel,* July 5, 1958.

[50] John H. Thomas, "The Academies of Indiana," in *Indiana Magazine of History,* 10 (1914):353.

[51] Fort Wayne *Sentinel,* September 26, 1846.

[52] *Ibid.,* September 13, 1849.

[53] *Ibid.,* December 26, 1846, July 17, 1847.

[54] Fort Wayne *Times,* August 22, 1850.

four years men attended the college under the title, "Collegiate Institute for Men," but in 1855 the two institutions were definitely merged into a coeducational college known officially as the Fort Wayne College.[55] By 1854 the enrollment was 256, 97 of whom were men.

Thus between the years 1836 and 1850, the progress of Fort Wayne in the field of private and parochial education was commendable. She had developed a whole system of private schooling from the elementary to the college level. *The People's Press* could boast, "the youth of this city, whether male or female, have no further need of going abroad to complete their education, their advantages at home being quite equal to those they can enjoy in other places."[56]

During this same period public education in Fort Wayne made virtually no progress. In 1836 the town trustees after discussing ways to raise funds for a common school allowed the matter to drop.[57] Occasional efforts were made in the early forties to interest the citizenry in the matter. In 1841 the press carried a few articles on the subject, yet Professor Caleb Mills of Wabash College attracted only a handful of people when he spoke on the need for public support of the schools.[58] By 1848, however, the residents of Allen County were prepared to cast an overwhelming vote in favor of free public schools. When the question was submitted to the voters of Indiana, Allen County's vote was 1,826 in favor and 440 opposed, while the state vote was only 78,523 in favor and 61,887

[55] The College was known by various names—The Fort Wayne Methodist College and the Old M. E. College. In 1890 it became Taylor University which later moved to Upland, Indiana.

[56] Fort Wayne *The People's Press,* September 10, 1844. In Indiana in 1850 Allen County ranked second only to Marion County in the number of academies. See *Compendium of the Seventh Census* (1850), 785-86.

[57] Report of the town trustees on December 21, 1835 and March 26, 1836, in Records of the Town Trustees, City Hall.

[58] Fort Wayne *Sentinel,* March 27, December 25, 1841.

opposed.[59] Therefore, over 80 per cent of the Allen County voters favored a public-supported school system, while only about 56 per cent of the voters throughout the state favored the concept. These statistics support the conclusion of Professor Wade that in the West, "the cities organized the movement for public schooling."[60] Actually nothing came of the statewide referendum, as the legislature failed to act; thus the struggle for free schools in Fort Wayne had to await the decade of the fifties.

Apart from the increasing educational opportunities for the youth of the town and the surrounding area, Fort Wayne offered certain other cultural advantages to its citizens. As it has been pointed out, "A remarkable characteristic of the westward migration was the speed and intensity with which the pioneers sought to reproduce the culture they had left behind."[61] It is true that the cultural opportunities offered in a new town the size of Fort Wayne were limited when compared to those offered in the urban centers of the East or even those of a larger western city such as Cincinnati. But just as the children of Fort Wayne had greater educational advantages than their rural counterparts of northeastern Indiana, so did the older residents enjoy a superiority over their country neighbors in other social and cultural matters.

For example, in 1844 the adults of the town could attend a night school which advertised that it taught "any of the branches of a good education" but specialized in writing and bookkeeping.[62] Again by the later forties, the townspeople could attend the annual winter series of weekly lectures. These

[59] Charles W. Moores, *Caleb Mills and the Indiana School System* (Indiana Historical Society *Publications,* Vol. 3, No. 6, Indianapolis, 1905), 539.

[60] Wade, "Urban Life in Western America," in *American Historical Review,* 64:25.

[61] Howard H. Peckham, "Books and Reading on the Ohio Valley Frontier," in *The Mississippi Valley Historical Review,* 44 (1958):651.

[62] Fort Wayne *The People's Press,* October 29, 1844.

lectures were sponsored by the Young Men's Literary Society organized in 1846. Outside speakers, the most noted of whom was Horace Mann, were brought to Fort Wayne or local citizens, such as Hugh McCulloch, addressed the society and its guests. The subject matter ranged all the way from the history of philosophy to zoology.[63]

Other societies also offered social opportunities to the people. For the military-minded young men there existed the "Fort Wayne Guards," which was organized in 1841 and later participated in the Mexican War. The oldest of the town's societies was that of the Masons, the Wayne Lodge being organized in 1823. Its membership included a number of the early American settlers, such as John Tipton, Alexander Ewing, Benjamin Cushman, and John P. Hedges. For almost two decades after 1833 the Fort Wayne Masonic Lodge was virtually disbanded due to the anti-Masonic sentiment throughout the nation.[64] Periodic attempts were made during this time to revitalize the lodge, but with little success until 1854.

In his interesting article on books and reading on the frontier, Howard Peckham writes:

> The general verdict about the dearth of books in frontier society is deceptively logical. We have assumed that in a rude society which had little time for reading there was no incentive to acquire books, and thus that the exceptional frontiersman who might wish to read found it difficult to obtain reading matter. Our attitude is

[63] See the Fort Wayne *Times,* issues for December, 1849, and January, February, 1850. Hugh McCulloch was one of the most popular speakers. As a man of varied intellectual and religious interests, McCulloch never devoted himself exclusively to banking. He corresponded with Professor Benjamin Pence of Harvard and a number of professors at Columbia University, as well as its president, Frederick A. P. Barnard. He also joined the State Historical Society of Wisconsin in 1858. See McCulloch Papers.

[64] It is interesting to note that two men directly implicated in the incident which touched off the anti-Masonic sentiment, that is the disappearance of William Morgan, came to Fort Wayne in the early thirties. One, Jared Darrow, settled on a farm outside the city, and another, Stephen Brown Bond, settled in the city itself. Robertson (ed.), *History of the Maumee River Basin,* 2:522-24.

reinforced, for example, by stories of young Abraham Lincoln eagerly borrowing books from his neighbors. But what we remember is the scarcity of books in the Lincoln cabin, rather than the fact that his Indiana neighbors had books to lend. Commonly, also, little distinction is drawn between frontier farms and frontier hamlets. . . . In general town living meant time and houseroom for books. . . . Frontier communities, at least in the Ohio Valley, offered a much wider range of reading matter. . . . [than did the rural areas].[65]

Good books were to be found at Fort Wayne even in the early period, being brought by individual settlers in most instances.[66] By the early 1830s books were being sent from publishers in the East and from book dealers in Cincinnati. The cost of transportation was very high, as was the case for all merchandise.[67] With the opening of the canal to the Great Lakes, these charges were considerably reduced. Travelers who came by way of the canal were also likely to carry books with them to their new homes or to purchase them along the way in order to while away their leisure hours on the slow-moving boats. One may find eastern publishers advertising regularly in the Fort Wayne papers by the early 1840s.[68] Agents for the publisher also carried books to the town periodically.[69] As the forties progressed, the local merchants started to carry and advertise books as a regular part of their stock. By 1848 Fort Wayne's first literary publication, *The Casket*, made its appearance. This was followed in the early fifties by

[65] Peckham, "Books and Reading on the Ohio Valley Frontier," *Mississippi Valley Historical Review*, 44:649-50.

[66] In 1764 an English officer, Captain Morris, was reading a volume of Shakespeare which he had purchased from an Indian when he was captured by a party of Miami within sight of the old French fort. See Poinsatte, A History of Fort Wayne, from 1716 to 1829, p. 23.

[67] Stephen Badin to Bishop Purcell, September 22, 1834, University of Notre Dame Archives.

[68] Fort Wayne *Sentinel*, April 10, 1841.

[69] One agent sold such works as *The Life of Emanuel Swedenborg* and *A Week in Wall Street* for fifty cents a volume. Fort Wayne *Sentinel*, November 20, 1841.

two more literary journals, *The Laurel Wreath* and *The Summit City Journal.*

Again, as Howard Peckham points out, it is interesting to note, "how early in the life of a community libraries were thought of and considered necessary."[70] In Fort Wayne provisions were made for a public library as early as 1824. Beginning in that year the county agents set aside 10 per cent of the income derived from the sale of lots donated to the county by Barr and McCorkle. These funds were to be used to support a county library. By 1842 approximately $1,700 had been raised in this fashion.[71] An act of 1831 provided that no more than $500 be invested in land or property apart from books.[72]

Due to the fragmentary nature of the county commissioners records, it is difficult to determine just when the library was established. It was certainly in existence no later than 1834, when at the request of Henry Rudisill the commissioners appointed three new trustees for the library.[73] Ten years later an inventory of the library's books was ordered, but we have no existing record of this inventory. In 1841 the Fort Wayne *Sentinel* published a list of books which had just been purchased by the library, including:

Madison Papers, Ferdinand and Isabella, Thiers' French Revolution, Russell's History of Europe, Marshall's Life of Washington, Gillies' Greece, Sismondi's Rome, Ferguson's Rome, Hallam's Middle Ages, Botta's History of the United States, DeTocqueville's Democracy in America, Steven's Greece, Steven's Arabia, Brougham's Statesmen, Plutarch's Lives, The Federalist, Bancroft's History of the United States, Don Quixote, Shakespeare's Works, Dryden's Works, Herodotus, Thucydides, Johnson's Works, Dicken-

[70] Peckham, "Books and Reading on the Ohio Valley Frontier," *Mississippi Valley Historical Review,* 44:657.

[71] John H. Jacobs, "Libraries of Allen County," in Robertson (ed.), *History of the Maumee River Basin,* 2:327. This provision for county libraries was set out in Article IX, section 5, of the first state constitution.

[72] *Ibid.,* 328.

[73] *Ibid.*

son's Works, Pope's Works, Irving's Columbus, Rollin's Ancient History, Say's Political Economy, Byron's Works.[74]

Such an impressive addition must have been welcomed by the readers of the county who were invited to use the books for a fee of only $1.00 a year or 25 cents per quarter.[75] Periodically men such as Hugh McCulloch, Henry R. Colerick, and Joseph K. Edgerton were called upon to select new works for the readers. There is no existing record of the total number of volumes in the library, but Henry Colerick later estimated it to be around five hundred.[76] In 1855 a decision of the county commissioners to divide the county into library districts and then to have the books circulate from one district to another virtually destroyed the county library system. A lack of centralized control and inadequate means of checking the volumes meant the eventual loss of most of the books. The rest of the volumes were appropriated by the newly created township libraries which had been brought into being as part of a state system in 1852. Thus in the city of Fort Wayne the Wayne Township Library replaced the Allen County Library in 1854.

In addition to sponsoring a lecture series, the Young Men's Literary Society supported a library for its members. The Society with its library was incorporated into the Workingmen's Institute and Library in 1855, maintaining not only a creditable number of good books but also the best in periodicals—*Harper's Monthly, The Atlantic, The Eclectic, North American Review, Blackwood's Edinburgh Magazine, Edinburgh Review, Westminster Review,* and the *London Quarterly Review.*

Indeed, to paraphrase Peckham, to look in on Fort Wayne as a representative community "in the Ohio Valley is to dis-

[74] Fort Wayne *Sentinel,* June 5, 1841.

[75] *Ibid.*

[76] Jacobs, "Libraries of Allen County," in Robertson (ed.), *History of the Maumee River Basin,* 2:328-29.

cover an unexpected level of reading interest and availability of books."[77] During the period under consideration its citizens not only initiated a county library but also began to lay the foundations for a number of personal libraries.[78] This literary interest was not limited solely to the more wealthy but also included the working class.

The availability of reading material in libraries was limited almost entirely to people within the town and its proximate vicinity. This was not true, however, of the Fort Wayne newspapers. These journals contained the weekly market prices for the farmers' grain, livestock, and produce as well as the advertising of the local merchants. Moreover, the news value was immeasurable to the more isolated farm family. Nevertheless, despite their importance to the farmers of northeastern Indiana, these journals on the frontier could not have existed apart from the community life of a town inasmuch as they needed the cash income derived from advertising by the local merchants and from subscriptions by the local citizens. The rural folk, lacking cash, quite often paid in kind for the subscription with such things as wood, vegetables, and meat in season. These items would sustain an editor, but they could not be used for purchasing type, machinery, and paper.

The establishment of the first newspaper, the *Sentinel,* followed by only one year the beginning of the canal construction. Clearly the new founded enthusiasm of the local leaders had to find some means of expressing the town's progress. The historian of American journalism, Frank Luther Mott, has written:

[77] Peckham, "Books and Reading on the Ohio Valley Frontier," in *Mississippi Valley Historical Review,* 44:649.

[78] The Allen Hamilton library would eventually number some six thousand books, and that of Hugh Hanna about two thousand. Franklin P. Randall not only had a fine collection of books, but a number of medieval and Renaissance manuscripts as well.

Wherever a town sprang up, there a printer with a rude press . . . was sure to appear as by magic. It was not magic, however; these pioneer towns all wanted and secured newspapers for both promotional and political reasons. In the first place they wanted them as 'boosters,' and the pioneers sent these sheets, filled with propaganda for the new country, back to the East, where they were effective in keeping up the flow of emigration.[79]

Activated by such consideration, Henry Rudisill, Dr. Lewis Thompson, Joseph Holman, C. W. Ewing, Allen Hamilton, and Francis Comparet invited Thomas Tigar and S. V. B. Noel, two printers from Indianapolis, to establish a newspaper in Fort Wayne. The above committee promised that they would contribute $500 to the enterprise. The press was to be held as security.[80] Apparently the money was not needed as Tigar and Noel had enough capital between them. S. V. B. Noel was the son of the Fort Wayne citizen, Smalwood Noel. Tigar was born in 1807 in Yorkshire, England, where he had learned his trade before coming to the United States in 1826.

The first difficulty of the publishers was in getting the hand press and other equipment to Fort Wayne from Indianapolis where it had been purchased from the *Indiana State Journal*. The road was almost impassable, and bridges had to be constructed to cross the rivers.[81] The initial issue appeared on July 6, 1833, and was received with enthusiasm by the townspeople although its news was somewhat limited. In fact, the Declaration of Independence took up a good deal of the first page.[82] Unlike Fort Wayne's later papers, the *Sentinel* obviously was not founded for political reasons, since the two publishers differed in party affiliation, Noel being a Whig while Tigar was an ardent Democrat. Apparently peaceful

[79] Frank Luther Mott, *American Journalism* (New York, 1941), 282.

[80] Willodeen Price, "Newspapers at Fort Wayne," MS in Fort Wayne—Allen County Public Library.

[81] Statement of Thomas Tigar, January 25, 1844, in *Letter of Col. John Spencer,* 40.

[82] Fort Wayne *Sentinel,* July 6, 1833.

co-operation with its neutral editorial policy soon proved impossible, and Noel retired from the venture within a year. Tigar immediately announced that the paper would champion the Democratic party. Except for a period of four years between 1837 and 1841, Tigar continued as the sole publisher of the *Sentinel* until 1865. It has been rightly said of this pioneer editor of northern Indiana,

He did not usually write much but he wrote well, and for years his party had not an abler editor in the state. He was particularly happy as a paragraphist, often condensing into a few sentences, pointed and expressive, the substance of a column in other hands. Had he been as ambitious as he was able, he might have risen to distinction as a party leader.[83]

While Tigar was a Jacksonian Democrat in every respect, he never intended the *Sentinel* to be simply a nonprofit-making party organ. Apart from his skill in his trade and as a journalist, Tigar had to have some managerial ability to make the publication of his four-page weekly a financial success. The odds seemed against him at first. The population of northeastern Indiana was still small in the 1830s, and the merchants of Fort Wayne who could advertise were also relatively few. As Tigar had probably foreseen, these conditions gradually improved with the continued construction of the canal. The growth of Fort Wayne may be seen in the increasing variety of advertising in the *Sentinel* through the years. Like other western publishers, Tigar devoted more than half of his paper to advertising. To obtain clients the *Sentinel*'s rates were kept relatively low.[84] In general, despite the Whig tendencies, the Fort Wayne merchants advertised in the

[83] Fort Wayne *News-Sentinel,* June 16, 1926 (Progress Edition), p. 20.

[84] Mott considers "fifty cents a square (about twelve lines of nonpareil) for the first insertion and half that for succeeding insertions" as a low rate for the period. Mott, *American Journalism,* 201. The *Sentinel* charged ten cents a line for three weeks (three issues) and five cents for each subsequent renewal when consisting of ten lines or more.

Sentinel. Only once did Tigar complain about certain merchants who for political reasons did not advertise in his paper.[85]

Other difficulties were not so easily overcome by Tigar and other early publishers. These were "first . . . to get paper . . . second to get news, and . . . third to get paid."[86] The completion of the canal did much to alleviate the periodic shortage of paper,[87] but as late as the mid-forties, the *Sentinel* had to limit its edition to one page on occasion. Although in short supply, the quality of the paper was good, still today retaining most of its color.

Until the telegraph came to Fort Wayne in 1848, the problem of obtaining news depended principally upon the delivery of other papers by mail. In 1833 the town received mail twice a week from the area to the northwest as far as Chicago, once a week from the East by way of the Maumee, twice a week from Logansport to the west, and once a week from Winchester to the south. The newspapers conducted vigorous campaigns for improvement in the mail service to Fort Wayne. The protest of a particular editor was most vigorous when the opposition party was in control of the postal system in Washington. In 1842 during a Whig administration the *Sentinel* complained that the mail which should have taken only four days between Indianapolis and Fort Wayne normally took seven to ten days.[88] The canal again was of some help in speeding up the service, but delays were still encountered. In 1848 the Whig paper complained about the lack of adequate

[85] Fort Wayne *Sentinel,* April 2, 1842.

[86] Mary A. Walker, *The Beginnings of Printing in the State of Indiana . . . to 1850* (Crawfordsville, 1934), 15.

[87] Fort Wayne *Sentinel,* February 10, 1844. In this issue the publisher announced that he would begin putting out a larger newspaper as the canal made possible a greater supply of paper.

[88] *Ibid.,* February 19, 1842.

mail deliveries.[89] What was extremely annoying to the Fort Wayne editor was his inability to verify news that reached the town by way of rumor. Often he could not risk rejecting untrustworthy stories on the chance that they might later prove true, especially since the paper appeared only weekly; therefore, these stories were printed with comments such as, "We suppose this to be a fabrication."

The third and greatest problem of the publisher was to get paid by his subscribers. The *Sentinel's* rates were two dollars per annum if paid in advance, $2.50 per annum if paid within six months, and $3.00 if paid at the end of the year. Wood, produce, etc. were also accepted by Tigar. Pleas for payment by the various publishers of Fort Wayne papers were too frequent to enumerate and varied from mild reminders to blunt statements of fact. In the May 8, 1841, issue the *Sentinel* warned its subscribers to pay or else there would be no paper. The September 11 issue did not appear, and the *Sentinel* notified its readers the following week, "Those who wish to know the reason can be informed by sending us the amount of their indebtedness."[90]

All the Fort Wayne publishers had difficulty in collecting their debts, but the hardest hit seems to have been Isaac Nelson. Nelson had purchased the *Sentinel* in 1840 from George W. Wood, who had previously bought the paper from Tigar in 1837. After eighteen months as publisher, Nelson increased the circulation somewhat, but by January, 1842, when he sold most of his interest in the *Sentinel* to Tigar, the subscribers were indebted to Nelson for $2,000.[91] Upon becom-

[89] Fort Wayne *Times*, April 20, 1848.

[90] Fort Wayne *Sentinel*, September 18, 1841.

[91] *Ibid.*, January 15, 1842. Apparently Isaac Nelson decided to reserve a few shares of the *Sentinel* as his son William R. Nelson later inherited these. After buying other shares William Nelson became part owner of the paper and gained experience in journalism which he later employed in Kansas City as owner of the Kansas City *Star*.

ing publisher again, Tigar announced that no more credit would be extended; but apparently he found its use still necessary because two years afterward he complained that 150 subscribers still had not paid during the entire period since he had returned.[92] One reason why publishers hesitated to drop delinquent subscribers was that certain governmental notices were awarded to the paper with the largest circulation.[93] These legal notices were even more profitable than advertising.[94] According to the law, the publisher could send the newspaper, if he desired, until the subscriber ordered his subscription to be cancelled. Hence it was better to carry some subscribers in the hope of being paid eventually than to drop them and risk losing valuable government contracts.

Despite its early problems the *Sentinel* not only survived but grew in size and number of subscribers in the period before the Civil War. By 1843 it could boast that it was the "oldest and largest" paper in northern Indiana;[95] by the 1850s it had a circulation of about seven hundred.[96] It could even afford the luxury of a strong competitor, the Fort Wayne *Times*. The latter paper was established by George W. Wood in 1841. During a very active life Wood had a variety of interests besides that of a printer. He was the first mayor of Fort Wayne, managed the telegraph office when it was first established, served as land agent for a time, and later as stock agent for the Ohio and Indiana Railroad. His last years were spent in managing the estate of Samuel Hanna. A native of New York, Wood came to Fort Wayne in 1836 and worked a year for Tigar before buying the *Sentinel*. He increased the

[92] Fort Wayne *Sentinel*, January 6, 1844.
[93] *Ibid.*, April 8, 1843.
[94] Mott, *American Journalism*, 202.
[95] Fort Wayne *Sentinel*, April 8, 1843.
[96] James H. Butler, "Indiana Newspapers, 1829-1860," in *Indiana Magazine of History*, 22 (1926):301.

size of the paper[97] then sold out to Isaac Nelson in 1840 after being elected mayor. This position did not satisfy Wood, who resigned in 1841 in order to establish the *Times*. As a Whig, Wood's purpose seems to have been as much political as financial. In 1843 he leased the *Times* to another Whig, Henry W. Jones, and a year later initiated another paper, *The People's Press,* which was to be published for eight months, or until after the election of 1844. All profits were to be used to send out free papers.[98] *The People's Press* actually lost money; by September, 1844, Wood had expended $1,000 and had collected only $50.[99] The worst blow, however, was Clay's defeat. After the election *The People's Press* was merged with the *Times* and conducted on a more businesslike basis. The advertisements in the *Times* equalled those of the *Sentinel,* even though the rates were somewhat higher than those of the latter paper.[100] While the two were similar in format, the *Times* was more attractive in appearance. There are no statistics available, but in 1848 the *Times* implied its circulation was about the same as the *Sentinel*'s and claimed that the combined circulation of the two papers equalled any other two in the state.[101] The competition between the two papers was carried at times beyond business and even politics into the personal arena, as Tigar and Wood battled one another in their editorials. Tigar used the stronger language in speaking of his opponent, whom he accused of being an eavesdropper and of plagarizing.[102] Wood's replies were a bit more subtle, for example, "We notice the *Sentinel* has been enlarged. It is now brought up again to the size

[97] Fort Wayne *The People's Press,* October 29, 1844.

[98] *Ibid.,* April 30, 1844.

[99] *Ibid.,* September 17, 1844.

[100] The initial charge was higher, $1.00 per square, but subsequent insertions were less costly than the *Sentinel*'s rates. Fort Wayne *Times,* April 20, 1848.

[101] *Ibid.,* October 26, 1848.

[102] Fort Wayne *Sentinel,* June 4, 25, 1842.

that we made it near six years ago, and what it was when we left it. We are glad to see this evidence of our neighbor's prosperity; for he, probably . . . needs it whether he deserves it or not."[103] There is reason to believe, however, that the rivalry between the two publishers was carried on without bitterness, for on one occasion Wood supplied Tigar with paper when the latter had exhausted his supply.[104] Probably these verbal battles also enabled the two printers to make copy when there was a shortage of news. This was often the case when Wood or Tigar engaged other small town editors from Indiana or Ohio in editorial duels. Such conflicts also grew out of the need to defend the honor of the community and surrounding area against charges of ill health, lack of progress, etc. In doing so the editor was simply fulfilling his duty, for one of the reasons for initiating and sustaining newspapers in towns such as Fort Wayne was to have a means of answering the charges of the rival western cities. After the opening of the canal, Fort Wayne's natural rivals were Lafayette and Toledo, and thus the local editors were expected to and did engage their counterparts in these two towns. Lesser rivals were Logansport, South Bend, and Muncie. Of course, at times these battles with out-of-town editors were also of a political nature.

The manner in which the political questions were treated in the two Fort Wayne papers of the period is rather interesting. In the 1830s and 1840s personalities on a national level were seldom, if ever, attacked; but issues were debated, and charges were leveled against the opponent's party. On a state level, however, the local candidates for Congress or for state offices received a good deal of personal abuse, the Democratic *Sentinel* being more inclined in this direction than the *Times*. Such

[103] Fort Wayne *The People's Press,* October 29, 1844.

[104] Fort Wayne *Sentinel,* December 5, 1846.

terms as "liar" and "scoundrel" or "white-livered demagogue" appeared often enough.[105] Charges that the candidate was proslavery or proabolitionist were frequent. In Fort Wayne especially the question of the candidate's attitude towards the immigrant and, to a lesser extent, towards Catholicism was introduced.[106]

Since the German vote was so important in the Fort Wayne area, Tigar, in 1843, decided to launch the first German newspaper in Indiana, *Der Deutsche Beobachter von Indiana.* The editor was Dr. Charles A. Schmitz. In a German editorial which appeared in the *Sentinel,* Schmitz pointed out that there was a need for a German newspaper in Indiana, and then stated:

> *Der Deutsche Beobachter* takes upon itself the duty . . . to defend the rights and freedom of the citizen, to preserve courageously the esteemed Democratic principles and to guard against the assaults and the *slanders* of the Whigs; to communicate the news from Europe and here to its readers, and for the benefit and pleasure of its lovely lady readers, to include stories, poetry and little puzzles.[107]

In the same issue Tigar explained to his English readers that although the Germans were well educated they do not read English; therefore they were "liable to be led astray by scheming demagogues." Tigar's efforts were premature, however, and after a few months *Der Deutsche Beobachter* was discontinued due to lack of support.[108] On the other hand,

[105] Fort Wayne *Sentinel,* March 4, 1843, July 24, 1847.

[106] One Catholic grew weary of these election-time appeals and wrote, "every true Catholic who loves his religion, scorns and despises the man who will tamper with it merely to accomplish political ends." Fort Wayne *Sentinel,* July 24, 1847.

[107] *Ibid.,* March 4, 1843 (Author's translation).

[108] There are no existing copies of *Der Deutsche Beobachter* as far as it is known. The first German newspaper to succeed in Fort Wayne was the *Zeitung* in 1856.

Wood admitted in 1844, "A large majority of our German fellow-citizens are against us."[109]

Tigar's attempt to establish *Der Deutsche Beobachter,* while premature, indicates the growing importance of the Germans in the community life of Fort Wayne. Their cultural and social significance may be seen in other respects as well. In the 1830s the Independence Day celebrations had brought forth all of the civic patriotism and ardor. The orators were especially eloquent, and the whole town after attending the ceremonies discussed the speeches for some time thereafter, just as the sermons of the Puritan ministers were topics for debate in seventeenth-century New England. By 1841, however, the fervor of the native Americans had declined. Concerning the celebration of the Fourth of July in that year, the *Sentinel* declared that the German citizens put others to shame.[110] Even the German oration surpassed all other efforts, "being replete with doctrines calculated to fan the flame of patriotism. . . ."[111] The following year, although the *Sentinel* had pleaded for a real celebration of the Fourth of July as was held ten years ago,[112] Tigar acknowledged afterwards that the Germans excelled the other citizens, fully one half of those present being German. The oration by Dr. Schmitz was "masterful," the German choir also performed, and the ladies were taken by canalboat to Hinton Grove.[113] It was suggested that one reason why the native Americans did not participate too actively was the Sunday School of the Presbyterian Church held its own celebration. It is quite likely that this was a deliberate move of the Temperance element inasmuch as the civic celebration was enlivened with thirteen official and a

[109] Fort Wayne *The People's Press,* October 29, 1844.

[110] Fort Wayne *Sentinel,* July 10, 1841.

[111] *Ibid.*

[112] *Ibid.,* June 4, 1842.

[113] *Ibid.,* July 9, 1842.

number of unofficial toasts.[114] The Germans delayed planning their celebration in 1845 until it was apparent that the native citizens were not going to do anything.[115] The following year the Irish and Germans were the only two groups to celebrate the day—separately of course. The "good old times when Fort Wayne was . . . but a small village" were dead, and the *Sentinel* implied that the Sunday schools were at fault.[116] While the editor of the *Times* agreed that the immigrants were the only ones who properly celebrated Independence Day, he also noted that many of them principally celebrated "the liberty to get drunk."[117]

To a great extent the Germans were also instrumental in promoting the cause of music in Fort Wayne. The Leipzig piano imported by Henry Rudisill was listened to with great pleasure by the citizens and by the farmers who came to hear his two daughters play it while he and his son accompanied them on their flutes.[118] The first musical instruments produced in Fort Wayne came from the hand of the immigrant Henry Hitzfield in 1845. Two years earlier the Germans of the city had organized a band.[119] However, in this case the German citizens were not the first, since the town leaders had organized the Kekiogue Band in 1842 and had subscribed $600 for its expenses.[120] Commenting on the efforts of the new musicians the *Sentinel* noted, "We . . . shall be happy when we can

[114] These numerous toasts became heavily charged with political overtones: "May God bless the farmer, laborer, and the mechanic, the champions of the resources of the country—Indian traders excepted." "A tariff for revenue and protection of American industry." "Free trade and equal rights." Fort Wayne *Sentinel*, July 9, 1842.

[115] *Ibid.*, June 28, 1845.

[116] *Ibid.*, July 11, 1846.

[117] Fort Wayne *Times*, July 11, 1850.

[118] Laura G. Detler, "Pioneer Days & Ways," in Robertson (ed.), *History of the Maumee River Basin*, 2:75.

[119] Fort Wayne *Sentinel*, April 15, 1843.

[120] *Ibid.*, February 26, 1842.

announce that their proficiency equals their zeal."[121] Six months later the Kekiogue Band gave its first concert. Besides selections from Mozart, Hoffmann, and Weber, the band played one number in the spirit of the contemporary conductor and showman, Pat Gilmore. Sleigh bells, whips, flat irons, rattles, straps, an anvil and horseshoes were all employed.

Dancing, once the favorite activity of the early French fur traders at the site of Fort Wayne, became a genteel tradition of the society of the 1840s. The hearty men at the early post who had reveled in the rondu until their feet were sore,[122] probably would have been amazed to learn that a French Dancing Academy under the direction of M. and M'me Casimir taught the later citizens of the town the refinements of the art.

Artists also found support in Fort Wayne by the early 1840s. A "Daguerrean artist," J. L. Hubbell, made his appearance in 1843, and in the same year, a "Mr. Richards" advertised his oil paintings.[123] In the course of the decade, H. Rockwell was able to establish himself permanently in Fort Wayne. He received commissions from the more prominent citizens and held regular exhibits of his paintings in Lasselle Hall.[124] Rockwell's exhibits were well received, for as G. W. Wood observed, "In the drapery [of his figures] Mr. R. has exhibited his usual good taste."[125]

Since one of the artists, Richards, also advertised stage scenery, it was suggested that this might be an opportunity to start a Thespian Society.[126] Although Fort Wayne was essen-

[121] Fort Wayne *Sentinel,* February 12, 1842.

[122] Poinsatte, A History of Fort Wayne, from 1716 to 1829, p. 36.

[123] Fort Wayne *Sentinel,* November 4, December 2, 1843.

[124] Receipt from H. Rockwell to Mrs. W. G. Ewing, October 29, 1837, Ewing Papers; Fort Wayne *Times,* December 11, 1851, April 15, 1852. He is listed as Cirael (or Carael) Rockwell in the 1850 census, age 43, born New York.

[125] Fort Wayne *Times,* April 15, 1852.

[126] Fort Wayne *Sentinel,* November 4, 1843.

tially non-Puritan, the majority of the people were not quite prepared to go *this* far. Touring theatrical companies were permitted to perform and did receive fairly good support, but a city license fee and taxes discouraged the actors.[127] Nevertheless, Fort Wayne was far more liberal than Rochester, New York, whose historian gave public thanks in 1838, that, "neither theatre nor circus can now be found in Rochester."[128] The theatrical companies were not only tolerated but circuses were warmly received in Fort Wayne. In addition, the showboat, "Dixie Boys Minstrel," provided entertainment for as many as one hundred persons in its elaborate cabin as it toured the Indiana section of the Wabash and Erie Canal. Admission was a mere 25 cents for a full evening's enjoyment.[129]

Of the arts, however, one might surmise that the functional ones were most appreciated in the Fort Wayne of the pre-Civil War period. Unknown craftsmen have left simple but sturdy examples of their work, especially in iron and furniture.[130] The first builders were simple carpenters. The construction of the fourth public building, the bank, was carried out by Tower and Tinkham who also built canalboats. Susan Man, who was to take up permanent residence in the bank building within a short time, wrote to her future husband, "do speak a good word in season about closets, clothes presses, etc. If you do not advise the Hoosiers, they will make nothing but

[127] Fort Wayne *Sentinel,* September 23, 1843.

[128] Richardson Wright, *Hawkers and Walkers in Early America* (Philadelphia, 1927), 202.

[129] Fort Wayne *Sentinel,* June 24, 1843, September 12, 1846.

[130] Many articles may be seen in the Allen County—Fort Wayne Historical Museum. A few good examples are to be found in the homes, one being the monumental ash bookcase in the Fleming Homestead. Built by a Fort Wayne cabinetmaker for William Rockhill with acanthus leaf and all, it is representative of the Greek Revival period. It is illustrated in Peter Certia, "The Fleming Homestead of Fort Wayne, Indiana," in *Old Fort News,* 24:no. 2 (April-June, 1961).

square rooms without halls, closets or anything of the sort."[131] Susan McCulloch later admitted that the bank in brick was "elegantly finished," but since it was "exceedingly inconvenient for a dwelling house," the McCullochs in 1843 built a new house just outside the city.[132] The McCulloch homestead was the first of two still extant homes built by Henry Williams, the so-called "southern architect" of Fort Wayne.[133] McCulloch's grandson spoke of the home with justifiable pride, "Architecturally, it was perfect. With the porch on the left, the greenhouse on the right, and square columns . . . it was a splendid house. . . . There was a tall white picket fence surrounding the entire estate. Its grounds were filled with fruit trees, and grapes. . . . Behind the house, down on the banks of the St. Mary's River, there were sycamore trees."[134]

The second mansion constructed by Henry Williams in the Greek Revival style was that of Samuel Hanna. Finished in 1844, the Hanna homestead had perfect symmetry. Its massive front was rather unique in that Williams employed two-story Doric pillars on each wing with only one-story pillars in the center of the home. The over-all appearance of the Hanna homestead is that of one of the Mississippi or Louisiana planters of his day. Indeed, after the railroad came to Fort Wayne in the 1850s, Hanna, like the southern planters who could board river boats from their own docks, had a special depot at the

[131] Susan Man to Hugh McCulloch, December 16, 1837, McCulloch Papers.

[132] Susan Man McCulloch, "Recollections," MS in the possession of the McCulloch heirs.

[133] A third house, the Hahn homestead, built by Williams in the style of the Greek Revival during the 1840s was but recently torn down. There is very little known about Williams. He is listed as living in Wayne Township according to the census of 1840. See Cleo Wilkins (comp.), *Index to the Sixth Census of the United States for Allen County, Indiana, 1840* (Allen County—Fort Wayne Historical Society, 1958).

[134] Statement of Ross McCulloch quoted in the Fort Wayne *News-Sentinel*, June 28, 1956.

Indiana State Library

SAMUEL HANNA HOME

Indiana Historical Society

HUGH McCULLOCH HOME

Indiana Historical Society

WILLIAM ROCKHILL HOME

Indiana State Library

rear of his estate, where as director of the railroad he could board or step off the train without a journey into town.

Built earlier than either the McCulloch or Hanna homesteads was that of Allen Hamilton. Begun in 1838, the home was not completed until 1841. Although it was changed considerably before being torn down in recent years, the home was originally designed as a replica of the ancestral home of the Hamiltons in Donegal, Ireland, "Mount Charles." Less imposing but well conceived in the Georgian style of the Middle Atlantic states was the home of Dr. Lewis Thompson built in 1835.

The two most impressive homes built by Fort Wayne citizens in the early 1850s were those of W. G. Ewing and William Rockhill. As yet both of these homesteads are still remarkably well preserved, although Rockhill's (better known as the Fleming Homestead) underwent a great deal of change in the period after the Civil War. The architecture of the Ewing home, built in 1854, remains virtually unchanged and is an excellent example of the balanced classical style of the northern states.

In studying the Fort Wayne homes built in the period between the late 1830s and the early 1850s, it is apparent that the architecture was not original but generally followed the national pattern. One may also agree (although not entirely) with Lewis Mumford's observation, "the pioneer jumped baldly from log cabin to White House, or its genteel and scroll-sawed equivalent; and the arts inherent in good building never had a chance to develop."[135] What is interesting in the present study, however, is the fact that some of the urban pioneers did make this jump within little more than a decade. The question which then arises is "was this change indicative of a social stratification developing within the town?"

[135] Mumford, *Sticks and Stones,* 84.

Professor Buley in speaking of the social conditions in the Old Northwest maintains that there was a greater contrast between the pioneer aristocracy and the log cabin dweller than that which exists today between the man of wealth and the wage earner.[136] If such a distinction may be noted in southern Indiana, for example, between the home and life of a William Henry Harrison and that of a Thomas Lincoln, one must consider as well the contrast between the homes of Hamilton, Hanna, Ewing, and McCulloch and the shanties along Canal Street in Fort Wayne or the average farmhouse of their rural neighbors. On the other hand, the anonymous writer of the series of letters to the *Sentinel* could say that in the Fort Wayne of 1842, there was no

> petty distinction in society. . . . The lawyer and the mechanic, the merchant and the farmer, move in the same circles and meet at the same parties on terms of the most perfect equality. . . . Nor is there here that deference paid to wealth, that subserviency to those upon whom fortune has been lavish of her favors, which I have frequently observed . . . in your eastern cities. Wealth has here (as it must everywhere) its influence and its power, but it is not with us a certain passport to respect and favor.[137]

Obviously the social lines emerging in Fort Wayne during this period were not as marked as in the East. It is also true that almost everyone in the town had certain common interests, such as the promotion of the canal. Nevertheless, by 1840 some economic differences were appearing. The early Indian traders and then the merchants had been the first to act collectively in an informal but effective manner. Now, however, the laborers of the town, pressed by the poor economic conditions of the late 1830s and early 1840s, organized their own society. Early in 1841 the craftsmen of the city met at the American House to form a Mechanic's Association.[138] Two

[136] Buley, *The Old Northwest,* 1:140.

[137] "Letters from Indiana, II," Fort Wayne *Sentinel,* April 23, 1842.

[138] Fort Wayne *Sentinel,* May 29, 1841.

weeks earlier they, together with the farmers of the region, had selected Andrew Kennedy, a former blacksmith, to run for Congress in the Fifth Congressional District, even though Kennedy had been in the race against Dr. Thompson for the nomination only a few weeks.[139] In one of its first meetings the Mechanics' Association called on the farmers and laborers of the area to boycott those merchants who purchased manufactured goods from the East rather than those which were produced in the Fort Wayne region. The Association argued that times were especially hard in Fort Wayne because these merchants refused to buy locally manufactured products. If the farmers also bought only the goods produced in Fort Wayne then the laboring man would be in a better position to buy more of the farmers' produce.[140] Two years later it was asked by a laboring man what good is the high tariff policy to the worker if the Fort Wayne merchants continue to buy their goods in the East. "This is hypocrisy!" cried the writer. "Reader look around—how many such hypocrites can you see?"[141] These harsh words may have been based on an over-simplification of the economic problem, but they reveal that at least some of the working men of the community had come to identify their interests as being distinct from the older merchant society.

During these same years the farmers also showed some resentment towards their urban neighbors. When Henry Rudisill, Samuel Hanna, and Dr. Thompson called for a meeting of the Agricultural Society,[142] a protest appeared in the *Sentinel*. Signed by six farmers representing a committee, the notice complained that the people of the city "make a practice of monopolizing all the institutions of the County. . . ."

[139] *Ibid.*, May 15, 1841.
[140] *Ibid.*, July 3, 1841.
[141] *Ibid.*, June 10, 1843.
[142] *Ibid.*, May 22, 29, 1841.

To prevent this "the REAL Farmers" were asked to meet at the American House.[143] It may be argued that Hanna owned a great deal of farm land and that Rudisill was also closely associated with the farming problems, but in the minds of many of the small farmers they were outsiders as was Dr. Thompson. The farmers' committee had no success in naming one of their members as a director of the Agricultural Society for Hanna and Rudisill were elected.[144] In the later 1840s William Rockhill, the "old-corn planter," was elected to head the society along with Hugh McCulloch.[145] Thus a balance was achieved, although as late as 1851 Samuel Hanna was still elected as president of the society. Therefore, it would seem that the Agricultural Society of Allen County was dominated largely by those men, who, although they held land, were primarily concerned with trade. At the same time, it is possible to see in this the close relationship that still existed between the rural and urban economies.

Finally we must not necessarily equate economic differences that appear during this period with social distinctions. In the early 1830s the various elements of Fort Wayne's limited society still mingled with relative ease. Although there was a certain distinction between the earlier French group and the later American settlers, at the same time there was intermarriage. By 1836 Susan Man referred to the American ladies when speaking of the "first society" of the town.[146] Still she attended an Irish wedding and a frontier "chevaree."[147] By the early 1840s she and other American ladies of the "first society" were employing German girls as servants. In 1850 Allen Hamilton gave a lavish party for 350 people, which even a guest from

[143] Fort Wayne *Sentinel,* June 12, 1841.

[144] *Ibid.,* July 3, 1841. It should be remembered that Rudisill was popular with the German farmers.

[145] Fort Wayne *Times,* March 29, 1849.

[146] Susan Man to Mrs. Frederick Halsey, July, 1836, McCulloch Papers.

[147] Susan Man to Mrs. Mary Hawkins, October 27, 1836, McCulloch Papers.

the East found magnificent with its exquisite variety of food and drink.[148] If on one hand Hamilton was one of the few citizens of the town who could afford such elegance, still in a city of only 4,282 people such a large number of guests could not have been drawn solely from the wealthy members of society. As late as the mid-fifties, the Young Men's Literary Society could merge with the Workingmen's Institute and Library.[149]

That there were definite cultural and social advantages from living in even a small western community such as Fort Wayne we may conclude from our study. That there were growing differences in economic interests is also true, but that there was fixed social cleavage is not yet apparent in the late 1840s and early 1850s.

[148] *The Old Fort Bulletin of the Allen County—Fort Wayne Historical Society* (September, 1956), no pagination.

[149] The latter was made possible by a grant from the estate of William Maclure, New Harmony scientist and educator, who wished to better the educational opportunities of the laboring man. Due to the very energetic leadership, especially that of Thomas Tigar, editor of the Fort Wayne *Sentinel,* the accomplishments of the Institute in Fort Wayne were of a very high order.

CHAPTER IX

COMMERCIAL AND INDUSTRIAL GROWTH: THE "HEY-DAY" OF THE CANAL 1843-1854

A life on the raging canawl, a home on the raging deep,
Where through summer, spring and fall, the frogs their revels keep.
Like a fish on a hook I pine, on this dull unchanging shore—
Oh give me the 'Red Bird' line, and the raging canawl's dread roar.

Fort Wayne *Sentinel,* July 3, 1847

Writing in 1865 the compiler of the *Fort Wayne Directory* summarized the reasons behind the city's development up to that time.

> The causes that produced this rapid growth, are apparent. The commanding situation of the town, in the center of a large and fertile scope of country that sought this point for trade, with no competing town, and the facilities for export and import. . . .
>
> By affording the means of shipping direct to the Lake, the canal drew the trade of a large region of country, north and south, immediately to this point. The water power resulting from this improvement, furnished facilities for the erection of mills and manufactories that were of great importance in its progress; and from this period it took a new start, and this impetus continued till the era of Plank Roads, in 1848. These roads were constructed with much energy and rapidity to a great distance in every direction, attracting an increased trade from a large and fertile section of the country. Lastly came the Railroads.[1]

Statistics bear out his analysis. In 1840, three years before the canal was opened to Lake Erie, the population of Fort Wayne may be estimated at about 1,500.[2] Ten years later the population was 4,282, an increase of 166 per cent.[3] By 1853 it

[1] C. S. Williams (comp.), *Williams Fort Wayne Directory,* 1864-65, pp. 10-11.

[2] See above, p. 44.

[3] *Compendium of the Seventh Census* (1850), 354. In the same ten-year period Indiana's population increased only 44.11 per cent. *Ibid.,* 98.

had risen to 6,500,[4] which was approximately four times the estimated population of 1840. In the eight years following the completion of the canal to the lake the assessed value of property within the limits of the city of Fort Wayne more than doubled. In 1842 it was valued at $424,185, while in 1850 it was assessed at a value of $891,912.[5]

Actually the possibilities of this growth had been foreseen in the ten years preceding 1843. Since work on the canal had originated at Fort Wayne certain immediate benefits had accrued to the town. The money spent in construction, the growth in population, and the phenomenal land sales of the period before 1837 were encouraging signs. The land, however, was not always turned into immediate production as it had been purchased by speculators in the belief that the canal would soon be completed. Since this was not the case, good land around Fort Wayne often remained undeveloped either by failure to clear it if wooded or to drain it if swampy. In a sense industry also had its real beginning in the period between 1832 and 1842, but as we have said, these were largely transitional years in which the economy was changing from one depending almost entirely on trade to one which was coming to depend equally as much on industry. Although at Fort Wayne water power from the canal was available from 1833 on, it was not employed to its maximum capabilities because of a lack of capital especially after 1837. Another and perhaps more important reason was that there was not a sufficient population to support more than the small industries that emerged prior to 1842. In other words, the market was not great enough nor were the raw materials available from the farms which were largely self-sufficient operations of the pioneers and did not produce a great surplus for export.

[4] *Compendium of the Seventh Census* (1850), 354.
[5] Fort Wayne *Daily Sentinel*, July 10, 1874.

The establishment of the Fort Wayne branch of the State Bank was financially very important, but commerce was still curtailed because of the high cost of transportation to the East. Consequently, during the uncertain years between 1838 and 1842 the temporarily revitalized fur trade and the profits from the last government treaties with the Miami helped to sustain Fort Wayne until the completion of the canal to Lake Erie.

The optimism generated by this event continued to activate the townspeople during the following years. Improvements were initiated throughout the city in the belief that Fort Wayne was destined to outstrip any other Indiana city.[6] The laborers found immediate employment when construction of over two hundred new buildings began in the spring of 1843.[7] By midyear this progress caught the attention of travelers in the tri-state region. The *Sentinel* reported:

> all unite in giving Fort Wayne the preference over any place they have seen in their travels. In addition to the beauty of its situation, there is a briskness, a liveliness, and appearance of business here far surpassing what they witness elsewhere. . . . There are more buildings under way in Fort Wayne, than in any other place in Indiana. . . . The opening of our canal has given more impetus to the growth of this place than the most sanguine had anticipated.[8]

Even at the end of the year the new construction had not caught up with the demand. All houses were occupied and at least fifty more were needed.[9] The new buildings which had been started included the large hotel of Michael Hedekin and a great number of three-story brick stores built along Columbia Street at the corners of Clinton, Calhoun, and Canal streets

[6] Fort Wayne *Sentinel,* April 8, 1843.

[7] *Ibid.* Even during the depression years construction of buildings had continued in Fort Wayne. Susan Man was astonished at the number of new buildings which went up in 1839 despite the hard times. See Susan Man to Mrs. Frederick Halsey, November 24, 1839, McCulloch Papers.

[8] Fort Wayne *Sentinel,* July 1, 1843.

[9] *Ibid.*

and usually running back to the Wabash and Erie Canal. These stores were owned by a number of firms such as Samuel Hanna, Hamilton and Taber, I. G. Jones and Co., Smith and Mason, and Miller and Wallace.[10]

The Hedekin House was built on Barr Street, where in canal days it was but a few steps to the docks. William Rockhill chose to build another four-story hotel at the western edge of the town, on the corner of Broadway and Main. When commenced in 1843 the *Sentinel* predicted that it would "be the largest and best constructed public house in the state."[11] In its day the sixty-five-room Rockhill House with its rural surroundings was one of the largest and most attractive hotels in Indiana.[12] The Hedekin House and Rockhill House were the most important hotels constructed during the 1840s. Prior to 1839 a number of taverns and hotels had been erected in anticipation of an early completion of the canal. These included the Palo Alto, the Custer, the Tremont, Talman Hotel, the Franklin, and the American. Together these hotels served as accommodations for the increasing number of passengers carried on the canal either by the slower-moving "lineboats" or by the fast-moving packets.

Oddly enough, the arguments advanced at Fort Wayne in favor of constructing the canal contained few if any references to the question of public travel, yet the number of passenger miles to and from Fort Wayne was surprisingly large after 1843. In fact, in the decade before the coming of the railroad it was about three times as great as the freight mileage.[13] By

[10] *Ibid.*

[11] *Ibid.*

[12] When the railroad depot was built at the other end of town the hotel proved to be a poor investment. It was sold to a Catholic society in 1868 and transformed into Fort Wayne's first hospital. For the history of the Rockhill House, see *"As I remember . . ." From the Winifred J. Randall Collections* (Allen County—Fort Wayne Historical Society, 1959), 4-5.

[13] Willis Richardson, "Finances and Commerce of the Wabash and Erie Canal," in *Old Fort News,* 14:nos. 3 and 4 (September-December, 1951): 6.

1844 the packet lines maintained regular schedules between Fort Wayne and Toledo, a distance of 104 miles, and by 1847 this service had been extended to Lafayette. Judging from the account of Charles Kiser, the youth of Fort Wayne viewed the packets in somewhat the same light as the young Mark Twain who watched the steamboats pass on the Mississippi.

> I can well remember when the packets used to run here on the Canal, and I recall my great anxiety to have a chance to ride on one of them. They seemed grand to us then. Talk about your Pullman packets, they had them in those days, but they were pulled by mules. The packets had a bell on them and a tin horn. They would ring the bell on coming into the city. The lock and bridge tenders were notified of the coming of the boat by means of the horn.[14]

The arrival of the packet was an occasion of great excitement according to all the accounts. David H. Colerick wrote:

> And with what pleasure did we frequently repair to the dock on her [the packet, "Indiana"] arrival (an event of no small interest to us isolated beings) which was always heralded by the clarinet and violin of Ed Parker and Bill Patchin, employes, as the boat emerged from the aqueduct and rounded the bend west of town. Sweeter music I think I never heard than these two men made.[15]

Once the boat docked the passengers mingled with the towns-people, chatting sociably and passing on the latest news. On the docks one might see fashionable women promenade as well as an occasional brawl between the crewmen.

According to the schedules advertised by the lines in Fort Wayne the packets averaged about eight miles an hour, a very fast speed for these boats at that time. The trip to Toledo from Lafayette, a distance of 242 miles, was scheduled for 56 hours.[16] Compared to other means of travel the packets appeared quite luxurious to the people of the town. The Fort Wayne *Times*

[14] Account of Charles Kiser in Lura Woodworth *et al., Reminiscences of Old Fort Wayne,* [34].

[15] Griswold, *Pictorial History of Fort Wayne,* 1:369.

[16] Fort Wayne *Times and Press,* October 21, 1847.

and Press boasted, "The boats are new, fitted up with great neatness and taste, fare low and commanded by the cleverest fellows in the world. What more could a fastidious public require? It is well worth while to make a trip to Cincinnati or Toledo just to enjoy the luxury of a passage in these boats."[17] This impression was not shared by the Bestes, an English family who made the trip in the summer of 1851. They found the food poor compared to that which they had received in the hotels of the region, and the sleeping conditions impossible due to overcrowding, the heat, and the mosquitoes.[18] The possibility of fever was quite likely especially for the uninitiated. Beste's son was mildly stricken but recovered with the aid of burnt brandy which his father secured at Fort Wayne.

Actually most of the travelers on the packets were people who had to arrive at their destination within the shortest possible period and were prepared to pay the higher fare, usually one or two cents a mile. These boats were especially beneficial to the merchant and professional classes of the city who were traveling from town to town or going East. Beste reported that the packet on which he and his family were traveling from Lafayette "had taken in a great number of passengers" after reaching Fort Wayne, "many of whom only used the boat for short stages, from town to town . . . many others now sought it as the only conveyance to the Lakes and the more busy districts we were here approaching."[19] The fast-moving packets also created the necessity of daily mail for the city. Speculators in grain, often hearing of price changes in the eastern markets, hastened to the city before the news arrived and bought at very favorable prices. This practice was largely checked by the establishment of a daily mail service in

[17] *Ibid.*, August 30, 1845.

[18] Beste, *The Wabash*, 2:192-98. Beste also thought the captain of the packet acted in a lordly fashion, disregarding the commitments made by the operators of the line.

[19] *Ibid.*, 2:212.

1843 between Toledo and Fort Wayne and between Lafayette and Fort Wayne.[20]

Despite their importance, in many respects the packets actually did not carry as many newcomers from the East to Fort Wayne as did the slower moving and less expensive line boats. It has been pointed out that one class of travelers on the canal "was composed of individuals or families who were removing permanently from their former homes to new locations in the West, and to whom time—measured in hours or days—was not of great importance."[21] Not only did the line boats move at a slower rate but the passengers were also expected to furnish their own food and sleeping accommodations. Compared to overland travel these were not serious inconveniences as food could be purchased at the towns along the route, and sleeping on the deck must have been almost as comfortable as sleeping in the crowded bunks of taverns and more secure than sleeping in the wilderness. Foreign immigrants accustomed to steerage passage on the ocean must have found such travel almost a pleasure. At times, nevertheless, they were cheated just as much by the operators of the canalboats as they often were in the earlier stages of their voyage. In 1846 the *Sentinel* reported:

> There have been a great many German Emigrants landed at this place this season, and in almost every instance, trouble and litigation have occurred between them and the captains of the canal boats, on account of the attempts of the latter to extort more than they had agreed to charge. The last case we have heard of was one where an engagement had been entered into with the captain and owners of the boat at Toledo to deliver the emigrants *and their*

[20] It should be mentioned here that the Wabash and Erie Canal also served a military purpose during the Mexican War. The contingents of troops which left Fort Wayne went by way of the canal to the Ohio River in 1846-47. This military use of the canal vindicated those who had argued for the Federal land grant in 1827 on the basis of national defense.

[21] Seymour Dunbar, *A History of Travel in America* (4 vols. Indianapolis, 1915), 3:851.

baggage at this place for a fixed price per head; and on their arrival here an attempt was made to charge freight on all baggage over a certain weight for each passenger; and failing in this, the goods were put in a warehouse, and four or five dollars extorted under pretence of storage![22]

Despite such unpleasantries all statistical evidence indicates that most immigrants who elected to travel inland did so by the all-water routes.[23] It is generally recognized that New York's predominance as a port of entry was confirmed with the completion of the Erie Canal. However, in the 1830s and 1840s the western canals were also important to the immigrant who wished to move inland from the Great Lakes. It is not surprising, therefore, that "the census atlas of 1870 shows a foreign born population from 1 to 4 persons to the square mile" throughout most of the United States, but "in parts, as around Ft. Wayne, the number increases to 8 and 10, and along the canal route eastward continues the same. . . . Back from this particular canal the density of the foreign born population is considerably less, being in fact less than one person to the square mile."[24] In 1848 the editor of the Fort Wayne *Times* claimed that one third of the city's population was foreign born.[25] Two years later the Federal census seemed to confirm this statement. Statistics are not available for Fort Wayne, but in Allen County there were 3,753 foreign born out of a total population of 16,919.[26] One may assume that Fort Wayne had a larger number of foreign born than the surrounding countryside by reason of its job inducements. In percentage of foreign born Allen County ranked second among the ninety-two counties of Indiana, being outnumbered

[22] Fort Wayne *Sentinel,* July 25, 1846.

[23] Benton, *The Wabash Trade Route,* 97.

[24] *Ibid.*

[25] Fort Wayne *Times,* October 26, 1848. George Wood, the editor, later took the Federal Census of 1850 in Allen County, and therefore, his estimate can be considered as fairly reliable.

[26] *Compendium of the Seventh Census* (1850), 225.

only by Vanderburgh County which included the large German settlements around Evansville.[27] This statistical evidence is confirmed by numerous contemporary accounts in the Fort Wayne papers and by the assertions of competent witnesses. According to one, "All the immigrants from the East came in by the canal; the boats would take grain to Toledo and bring immigrants and their goods by the hundred."[28]

In the 1840s the Germans assumed complete numerical dominance over other foreign immigrants to Fort Wayne. Some Irish continued to come from the East as boatmen for the canal, such as William H. Ward, captain of the packet "Indiana." Other Irish boatmen had come in the 1830s or early forties as laborers and now simply remained to work on the canal in their new capacity. A few new Irish immigrants continued to find work in the city or in repairing the canal. After 1843, however, most of the new canal diggers were working beyond Lafayette.

In the mid-forties the Irish vote at Fort Wayne was sufficiently large for the political parties to make definite appeals to them,[29] and as an ethnic group they were second only to the Germans. Often the Irish settlers who came in this period were men who had achieved some success in the United States such as Bernard O'Connor, builder of the first telegraph line in the United States, or Peter Moran, Fort Wayne's first ice dealer. While the citizens of Fort Wayne took an interest in aiding the cause of Irish relief during the great famine of the late 1840s, there was no effort to attract these destitute individ-

[27] *Compendium of the Seventh Census* (1850), 225, 231.

[28] Statement of a contemporary, quoted in Benton, *The Wabash Trade Route,* 98. In 1850, 3,419 canal passengers arrived at Fort Wayne; in 1851 the number was 3,083. Dunbar, *A History of Travel in America,* 3:843.

[29] Fort Wayne *Sentinel,* July 1, August 12, 1843, May 18, 1844.

uals to the city.[30] A few families such as that of William Fleming did reach Fort Wayne during this time. Arriving in Quebec in 1848 William Fleming's father and four of his children had died in quarantine. William's mother then brought her three remaining children to Fort Wayne where they were assisted by relatives. Unlike most of the Irish immigrants of the day, William Fleming had received a fairly good education in Ireland. After teaching school for a short time in Fort Wayne he rose rapidly in political and business circles, being elected to a number of county and state offices on the Democratic ticket and serving on the boards of directors for a number of firms, including the Nickel Plate Railroad. He ultimately became editor and publisher of the Fort Wayne *Sentinel.*

In addition to the Irish, the British Isles also furnished a handful of craftsmen and clerks from England, Wales, and Scotland. A few French immigrants also continued to settle in Fort Wayne in the 1840s, such as Peter Bobay, Delphos Martin, and Frank Pevert. Many were fairly well off financially, being either craftsmen or merchants. In the latter group were Claude A. Cour, Claude F. Eme, and the Jewish banker-merchant, Isaac Lauferty. As late as the 1850s French was still spoken by a few of the oldest families of Fort Wayne,[31] and for a long time a section of Hanna's addition retained the name "Frenchtown."

The foreign language heard most frequently on the streets of Fort Wayne was German. Ernest G. Sihler wrote:

> Although the bulk of the German settlers came from Westphalia and Hanover, *every* part of Germany was represented, from East

[30] A public meeting was held at the courthouse at which David Colerick, Allen Hamilton, Robert E. Fleming, and others spoke in favor of raising funds. A dinner was given at the Hedekin House sponsored by Hamilton, Henry Colerick, and Hugh McCulloch, and appeals were made in various churches. Altogether $1,200 was raised for relief. See Fort Wayne *Sentinel,* February 27, March 13, 20, 27, 1847.

[31] Ernest B. Sihler, *From Maumee to Thames and Tiber: The Life-Story of an American Classical Scholar* (New York, 1930), 14.

Prussia to the Rhine, from Bremen to the Black Forest; so that as a young boy I became familiar with the dialects of Mecklenburg and Pomerania, of Bremen and Minden—the latter a veritable hive of ever more newcomers—of Bavaria and with the guttural articulation of the Swiss. All this was especially notable on market days, particularly on Saturdays. . . .[32]

Like the earlier German settlers these newcomers were attracted by the availability of good wooded land at reasonable prices and by the growing industrial opportunities in the city itself. Moreover, the fact that there was already a successful German community in existence at or near Fort Wayne undoubtedly led others to come here. Organizational efforts are also indicated by the fact that the canalboats often brought an entire group of German settlers. In the summer of 1842 one boat loaded with German immigrants arrived at sunrise. As it neared Fort Wayne the citizens were awakened by the *Lieder* being sung by the immigrants. "The effect, in the calm stillness of a dewy morning . . . was almost sublime."[33] While the greatest number of Germans came by way of the Great Lakes, others came up from New Orleans by way of the Mississippi and Ohio rivers to the Wabash and Erie Canal or by way of Cincinnati and the Ohio canals and then overland.

Any list of German settlers who came during this period would be too extensive for this study. Suffice to say that besides the farmers who came into the region they represented almost all of the then existing trades and professions except law. For example, John G. Thieme, a Saxon tailor, Christian Schiefer, a Hamburg shoe merchant, William Paul, a canalboat captain and contractor from Hanover, Frederick J. Beach, a hardware merchant from Berlin, Christian Tresselt, a miller from Thuringia, are representative for the year 1846. Others who

[32] *Ibid.*, 16. Sihler, later an internationally known classicist, was the son of the Lutheran minister at Fort Wayne, Wilhelm Sihler. It is interesting to note that both Ernest Sihler and Edith Hamilton, one of America's greatest classicists, were tutored by the instructors of St. Paul's Lutheran Church in Fort Wayne.

[33] Fort Wayne *Sentinel,* August 6, 1842.

came in 1850 were Fort Wayne's pioneer dentist, Dr. Von Bonhurst, Charles Reese, city weighmaster from Westersoda, Germany, Gustave Spiegel, retail boot and shoe merchant, Charles Pape, manufacturer and later city councilman, Charles F. Diether who engaged in the lumber trade, and Henry Tons, insurance broker.

For the most part the citizens of Fort Wayne welcomed these arrivals; however there were exceptions. Ernest Sihler recalled that in his youth during the Know-Nothing movement of the 1850s, "it was not a rare experience that boys on the street hooted after me, 'Damned Dutchman!' "[34] On the other hand, when German immigration to Indiana declined in the years 1849 and 1850, despite an increase in the total number of Germans coming to the United States in these same years, a committe from Fort Wayne petitioned the state to send an agent to Germany to encourage immigration to Indiana. The committee consisted of Samuel Brenton, Elza A. McMahon, and Anthony Yeager, only the latter member being of German descent.[35] It was argued that other states maintained such agents and that unless Indiana did so she would continue to fall behind.

Fort Wayne never developed a strong nativist movement even during the 1850s. In 1854 John W. Dawson, then editor of the Fort Wayne *Times,* became closely associated with the American party in Indiana, but by the midpoint of the campaign of 1856 he had deserted the Know-Nothings for the Republican party.[36] During the 1840s even the Whig paper, *The People's Press,* defended the Irish, saying, "Give these people work and they will not be found in your Alms-House."[37] At the state constitutional convention of 1850 Allen Hamilton

[34] Sihler, *From Maumee to Thames and Tiber,* 26.

[35] Fort Wayne *Times,* February 20, 1851.

[36] Carl F. Brand, "The History of the Know-Nothing Party in Indiana," in *Indiana Magazine of History,* 18 (1922): 79, 201, 281. See also the Fort Wayne *Times* for the years 1853-56.

[37] Fort Wayne *The People's Press,* May 7, 1844.

was one of the most outspoken of the Whigs who defended the immigrants. He never trespassed much upon the delegates' attention with lengthy remarks, but on one occasion, when he believed an attack had been made upon the immigrants, he found a ready vocabulary.

What does the gentleman from Delaware say in explanation of his former remarks. . . .? That he meant foreigners who did not speak our language. Well, sir, who are they to whom he thus alludes. I presume they are principally emigrants from Germany—a country where education is almost universal. How many, sir, from that country, has he or any other gentleman ever known, who have not received the benefit of an education to some considerable extent. To them—say in this day of letters . . . that our institutions and the benefits they confer on mankind are unknown, is what I cannot believe. What has caused the countries in the Old World, during the few past years, to be shaken to their very centre, and the thrones of tyrants there to totter. It was the knowledge there possessed of our institutions; their liberality and justness in contrast with their own. And what has experience taught us. . . . It is this: The moment a foreigner reaches our shores, whether from France, Germany, or the Green Island, the place of my own nativity, and our country needs his service, does he await to be naturalized, if his adopted country invites him to the field of danger. No, sir, far from it. He at once enters our ranks, rushes to the battle field to fight under the stars and stripes—the flag of the land of his voluntary adoption. Is this not so. Let the plains of Chippewa in the war of 1812, and that of Buena Vista and Mexico, in the recent war, speak. . . .

. . . Then, sir, as a citizen of this country, as an adopted citizen, as one who owes much gratitude to your laws and institutions which induced him in early life to emigrate from the land of oppression to the land of freedom—being in the language of the gentleman from Delaware, 'a foreigner by birth,' but an American by adoption, I will say to that gentleman that while I may concede to him a higher degree of intelligence than I can boast, I will not concede to him more of moral rectitude or patriotism; and I will tell him further that should this country ever be in danger, and call her citizens to the field, I will not be behind that gentleman in defending her rights.[38]

[38] *Debates and Proceedings of the Convention,* 1: 909, 910.

If foreigners were generally well received by the people of Fort Wayne in the late forties and early fifties, one can surmise that the native Americans from other states were equally or even more welcome. The trend of immigration to Fort Wayne from the North, especially the Middle Atlantic and North Central states, which began in the 1830s continued to mount in the decade following the completion of the canal to Lake Erie. Exact statistical evidence is lacking but any accounting of the known individuals coming to Fort Wayne during this period reveals that the great majority were from the northern states. New York and Ohio ranked first, followed by Pennsylvania and the New England states. The few immigrants who came from the South were almost in every case from Kentucky or Maryland, some of these having sojourned in southern Indiana. There is no evidence of any movement eastward to Fort Wayne from the states further west except for a handful of individuals who returned after disappointments in California or Oregon.

From Ohio came such representative newcomers as Pliny Hoagland, former engineer on the Ohio branch of the Wabash and Erie Canal, who was to take a leading role in bringing the first railroad to Fort Wayne. Later he succeeded Hugh McCulloch as president of the Fort Wayne branch of the State Bank and also served as director of two Fort Wayne railroads. Lemuel R. Hartman also became prominent as a banker. Other Ohioans who settled in Fort Wayne between 1843 and 1853 included Hugh B. Reed, a druggist, Elza A. McMahon, lawyer and judge, Samuel Bigger, former governor of Indiana, but originally from Ohio, Calvin Anderson, landlord of the Hedekin House and his son, E. G. Anderson, coffee and tea merchant, Solomon Bash, miller and grain dealer, and Charles Case, lawyer and Congressman.

The number of settlers from New York during this period was almost as numerous, but with the exception of Alexander

C. Huestis, wholesale grocer and president of the Methodist College, Chauncey B. Oakley, later mayor of Fort Wayne, and Judge Peter P. Bailey, railroad director, banker and editor of the *Republican,* they did not achieve as much prominence in civic or business affairs. James H. Robinson came to Fort Wayne from New York City, but most of his life had been spent in New Jersey, where he had amassed a fortune only to lose it in the Panic of 1837. Still young, he then became active in the Whig party as a close associate of Theodore Frelinghuysen before he decided to move West to enter the wholesale boot and shoe business in Fort Wayne in which he was quite successful.

After 1843 the influence of the completed canal was reflected in the relative decline from previous years in the number of settlers from Pennsylvania as compared with those from New England. Among the latter the most important citizen to come to Fort Wayne in the decade following 1842 was Joseph K. Edgerton. Born in Vermont, Edgerton had studied law in New York and then moved to Fort Wayne in 1844. He played a leading role in bringing the first railroads to Fort Wayne and gained a reputation as one of the foremost railroad promoters of the Midwest. He ultimately entered politics and was elected to Congress. Other New Englanders to come in the 1840s included James L. Worden, later mayor of Fort Wayne and state Supreme Court justice, and Dr. Benjamin S. Woodworth, prominent physician, both of whom were born in Massachusetts.

While there were but a few settlers from the southern states who came to Fort Wayne in these years, the Bass family from Salem, Kentucky, deserves some attention. Sion S. Bass arrived in 1848 and was followed by his brother John H. Bass in 1852. The following year Sion Bass along with W. H. Jones initiated a company which ultimately became one of the foremost industries of the city in the second half of the nineteenth century, the Bass Foundry and Machine Works.[39] In 1858 John H. Bass was taken into partnership in the reorganized company and after the heroic death of Colonel Sion Bass at Shiloh, eventually became president of the firm.

While the Wabash and Erie Canal served as the principal means of supplying the increasing population for Fort Wayne, it also made the increase of population possible by encouraging commerce, agriculture, and industry. Without any visible sign of a canal today it may be difficult for some to picture Fort Wayne commercially as a canal port. The shipping and warehouse area extended from Calhoun to Lafayette streets, along the south bank of the canal. Some of these old warehouses which once faced the dock stood until recently with their "half obliterated signs" proclaiming "that here were received imports of teas, coffees and spices, cloth of domestic and foreign manufacture."[40]

The first large warehouse was built in the early 1840s by a "Mr. Nichols" from La Grange County.[41] By 1842 Nichols was shipping regularly to the merchants of Kosciusko, Elkhart, La Grange and Steuben counties as well as to counties in southern Michigan. Other commission houses were soon established by Royal W. Taylor, Joseph J. and David Comparet, Samuel and William Edsall, Peter P. Bailey, Jesse L. Williams, and the Ewings. The following is a complete list of articles and produce handled at the port of Fort Wayne in the year 1848, giving some idea of the commerce of the city.[42]

The year 1848 was selected because it represents an average year in the period between 1842 and 1855 from the standpoint

[39] By the 1870s the Bass Foundry and Machine Works was the leading producer of railroad wheels in the world. Fort Wayne *Daily Sentinel,* June 6, 1871.

[40] Benton, *The Wabash Trade Route,* 100.

[41] Fort Wayne *Daily Sentinel,* July 10, 1874.

[42] Report of the Trustees of the Wabash and Erie Canal in Indiana *Documentary Journal,* 1848-49, pt. 2, no. 5, p. 269.

RECAPITULATION

Of the business done upon the Wabash and Erie Canal, from the commencement to the close of navigation in the year 1848.

FORT WAYNE

	Total	Total pounds	Total tons
Miles boats run,	202,773	....	.....
Miles, passengers,	564,856	....	.....
Barrels of flour,	28,132	6,104,644	3,052
Bushels of wheat,	109,488	6,569,280	3,285
Bushels of corn,	32,349	1,811,544	906
Bushels of oats,	2,823	93,159	47
Bushels of rye,	50	2,800	1
Bushels of barley,	581	27,888	14
Bushels of seeds,	1,195	71,700	36
Bushels of beans,	....	....	.....
Bushels of mineral coal,	5,023	401,840	201
Barrels of whisky,	2,176	760,600	380
Barrels of salt,	61,743	18,522,900	9,261
Barrels of fish,	1,266	379,800	190
Barrels of oil,	286	85,800	43
Barrels of lime,	93	27,900	14
Barrels of pork,	3,633	1,268,560	634
Pounds of lard,	....	175,484	88
Pounds of bacon,	....	157,235	79
Pounds of live hogs,	....	....	.....
Pounds of beef and tallow,	....	....	.....
Pounds of hair and bristles,	....	....	.....
Pounds of deer and coon skins,	....	....	.....
Pounds of feathers,	....	....	.....
Pounds of wool,	....	....	.....
Pounds of cranberries,	....	531,321	266
Pounds of merchandize,	....	7,541,818	3,771
Pounds of sugar and molasses,	....	1,206,306	603
Pounds of coffee,	....	1,481,006	740
Pounds of tobacco,	....	553,470	277
Pounds of glass ware and white lead,	....	522,818	261
Pounds of iron, nails, castings, &c.,	....	3,177,857	1,589
Pounds of furniture,	....	937,961	469
Pounds of agricultural implements,	....	73,054	37
Pounds of wood ware,	....	106,610	53
Pounds of marble and mill stones,	....	543,075	272
Pounds of butter,	....	139,902	69
Pounds of cheese,	....	85,036	43

RECAPITULATION—Continued

FORT WAYNE

	Total	Total pounds	Total tons
Pounds of hides,	....	4,9 5	2
Pounds of pearl and pot ash,	....	401,417	200
Pounds of staves, hoop-poles, &c.	....	189,210	95
Cords of wood,	1,969	9,845,000	4,923
Perches of stone,	3,206	12,824,000	6,412
Feet of lumber,	1,410,392	4,936,372	2,468
Number of laths,	45,000	15,000	8
Thousands of shingles,	6,173	1,851,900	926
Feet of timber,	....	....	.....
Number of posts and rails,	....	....	.....
Kegs of beer,	422	42,200	21
Pounds of stone ware,	....	85,638	43
Pounds of leather,	....	247,304	124
Pounds of saleratus,	....	79,603	40
Pounds of beeswax and roots,	....	46,443	23
Pounds of miscellaneous,	....	1,287,976	644

of total income earned by the canal.[43] It must be remembered, therefore, that there were variations in certain items and produce after that year; for example, various kinds of skins would decline with the fur trade, while farm produce increased in quantity. In the way of individual items pounds of merchandise consistently led all others, with the exception of the bulky items such as wood and stone, thus indicating the importance of Fort Wayne as a wholesale center. In merchandise tonnage Fort Wayne was far ahead of the combined total of the other ports. Goods were brought from the East by way of Toledo and Cincinnati. Items were shipped from the latter city up the Miami Canal to Defiance, Ohio, where they were then sent down the Wabash and Erie Canal to Fort Wayne. Prices for merchandise at Fort Wayne varied only slightly from those charged at Cincinnati. For example, before the opening of the canal salt sold at Fort Wayne for ten to twelve dollars per

[43] See the table of yearly revenue in Benton, *The Wabash Trade Route,* 76.

barrel. Within two years the price dropped to $1.50 per barrel.[44]

As might be expected agricultural goods surpassed in tonnage all other items shipped from Fort Wayne. There can be no doubt that the completion of the canal hastened the development of agriculture in the region of Fort Wayne. As noted previously, there was an abundance of good farm land still available within the area of the city as late as 1843. In that year the *Sentinel* pointed out that land which had cost the speculators of the mid-thirties "at least ten to fifteen dollars an acre can now be had from twelve shillings to five dollars. . . ."[45] The usual price for uncleared land was between $2.50 and $5.00 an acre. One reason for this relatively low price was the fact that government land was still available, and some good land had reverted to the state because of the nonpayment of taxes in the years 1839 to 1842 and therefore was available to new settlers.[46] Furthermore, in 1845 the last sections of land which had been reserved for the Miami were now thrown open for settlement. There were some thirty thousand acres of these lands in Allen County alone.[47] Although it was reported that pioneer farmers arrived daily by the canal and that others passed through the city with their "flocks and herds," the people of Fort Wayne were still anxious to have the lands sold even more rapidly.[48] The Miami lands were not opened up for sale fast enough to please them. In this connection an editorial quoted in the *Sentinel* argued, "The civilized world is now filled with reformers, but the best way to get rid of crime and poverty is to give the poor a place to

[44] Statement of a contemporary merchant quoted in the Fort Wayne *Daily Sentinel,* July 10, 1874.

[45] Fort Wayne *Sentinel,* April 8, 1843.

[46] See Fort Wayne *Sentinel* during the year 1842 for numerous land sales by the sheriff of Allen County for nonpayment of taxes.

[47] *Ibid.,* March 2, 1844.

[48] *Ibid.,* October 28, 1843.

settle."[49] Those speculators who refused to sell were told that they hindered the development of the community.[50]

With reasonably cheap lands still available for the farmer and with a means of marketing their products, the clearing of the undeveloped region around Fort Wayne moved forward very rapidly during this period. This is indicated by the quantity of lumber and other wood products as well as pot and pearl ashes shipped from Fort Wayne by way of the canal. This waterway was especially valuable for such bulky items that heretofore had gone to waste. The settlers who had improved their land soon turned to grain and livestock. Whereas in 1841 wheat sold for only fifty cents a bushel in Fort Wayne, within a year it was selling for seventy-five cents.[51] Fort Wayne's increasing importance as a market was noted by the Cincinnati *Enquirer* which reported that in 1837 a traveler on the roads north of Fort Wayne met only Indians and a few whites, but now on one road alone he saw over fifty wagons all laden with wheat for the Fort Wayne market.[52] In 1843 Samuel Hanna began financing large scale slaughtering operations at Fort Wayne.[53] By 1848 up to eight thousand hogs a season were being packed there.[54]

The canal had opened up for the Fort Wayne market an agricultural hinterland which ranged from sixty miles north to Sturgis, Michigan, sixty miles northwest to Goshen, Indiana, fifty miles south to Muncie, Indiana, and some fifty-five miles southeast to St. Mary's, Ohio. However, the increase of agricultural products seeking a market at Fort Wayne also created the vital necessity of improving the roads leading to the city. As

[49] *Ibid.*, December 6, 1845.

[50] *Ibid.*, October 28, 1843.

[51] *Ibid.*, April 10, 1841, May 6, 1842.

[52] Article from the Cincinnati *Enquirer* reprinted in *ibid.*, November 29, 1845.

[53] Fort Wayne *Sentinel*, December 9, 1843.

[54] Fort Wayne *Times*, December 28, 1848.

early as 1842 the *Sentinel* had called attention to the fact that the roads to the north and northwest should be improved, that in reality such a project was more important than the proposed canal from Fort Wayne to Lake Michigan.[55] In the following year the business interests of the city subscribed $1,000 to improve the Goshen and Mongoquinong roads which had been opened in 1841.[56] However, as the traffic multiplied in the next three years, the rut-lined dirt roads became almost impassable for heavy wagons except in dry weather. The need for some better type of road was generally recognized.[57] This became more apparent as rival marketing centers started to threaten Fort Wayne's position in the tri-state region. After 1845 Hillsdale, Michigan, in particular posed a distinct problem. The Michigan Railroad had been constructed between Hillsdale and Lake Erie. On this wooden railroad horse-drawn cars carried the grain directly to the lake. Early in 1845 the *Sentinel* warned its readers:

> The miserable state of the roads in this part of the country has not only greatly retarded the growth and prosperity of our town, but will if not speedily improved, be the means of forever diverting a large amount of trade to other points. . . . It is a notorious fact that a large portion of the produce of the northern counties, is now forced to find an outlet to the east by the Michigan railroad and the St. Joseph river, which would, if the roads were passable, be brought here. This is considered the natural market for the northern counties, and is the point at which the citizens of that rich wheat growing region wish to do their business; but the impossibility of reaching here with loaded teams, drives them to seek a more accessible market. This may perhaps eventually . . . be remedied, but in the mean time the trade may have settled into another channel from which it cannot be removed.[58]

[55] Fort Wayne *Sentinel,* November 5, 1842.

[56] Thomas B. Helm, *History of Allen County with Illustrations and Biographical Sketches of Some of its Prominent Men and Pioneers* (Chicago, 1880), 58.

[57] W. G. Ewing to David B. Herriman, November 9, 1845, Ewing Papers.

[58] Fort Wayne *Sentinel,* February 15, 1845.

The editor then recommended the construction of a new type of road then being built in Canada, the plank road, from Fort Wayne to La Grange and Elkhart counties. Quoting an engineer who had visited Canada the editor described the plank road as follows:

> The road is graded uniformly thirty-five feet wide, slightly convex, and the centre raised to three feet and a half above the bottom of the side ditches, which are made sufficiently large to carry off the water readily. The verdical [*sic*] line of the road is made to conform as nearly as may be to the natural surface by frequent changes. . . .
>
> Upon this road thus graded, the superstructure is placed, by laying down longitudinally with the road, five pieces 4x6 scantling equidistant from each other. These are firmly bedded in the earth, and the spaces between them compactly filled even with the surface. Upon these a course of three inch plank is laid edge to edge, and the ends secured by seven inch spikes. About one foot of each end of the plank is then covered with earth, to the depth of three inches and the remainder of the plank covered with sand, to the debth [*sic*] of two inches. The same protects the plank from wear, and is kept in place by the deeper covering of earth on each side. From the covering on the ends of the plank, the slope to the side ditches is sufficient to carry off the falling water. The water that settled beneath the planking is discharged into the side ditches by frequent cross drains.
>
> Through and in the vicinity of the principal towns, the plank are sixteen feet long, forming two road ways; but where the travel is less, the plank are twelve feet long, forming only a single track.[59]

Again in May the *Sentinel* called for citizens to promote the building of either plank or charcoal roads. This article went on to point out that as times were bad no help could be expected from the government, but on the other hand construction costs were low and that those who subscribed would get the most for their dollars.[60]

[59] Fort Wayne *Sentinel,* February 15, 1845.

[60] *Ibid.,* May 24, 1845. Although the Indiana General Assembly had called for better roads in northern Indiana, nothing came from this action in the way of actual appropriations. See *Laws of Indiana,* 1843-44 (general), p. 79.

It is conceivable that these articles were instigated by Samuel Hanna, who about this time turned his attention to the construction of plank roads. Jesse Vermilya, who had visited Canada in order to inspect the plank roads, reported favorably to Hanna and others.[61] There were a number of reasons for favoring plank roads over other types. They cost less and were easier to repair than Macadamized roads, and it was also said that horses could draw twice the load on the plank roads.[62] The most important reason was the accessibility of a plentiful supply of lumber from the land then being cleared.

After a mass meeting held in November, 1845, Hanna, Allen Hamilton, Samuel Edsall, Peter Bailey, and others began a drive to raise subscriptions for a plank road north to Lima, Indiana.[63] By 1847 the Fort Wayne and Lima Plank Road Company was organized with Samuel Hanna as president. The citizens of Fort Wayne subscribed $40,000 which "was to be paid in goods and land of every description."[64] Farmers north of Fort Wayne promised labor and lumber. Merchants and property owners in the county who refused to contribute to the road were "persuaded" by threatening publication of their names in the two Fort Wayne newspapers.[65] Samuel Hanna, Allen Hamilton, and the Ewings each contributed about $4,000 in land.[66] Yet of the $40,000 pledged by the people of the city only $300 was promised in cash, a clear indication that ready capital was still extremely scarce at Fort Wayne. Hanna proposed that the state legislature be petitioned to grant authority to the county commissioners to buy stock in the proposed road.[67] It is interesting to observe that although noth-

[61] Brice, *History of Fort Wayne*, p. 8 of the appendix.
[62] Fort Wayne *Sentinel*, May 24, 1845.
[63] *Ibid.*, November 15, 22, 29, 1845.
[64] Fort Wayne *Daily Sentinel*, July 10, 1874.
[65] Fort Wayne *Sentinel*, September 4, 1847.
[66] Fort Wayne *Daily Sentinel*, July 10, 1874.
[67] Fort Wayne *Sentinel*, September 4, 1847.

ing came of this proposal, a similar plan was approved when the county later subscribed to the building of the first railroad to Fort Wayne.

With only $300 in cash available contractors were unwilling to offer bids for the proposed road. Their reluctance is even more understandable when it is remembered that many contractors had so much difficulty in securing payment from the state for their work on the canal between 1838 and 1841. Fortunately the Fort Wayne branch of the Bank of Indiana extended credit to the Fort Wayne and Lima Plank Road Company. Within eighteen months northern Indiana's first plank road was completed to Kendallville and eventually was extended beyond Lima, Indiana, to Sturgis, Michigan, a distance of some sixty miles. When completed the Lima Plank Road assured Fort Wayne of the farm produce of the area lying to the north as far as southern Michigan.[68]

Even before the road was completed to Lima the people of Fort Wayne realized its value and redoubled their efforts to build plank roads. The road south to Bluffton was hastened when a convention at Muncie voted to make Bellefontaine, Ohio, rather than Fort Wayne, the northeastern terminus of a proposed rail line from Indianapolis to the East.[69] The Fort Wayne delegation composed of Hanna, McCulloch, and Rockhill returned from Muncie convinced that unless the Bluffton Road was constructed the rich farm land to the south, especially Wells County, would be lost for the Fort Wayne market. The Edsall brothers, having just put up a steam-power sawmill in Fort Wayne, agreed to build the road for $40,000.[70]

[68] Benton, *The Wabash Trade Route,* 101.

[69] Fort Wayne *Sentinel,* August 28, 1847. The Muncietown and Fort Wayne Railroad had been chartered in 1841, but although there were periodic meetings nothing had been really accomplished by 1847.

[70] Fort Wayne *Times,* January 24, 1850. In an interesting letter addressed to the farmers south of Fort Wayne, Samual Edsall pointed out the real advantages which would accrue to them from the construction of the Bluffton Road.

The Bluffton Road was completed in 1850, and within the same year the plank road to Piqua, Ohio, via Decatur, Indiana, was under construction and soon completed. In 1850 plans were also laid for plank roads to Columbia City, Goshen, and Huntington. Although construction began on the road to Goshen it was eventually abandoned in favor of the Fort Wayne and Chicago Railroad. Samuel Hanna's name usually appeared as one of the leading promoters of all these roads.[71]

Over-all the plank roads, together with the improved dirt roads, gave the farmer more accessible routes to Fort Wayne and undoubtedly improved the position of the city as a commercial port on the canal. These roads also contributed to the industrial growth of Fort Wayne by extending the radius of the city's potential market. However, the market for Fort Wayne's industrial products also increased considerably for two other reasons. First, there was the augmented demand made possible simply by the growing population of the surrounding area and of the city itself. What is equally significant is the fact that as the farmers within the trade region of Fort Wayne turned from a subsistence to a specialized type of agriculture, they had more money with which to buy the city's manufactured goods. Naturally they purchased these items in Fort Wayne where they marketed their produce. Also as the farmer moved in the direction of specialized production he made less in the way of home manufactured goods; consequently, he was forced to look to the city for more of his supplies.

Richard Wade has written, "Of all indices of urbanization probably none is more important than the separation of work from home."[72] Unfortunately, in this respect, there are no statistics available for 1840. However, those of 1850 are very significant. In that year the families of Allen County produced

[71] Fort Wayne *Times,* April 4, 11, 1850.
[72] Wade, *The Urban Frontier,* 308.

in their homes only $6,341 worth of manufactured goods, compared to $701,300 worth of manufactured goods produced in establishments outside the home.[73] By 1860 the value of products manufactured in the homes of Allen County had dropped to $6,113 despite a population increase to 29,328.[74]

The demand for goods was not limited solely to items previously manufactured in Fort Wayne such as shoes and leather products. New items directly connected with the needs of the farmer appeared. In 1843 the Fort Wayne Foundry advertised that from henceforth they would specialize in the production of "Wood's Cast Iron Ploughs."[75] Nine years later Adam D. Reid began the manufacture of steel plows.[76] One of the most important and interesting of the new industries was the manufacture of tile. Isaac De Groff Nelson, the former publisher of the *Sentinel,* had been experimenting with various methods of draining the lowlands. Finding hollowed-out logs satisfactory but too expensive, he conceived the idea of manufacturing tile in Fort Wayne. With Nelson's financial backing, Samuel Lillie, a Scot craftsman, began producing drainage tile. By this means thousands of acres, especially southwest of Fort Wayne, were reclaimed. For the settlers of this region tile became as important as the axe had been to the woodsman.

Apart from furnishing Fort Wayne industry with wider markets, the expansion of agriculture in the region meant more raw materials for the city's manufacturers. More wood was available for the sawmills, grain for the flour mills and distilleries, leather for the tanneries and wool for textile production. In addition to its importance as a regional center of trade, Fort Wayne had two other advantages, industrially

[73] *Compendium of the Seventh Census* (1850), 228-29.

[74] United States Bureau of Census, *Eighth Census* (1860), *Agriculture,* 40-41.

[75] Fort Wayne *Sentinel,* September 3, 1842.

[76] Helm, *History of Allen County,* 113.

speaking. First, as mentioned earlier in this chapter, Fort Wayne profited from the water power of the canal. Secondly, the German craftsmen furnished Fort Wayne with a skilled and reasonably inexpensive labor supply.

It is impossible to give an exhaustive presentation of all the industrial enterprises initiated in the decade following 1842. In 1850 flour milling was the most important type of industry from the following standpoints: annual value of its products, $163,000, annual value of raw materials used, $146,500, and capital invested, $45,000.[77] Two new flour mills were established in the period between 1842 and 1845, both of these employing water power from the canal. The first of these was constructed by Samuel Edsall by 1844.[78] In 1850 this mill led all other Fort Wayne grist mills with a yearly output of flour valued at $80,000.[79] The other grist mill was financed by Allen Hamilton and Jesse L. Williams. In 1850 the flour produced at this mill was valued at $63,000.[80] Ten years later the grain processed amounted to 88,000 bushels valued at $103,000.[81] This mill was very popular for the visiting farmers since it was located in the business section of the city where they could shop while waiting for their wheat to be ground.

Other types of mills relying on steam as well as water power made their appearance during this period. One of the most important of these was the oil and woolen mill originally built through the efforts of Henry Rudisill and Louis Wolke.

[77] Original Returns of the Seventh Census (1850), Manufactures, Wayne Township, Allen County, Indiana, microfilm in Indiana University Library, and in Archives Division, Indiana State Library.

[78] Bates, "The Water-Powered Mills of Allen County, Indiana," in *Old Fort News,* 7: no. 1: 21.

[79] Original Returns of the Seventh Census (1850), Manufactures, Wayne Township.

[80] *Ibid.*

[81] Bates, "Water-Powered Mills of Allen County," in *Old Fort News,* 7: no. 1:23.

MANUFACTURING ESTABLISHMENTS IN WAYNE TOWNSHIP, 1850

12

SCHEDULE 5.—Products of Industry in Wayne Township in the County of Allen State of Indiana during the Year ending June 1, 1850, as enumerated by me, P. W. Wood Ass't Marshal.

	Name of Corporation, Company, or Individual, producing Articles to the Annual Value of $500.	Name of Business, Manufacture, or Product.	Capital invested in Real and Personal Estate in the Business.	Raw Material used, including Fuel. Quantities.	Kinds.	Values.	Kind of motive power, machinery, structure, or resource.	Average number of hands employed. Male.	Female.	Wages. Average monthly cost of male labor.	Average monthly cost of female labor.	Annual Product. Quantities.	Kinds.	Values.
	1	2	3	4	5	6	7	8	9	10	11	12	13	14
1	John Burt	Brickmaker	1000		Clay	25								
				100 cords	Wood	125	Horse	3		55		250,000	Brick	1,000
2	Smith & Shuttzman	Brewers	3000	3000 bu	Barley	2,000								
				50 cords	Wood	75	Hand	2		40		700 bbls	[illegible] Beer	3,500
3	Albert Arnold	Joiners	500	30,000 ft	Lumber	300	Hand	3		90			Joiner Work	1,500
4	[illegible] & Cocanour	Joiners	600	40,000 ft	Lumber	400	Hand	6		180			Joiner Work	3,000
5	John Cochran	Joiner	700	25,000 ft	Lumber	250	Hand	4		120			Joiner Work	2,000
6	James Humphrey	Stone Cutter	1,600	70 perch	Stone	140							~~[illegible]~~	2,000
				700 feet	Marble	700	Hand	6		180			Marble Work	3,000
7	Wm Bowen	Sadler	1000	200 sides	Leather	600								
					Hardware	60	Hand	4		80			Saddlery	2,500
8	L & F Baker	Blacksmiths	300	2 tons	Bar Steel	160								
				800 bu	Coal	40	Hand	2		50			Iron Work	1,000
9	Charles Baker	Wagon Maker	300		Timber									
					Lumber	80	Hand	2		80			Wagons	800
10	Drake & Hurd	Joiners	800	50,000 ft	Lumber	500	Hand	2		60			Joiner Work	1500
11	John [illegible]	Rope Maker	200	5 tons	Hemp	500	Hand	3		60			Ropes	1,500
12	Joseph Ellsworth	Boat Yard	500	35,000 ft	Timber									
					Lumber	1,000	Hand	17		300			Boats	6,000
13	Bryant & Lowe	Joiners	300	50,000 ft	Lumber	500	Hand	2		50			Joiner Work	1,500
14	John Smith	Glue Factory	500	12,000 lbs	[illegible]	20	Hand	2		[illegible]		8000 lbs	Glue	1,000
15	Wm G. Shaffer	Joiner	400	25,000 ft	Lumber	250	Hand	2		50			Joiner Work	1,200
16	Jos P. Edsall	Saw Mill	4000	3000	Logs	2400								
				300 cords	Wood	400	Steam	5		125		600,000 ft	Lumber	5,500
17	Thomas Baldock	Joiner	300	30,000 ft	Lumber	300	Hand	3		90			Joiner Work	1,800
18	John [illegible]	Cooper	1,300	200,000	Staves									
	~~[illegible]~~	~~[illegible]~~	[illegible]	[illegible]	Poles	900	Hand	7		140			Barrels	3,500
19	Alexr H. [illegible]	Boat Yard	2000	20,000 ft	Timber								[illegible]	
					Lumber	1,000	Hand	5		125			Repairing	3,500
20	Philip [illegible]	Brewer	2,500	2000 bu	Barley	1000								
				40 cords	Wood	60	Hand	2		40		600 bbls	Ale & Beer	3000
21	[illegible] & Morrison	Saw Mill	2,500	2,000	Logs	1,600	Water	3		75		600,000 ft	Lumber	3,500
			[illegible]			[illegible]		[illegible]		[illegible]				[illegible]

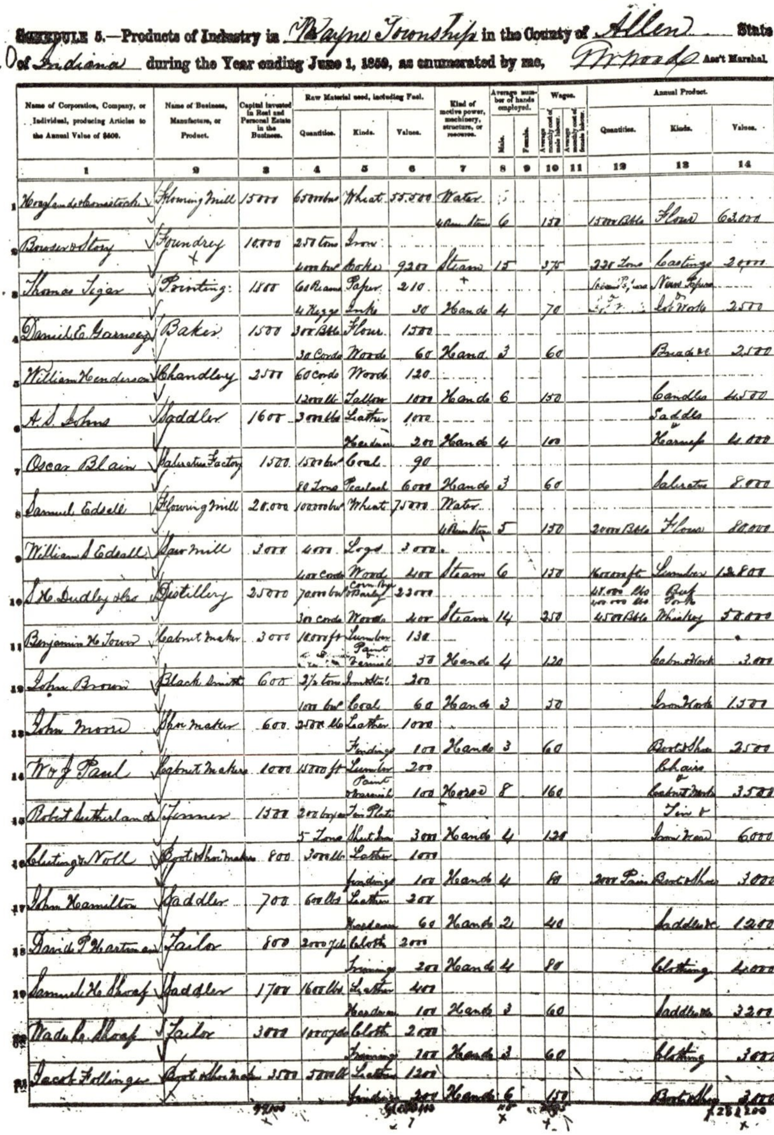

20 SCHEDULE 5.—Products of Industry in Wayne Township in the County of Allen State of Indiana during the Year ending June 1, 1850, as enumerated by me, P. W. Woods Ass't Marshal.

	Name of Corporation, Company, or Individual, producing Articles to the Annual Value of $500.	Name of Business, Manufacture, or Product.	Capital invested in Real and Personal Estate in the Business.	Raw Material used, including Fuel. Quantities.	Kinds.	Values.	Kind of motive power, machinery, structure, or resource.	Average number of hands employed. Male.	Female.	Wages. Average monthly cost of male labor.	Average monthly cost of female labor.	Annual Product. Quantities.	Kinds.	Values.
	1	2	3	4	5	6	7	8	9	10	11	12	13	14
1	Hoagland & Comstock	Flouring Mill	15000	650000 bu	Wheat	55,500	Water 4 Run Stone	6		150		15000 Bbls	Flour	63,000
2	Bowser & Story	Foundrey	10,000	250 tons 4000 bu	Iron Coke	9200	Steam	15		375		230 Tons	Castings	20,000
3	Thomas Tigar	Printing	1800	60 Reams 4 Kegs	Paper Ink	210 30	Hands	4		70		[illegible]	News Paper & Job Work	2500
4	Daniel E. Garnsey	Baker	1500	300 Bbls 30 Cords	Flour Wood	1500 60	Hand	3		60			Bread &c	2500
5	William Henderson	Chandlery	2500	60 Cords 12000 lbs	Wood Tallow	120 1000	Hands	6		150			Candles	4500
6	A. S. Johns	Saddler	1600	3000 lbs	Leather Hardware	1000 200	Hands	4		100			Saddles & Harness	4000
7	Oscar Blain	Saleratus Factory	1500	1500 bu 80 Tons	Coal Pearlash	90 6000	Hands	3		60			Saleratus	8000
8	Samuel Edsall	Flouring Mill	20,000	100000 bu	Wheat	75000	Water 4 Run Stone	5		150		20000 Bbls	Flour	80,000
9	William S. Edsall	Saw Mill	3000	4000 400 Cords	Logs Wood	3000 400	Steam	6		150		[illegible] ft	Lumber	12,800
10	S. H. Dudley & Co	Distillery	25000	70000 bu 300 Cords	Corn, Rye & Barley Wood	23000 400	Steam	14		250		48,000 lbs 400 000 lbs 4500 Bbls	Beef Pork Whiskey	58,000
11	Benjamin H. Tower	Cabinet Maker	3000	10000 ft [illegible]	Lumber Paint & Varnish	130 50	Hands	4		120			Cabinet Work	3000
12	John Brown	Black Smith	600	2½ tons 1000 bu	Iron & Steel Coal	200 60	Hands	3		50			Iron Work	1500
13	John Moore	Shoe maker	600	2500 lbs	Leather Findings	1000 100	Hands	3		60			Boots & Shoes	2500
14	Wm J. Paul	Cabinet Maker	1000	15000 ft	Lumber Paint & Varnish	200 100	Horse	8		160			Chairs & Cabinet Work	3500
15	Robert Sutherland & Co	Tinner	1500	200 boxes 5 Tons	Tin Plate Sheet Iron	3000	Hands	4		120			Tin & Iron Ware	6000
16	Clutting & Noll	Boot & Shoe maker	800	3000 lbs	Leather findings	1000 100	Hands	4		80		2000 Pairs	Boots & Shoes	3000
17	John Hamilton	Saddler	700	600 lbs	Leather Hardware	200 60	Hands	2		40			Saddles &c	1200
18	David P. Hartman	Tailor	800	2000 yds	Cloth Trimmings	2000 200	Hands	4		80			Clothing	4000
19	Samuel H. Shoaf	Saddler	1700	1600 lbs	Leather Hardware	400 100	Hands	3		60			Saddles &c	3200
20	Wade C. Shoaf	Tailor	3000	1000 yds	Cloth Trimmings	2000 100	Hands	3		60			Clothing	3000
21	Jacob Follinger	Boot & Shoe Maker	3500	5000 lbs	Leather findings	1200 200	Hands	6		150			Boots & Shoes	3000
			97100			[illegible]		[illegible]		[illegible]				252,200

21

SCHEDULE 5.—Products of Industry in *Wayne Township* **in the County of** *Allen* **State of** *Indiana* **during the Year ending June 1, 1850, as enumerated by me,** *D. W. Wood* **Ass't Marshal.**

	Name of Corporation, Company, or Individual, producing Articles to the Annual Value of $500.	Name of Business, Manufacture, or Product.	Capital invested in Real and Personal Estate in the Business.	Raw Material used, including Fuel. Quantities.	Kinds.	Values.	Kind of motive power, machinery, structure, or resource.	Average number of hands employed. Male.	Female.	Wages. Average monthly cost of male labor.	Average monthly cost of female labor.	Annual Product. Quantities.	Kinds.	Values.
	1	2	3	4	5	6	7	8	9	10	11	12	13	14
1	Benj'n Saunders	Baker	3000	200 bbls	Flour	900								
				20 cords	Wood	40	Hand	3		60			Bread &c	2,000
2	Jacob King	Blacksmith	1000	2 tons	Iron & Steel	160								
				800 bu	Coals	40	Hand	2		40			Iron Work	1,000
3	Conrad Nill	Shoe Maker	600	2500 lbs	Leather	1000								
					Findings	80	Hand	3		60			Boots & Shoes	2,500
4	James M. Blossom	Tailor	1200	2000 yds	Cloth	2,000								
					Trimings	150	Hand	4	2	80	16		Clothing	4,000
5	Michael Graffe	Cab't Makers	1,200	8000 ft	Lumber	120								
					Rose wood & Mahogany	120	Hand	2		60			Cabinet Work	2,000
6	John Hoke	Brewer	600	1000 bu	Barley	500								
				30 cords	Wood	50	Hand	2		36		300 bbls	Ale & Beer	1,500
7	Andrew Phlegar	Potter	500		Clay	20								
				40 cords	Wood	80	Hand	3		45			Potters ware	1,200
8	Jas. H. Robinson	Leather & Shoe Manufactory	15,000 (9.50 Tan)	350 cords	Bark	700						4000 sides	Leather	
				2000	Hides	4000	Hand	14		300		4000 prs	Boots & Shoes	15,000
9	Charles Fink	Cab't Maker	1200	15,000 ft	Lumber	200								
					Trimmings	100	Hand	6		100			Furniture	2,500
10	John Snively	Joiner	500	20,000 ft	Lumber	200	Hand	2		50			Joiner Work	1,400
11	Joseph Hartel	Blacksmith	700	2 tons	Iron & Steel	160								
				800 bu	Coal	40	Hand	2		50			Iron Work	1,400
12	Augustus C. Beaver	Fan Mill Maker	800	10,000 ft	Lumber	100	Hand	2		50		80	Fanning Mills	1,600
13	John Johnson	Cooper	600	100,000	Staves	600								
				30,000	Poles	150	Hand	10		200		5000	Barrels	4,000
14	John Brown	Lime Kiln	500	500 perch	Stone	450								
				100 cords	Wood	150	Hand	4		80		3000 bbls	Lime	2,000
15	George Black	Blacksmith	400	3 tons	Iron & Steel	240								
				1000 bu	Coals	50	Hand	2		50			Iron Work	1,000
16	Lewis Pelkey	Cab't Maker	1000	40,000 ft	Lumber	500								
					Trimmings	100	Hand	2		50			Cabinet Work	1800
17	Eli Broom	Wagon Maker	700		Timber & Lumber	100								
					Paints &c	40	Hand	3		75			Wagons	1,500
18	Joseph Cutler	Blacksmith	300	1½ tons	Iron	120								
				800 bu	Coals	40	Hand	1		30			Iron Work	800
19	John Miller	Cabinet Maker	2000	30,000 ft	Lumber	1500								
					Veneering & Varnish &c	1000	Horse	12		360			Furniture	8,000
20	Conklin & Stanley	Wagon Makers	500		Timber	75								
					& Lumber	125	Hand	3		90			Wagons	2,300
21	Charles Burt	Brick Maker	500		Clay	50								
				200 cords	Wood	200	Horse	4		70		400,000	Bricks	1,600
			$33800			$15390		80	2	1988	16			39,100

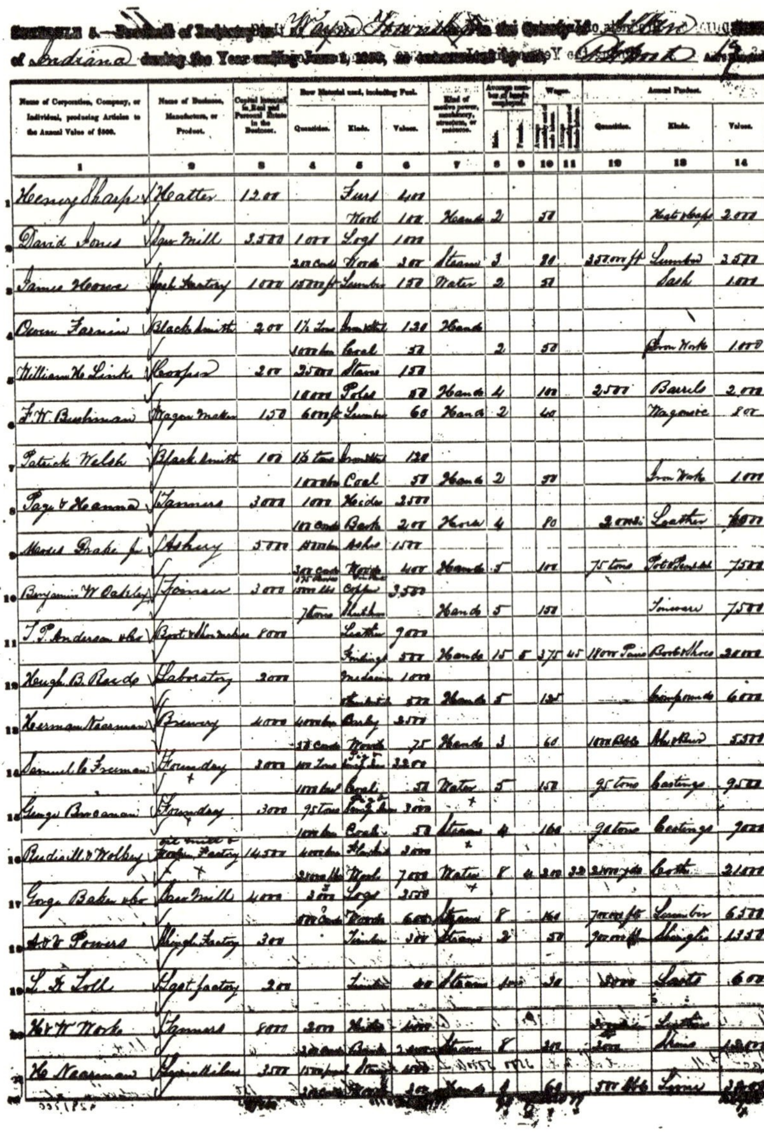

SCHEDULE 5.—Products of Industry in Wayne Township in the County of Allen, State of Indiana during the Year ending June 1, 1850, as enumerated by me, R. Brook

Name of Corporation, Company, or Individual, producing Articles to the Annual Value of $500.	Name of Business, Manufacture, or Product.	Capital invested in Real and Personal Estate in the Business.	Raw Material used, including Fuel. Quantities.	Kinds.	Values.	Kind of motive power, machinery, structure, or resource.	Average number of hands employed. Male.	Female.	Wages. Average monthly cost of male labor.	Average monthly cost of female labor.	Annual Product. Quantities.	Kinds.	Values.
1	2	3	4	5	6	7	8	9	10	11	12	13	14
1 Henry Sharp	Hatter	1200		Furs	400								
				Wool	100	Hand	2		50			Hats & Caps	2.000
2 David Jones	Saw Mill	3.500	1000	Logs	1000								
			200 Cords	Wood	200	Steam	3		80	350.000 ft	Lumber	3.500
3 James Howe	Sash Factory	1000	15000 ft	Lumber	150	Water	2		50			Sash	1.000
4 Owen Farnin	Blacksmith	200	1½ Tons	Iron & Steel	130	Hand							
			1000 bu	Coal	50		2		50			Iron Work	1.000
5 William H. Link	Cooper	200	25000	Staves	150								
			10000	Poles	50	Hand	4		100		2.500	Barrels	2.000
6 F. W. Bushman	Wagon maker	150	6000 ft	Lumber	60	Hand	2		40			Wagons &c	800
7 Patrick Welsh	Blacksmith	100	1½ tons	Iron & Steel	120								
			1000 bu	Coal	50	Hand	2		50			Iron Work	1.000
8 Page & Hanna	Tanners	3000	1000	Hides	2.500								
			100 Cords	Bark	200	Horse	4		80		2000 sides	Leather	4000
9 Marcus Drake jr	Ashery	5.000	[illegible] bu	Ashes	1500								
			300 Cords	Wood	400	Hand	5		100		75 tons	Pot & Pearl ash	7500
10 Benjamin W. Oakley	Tinner	3000	175 boxes / 5000 lbs	Tin Plate / Copper	3.500								
			7 tons	Sheet Iron		Hand	5		150			Tinware	7500
11 T. P. Anderson & Co	Boot & Shoe maker	8000		Leather	7000								
				Findings	500	Hand	15	5	375	45	11000 Pairs	Boots & Shoes	20000
12 Hugh B. Reed	Laboratory	2000		Medicines	1000								
				[illegible]	500	Hand	5		125		—	Compounds	6000
13 Herman Nierman	Brewery	4000	4000 bu	Barley	2.500								
			50 Cords	Wood	75	Hand	3		60		1000 Bbls	Ale & Beer	5.500
14 Samuel C. Freeman	Foundry	3000	100 Tons	Pig Iron	3200								
			1000 bu	Coal	50	Water	5		150		95 tons	Castings	9500
15 George Bowman	Foundry	3000	95 Tons	Pig Iron	3000								
			1000 bu	Coal	50	Steam	4		160		90 tons	Castings	9000
16 Rudisill & Wolke	Grist Mill & Woolen Factory	14.500	4000 bu	Flaxseed	3000								
			25000 lbs	Wool	7000	Water	8	4	200	32	25000 yds	Cloths	21000
17 George Baker & Co	Saw Mill	4000	3000	Logs	3500								
			500 Cords	Wood	600	Steam	8		160		700.000 ft	Lumber	6.500
18 A & J Powers	Shingle Factory	300		Timber	300	Steam	2		50		900.000	Shingles	1350
19 L. F. Toll	Last factory	200		Timber	40	Steam	[illegible]		30		[illegible]	Lasts	600
20 H & W Work	Tanners	8000	2000	Hides	4000						[illegible]	Leather	
			200 Cords	Bark	[illegible]	Steam	8		200		2000	Skins	12000
21 H. Nierman	Gypsum Kilns	2500	1500 pounds	Stone	600								
			200 Cords	Wood	200	Hand	[illegible]		60		500 Bbls	Lime	3000

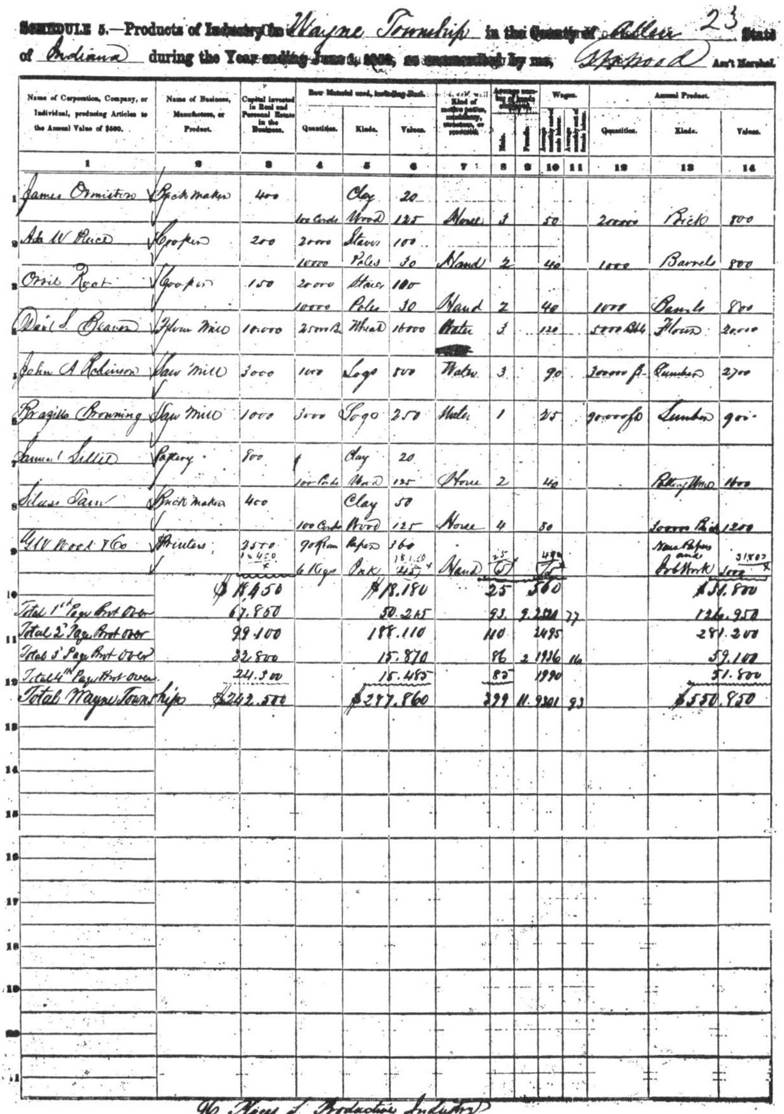

SCHEDULE 5.—Products of Industry in *Wayne Township* in the County of *Allen* 23 State of *Indiana* during the Year ending June 1, [illegible], as enumerated by me, *[illegible]* Ass't Marshal.

	Name of Corporation, Company, or Individual, producing Articles to the Annual Value of $500.	Name of Business, Manufacture, or Product.	Capital invested in Real and Personal Estate in the Business.	Raw Material used, including Fuel. Quantities.	Kinds.	Values.	Kind of motive power, machinery, structure, or resource.	Average number of hands employed. Male.	Female.	Wages. Average monthly cost of male labor.	Average monthly cost of female labor.	Annual Product. Quantities.	Kinds.	Values.
	1	2	3	4	5	6	7	8	9	10	11	12	13	14
1	James Ormiston	Brick maker	400		Clay	20								
				100 Cords	Wood	125	Horse	3		50		200000	Brick	800
2	Asa W Pierce	Cooper	200	20000	Staves	100								
				10000	Poles	30	Hand	2		40		1000	Barrels	800
3	Orril Root	Cooper	150	20000	Staves	100								
				10000	Poles	30	Hand	2		40		1000	Barrels	800
4	David S. Beaver	Flour Mill	10.000	25000 Bu.	Wheat	16000	Water	3		120		5000 Bbls	Flour	20.000
5	John A Robinson	Saw Mill	3000	1000	Logs	800	Water	3		90		300000 ft.	Lumber	2700
6	Brazilla Browning	Saw Mill	1000	3000	Logs	250	Water	1		25		90000 ft	Lumber	900
7	Samuel Sillit	Pottery	800		Clay	20								
				100 Cords	Wood	125	Horse	2		40			Pottery Ware	1600
8	Silas Farr	Brick maker	400		Clay	50								
				100 Cords	Wood	125	Horse	4		80			300000 Brick	1200
9	G W Wood & Co	Printers	3500 / 18450	90 Ream	Paper	360							News Papers and	
				6 Kegs	Ink	18180 / 45	Hand	25 / 6		490 / 70			Job Work	31800 / 5000
10			$18.450			$18.180		25		560				$51.800
	Total 1st Page Brot Over		67.850			50.245		93.	9.	2301	77			126.950
11	Total 2d Page Brot Over		99.100			188.110		110		2495				281.200
	Total 3d Page Brot Over		32.800			15.870		86	2	1936	16			59.100
12	Total 4th Page Brot Over		24.300			15.485		85		1990				51.800
	Total Wayne Township		$242.500			$287.860		399	11.	9301	93			$550.850
13														
14														
15														
16														
17														
18														
19														
20														
21														

96 Places of Productive Industry

By 1854 this mill employed both water and steam as its source of power to drive its carding machinery and looms.[82] The opportunities provided by the building of the plank roads led to the construction of two steam-powered sawmills in 1848. The first of these was owned by George Baker and his sons; the second mill was operated by William Coombs and Samuel Edsall. In 1843 Samuel Hanna financed the building of a tannery which originally employed water power; however, five years later, after the first building was destroyed by fire, Hanna turned to steam power for the new tannery which he built. In 1846 the three largest mills operating along the entire length of the canal were located at Fort Wayne or in its immediate vicinity.[83]

While the early merchants of Fort Wayne invested a good deal of their available capital in these power-driven industries, most of the opportunities for the laboring man still called for some specialized skill. Of the seven types of industry which gave employment to twenty or more men in 1850, all but one required some marked degree of specialization.[84] The boot and shoe industry, for example, employed more workers than any other in the city, forty-five men and five women. Next in importance was cabinet making which employed thirty-four people.[85] With skilled labor available for relatively moderate wages,[86] Fort Wayne was in position to supply the surrounding

[82] Fort Wayne *Daily Sentinel,* November 18, 1871.

[83] Engineer's report in Indiana *Documentary Journal,* 1846, pt. 1, no. 8, pp. 234-35.

[84] Original Returns of the Seventh Census (1850), Manufactures, Wayne Township.

[85] *Ibid.*

[86] In 1850 the average daily wage without board for a carpenter in Indiana was $1.30. Indiana ranked only 23d out of the 32 states in this respect. At Fort Wayne the average monthly wage for a joiner was $28.75, and for a cabinet-maker only $25.00. *Compendium of the Seventh Census* (1850), 164; Original Returns of the Seventh Census (1850), Manufactures, Wayne Township.

agricultural region with many of its needs. Thus German carpenters and leather craftsmen, such as John Baker and Christian Schiefer, furnished the farmers with wagons, furniture, harness, and shoes, while the power mills cut the lumber and ground the grain. In an era when American industry was changing from the handicraft system to one depending on power-driven machinery, Fort Wayne was no exception. Although steam and water power were being put to use and were employing more capital than other enterprises, the true factory system had not yet arrived at Fort Wayne if one uses the criteria for such established by Victor S. Clark.[87] It would take the advent of the railroads in the early 1850s to create the foundations for such a system which would appear in the latter part of the decade and in the early 1860s with the growth of such industry as the Bass Foundry and Machine Works.

Nevertheless, by the early 1850s Fort Wayne had kept pace industrially with its growing population and commerce. While the population of the city had increased approximately 166 per cent, the capital invested in manufacturing in Allen County had jumped from $67,300 in 1840 to $298,850 in 1850, an increase of 343 per cent.[88] Of Allen County's capital investments in manufacturing in 1850, Wayne Township had $242,500 or 81 per cent.[89] Wayne Township also accounted for 410 of the 491 men and women employed in manufacturing.[90] We may safely assume that the industrial progress of Allen County was largely that of Fort Wayne. In terms of manufacturing capital, Allen County ranked seventh among the ninety-two counties of the state, whereas in 1840 she had ranked twenty-second

[87] Victor S. Clark, *History of Manufactures in the United States, 1607-1860* (2 vols. Carnegie Institution of Washington, *Publications,* 1916), 1:450.

[88] *Compendium of the Sixth Census* (1840), 297; *Compendium of the Seventh Census* (1850), 228-29.

[89] Original Returns of the Seventh Census, Manufactures, Wayne Township.

[90] *Ibid.; Compendium of the Seventh Census* (1850), 228-29.

among 87 counties.[91] Although there are no statistics available for the midpoint of the 1850s, it is evident from the census of 1860 that industrial progress must have continued throughout the early fifties. By 1860 Allen County in comparison with the other counties of Indiana ranked second in number of industrial establishments, eighth in value of raw materials used, third in number of male workers employed, and eighth in annual value of industrial products.[92]

Considering the growth of Fort Wayne's population as well as its increasing industry and commerce, one might well call the decade following 1842 the "Hey-day of the Canal Era for Fort Wayne."[93] The year 1850 was a turbulent one for the nation, but the great issue of slavery seemed to be resolved by the Compromise of that year. After calling attention to the fact that the nation had survived the recent crisis and had annexed new land, George Wood, editor of the Fort Wayne *Times,* predicted that the United States was now prepared to expand internally to a greater extent than ever before and that Fort Wayne was ready to play its role in this expansion.[94]

[91] *Compendium of the Seventh Census* (1850), 229, 235; *Compendium of the Sixth Census* (1840), 292-97.

[92] United States Bureau of Census, *Eighth Census* (1860), *Manufactures,* 142-43.

[93] In his monograph on the Wabash and Erie Canal, E. J. Benton speaks of the period from 1847 to 1856 as "the hey-day of the canal." Benton, *The Wabash Trade Route,* 76. This is correct insofar as he is viewing the canal as a whole, but from the standpoint of Fort Wayne's development the canal was most important from the time it linked Fort Wayne with Lake Erie in 1843 until the coming of the railroad in 1854.

[94] Fort Wayne *Times,* October 10, 1850.

CHAPTER X

THE END OF AN ERA: THE CANAL GIVES WAY TO THE RAILROADS 1852-1855

There can be no place justly entitled to the appellation "city" unless she has a Railroad.

Although the eastern half of the Wabash and Erie Canal was completed in 1843, work on the waterway continued southwest of Lafayette until ultimately the Ohio River was reached at Evansville, Indiana, in 1853. By that year it had become the longest canal in the United States, running a distance of 458$\frac{3}{8}$ miles.[1] It should not be surprising, however, to learn that the newspapers as well as the people of Fort Wayne paid little attention to this achievement for the extension of the canal beyond Lafayette had little practical effect on the prosperity of the city. If anything, by saddling the revenues of the canal with the additional cost of this construction and with the expense for its upkeep, this action probably brought about the early demise of the canal.[2] The real reason behind the disinterest of the Fort Wayne citizenry, however, was the fact that they were already engaged in constructing their first railroad, the Ohio and Indiana, which would link the city with Pittsburgh and the East by November 1, 1854. Within another year the packet lines would cease to operate on the canal, and the over-all canal tolls would decrease almost 50 per cent.[3] By 1856, when the Wabash Railroad linked Fort

[1] Benton, *The Wabash Trade Route,* 76.

[2] *Ibid.,* 78; Harlow, *Old Towpaths,* 277-78.

[3] Fort Wayne *Daily Sentinel,* July 10, 1874; Benton, *The Wabash Trade Route,* 79.

Wayne with Toledo to the East and Lafayette to the southwest, thus actually paralleling the Wabash and Erie Canal, there was little need any longer for the waterway. The following year clearances at Fort Wayne and Lafayette scarcely amounted to one fourth of those issued at the same points in 1854.[4] Line boats which still carried some bulky products to Toledo from Fort Wayne now returned empty—without passengers or without manufactured goods from the East. As early as September, 1850, the Ewings with characteristic business sagacity decided to sell the canalboats in which they had an interest.[5]

The action of the Ewings was an isolated incident in 1850, but the evidence of the canal's rapid decline after 1854 is abundant and clear. The reasons why the people of Fort Wayne and vicinity so readily abandoned the old for the new are also apparent. In 1834-35 when the Indiana House of Representatives debated the Mammoth Internal Improvements Bill the question of railroads vs. canals was raised. The following advantages and disadvantages of both were mentioned during the course of the discussions:

Advantages of Canals

First—Cheapness of construction, when compared with their utility and durability.
Second—The cheapness, safety, and indeed facility, with which the heavy productions of the soil, as well as all other bulky articles, may be conveyed upon them, and the advantages they afford to farmers to use their own means of conveyance.
Third—Their permanency. There are canals now in use, that have been channels of extensive commerce for centuries, and which, with trifling repairs, will remain as useful for centuries to come.
Fourth—The money that is expended in their construction, is circulated amongst us, while many things necessary in the construction of a rail-way—such as iron for rails, &c.—is brought from a distance. . . .

[4] Benton, *The Wabash Trade Route,* 80.

[5] W. G. Ewing to G. W. Ewing, September 16, 1850, Ewing Papers.

Fifth—The repairs in canals, unlike rail-ways, become less expensive the longer they are in use, excepting the rebuilding the wooden structures when that material must necessarily be used.
Sixth—The water privileges created for hydraulic purposes, are not only a source of revenue to the State, but great convenience to the community at large.

Objections to Canals

First—Boats cannot move with sufficient velocity to suit the commercial transactions of the country.
Second—They do more injury to the farms through which they pass, and by some have been supposed to be productive of bad health.
Third—The frequency of breaches produces interruptions in the trade of the country.

Advantages of Rail-roads.

First—Velocity
Second—They can be used during seasons of the year when canals will be closed by ice.
Third—Steam power may be used advantageously upon them.

Objections to Rail-roads.

First—If double tracks are used, and it is believed none other will answer the purpose, they are as expensive as canals.
Second—Both cost and hazard is greater on roal-roads [*sic*] than on canals. . . .
Third—The track, except the iron, must be composed entirely of wood; for stone has not been found to answer the purpose—and will decay so as to require an entire renewal as often as once in eight or ten years; and in addition to this, the annual repairs are great.
Fourth—Much of the money expended in construction, must of necessity be sent out of the country, and when completed, the farmers must be dependent on a monopoly for the transportation of the fruits of their toil.[6]

After a careful reading of the above it becomes apparent that some of the suggested advantages of the canal did not materialize, for example, the belief that the farmers would use their own canalboats.[7] Other "advantages" of the canal became

[6] Indiana *House Journal*, 1834-35, pp. 346-47.

[7] On the other hand, one must admit that there was intelligent foresight in the fourth objection to the railroads.

less important as industry and commerce changed. Water power could be, and gradually was, replaced by steam power, therefore the advantages of the canals diminished while their disadvantages increased. On the other hand, the reverse was true for the railroads. Furthermore, while they were still more hazardous than canals, the railroads were far more safe for travel in the 1850s than they had been in 1835.

The changing viewpoint is quite evident in a letter published in the Fort Wayne *Times* in 1851.[8] The writer asked, "Why a railroad, since we have a canal at Fort Wayne?" He listed seven reasons which may be summarized as follows: (1) The canal operated fairly efficiently only six months of the year. During the other months it was either frozen or the water was too low. (2) The canal is closed in the winter just when it is more convenient to ship grain because the farmers have more time and when the price of grain is higher in the East. (3) The transportation on the canal is too slow. Often the prices in the East rise suddenly, but buyers are afraid to buy from Fort Wayne because it takes three to four weeks to ship the products. (4) The railroad will increase property values. (5) The railroad will stimulate business and mean more work for the laboring man. (6) Most of the money for construction will be spent in Allen County. (7) The railroad, unlike the canal, will be subject to taxation and will pay (it was estimated) one tenth of the county's property tax in the future. Other defects of the canal may be found by reading the papers of the period. Floods, for example, frequently made breaches which resulted in delay and costly repairs as well as causing damage to the surrounding farm lands.[9]

[8] Fort Wayne *Times*, February 13, 1851.

[9] Fort Wayne *Sentinel*, June 17, 1843 and January 16, 1847; Fort Wayne *The People's Press*, September 10, 1844. Concerning the lack of water power, see Fort Wayne *Sentinel*, August 23, 1845.

As the city entered the fifties with greater maturity, shortcomings of the canal which were formerly overlooked or soon forgotten in the excitement of first love now became more apparent. In one sense, therefore, the canal failed to a great extent because it did succeed.[10] In the words of Joseph K. Edgerton, one of Fort Wayne's most active railroad promoters, "It [the canal] had done much, but not all that was required. . . . It had helped Fort Wayne to grow from an Indian frontier trading-post, to a thriving county town . . . but with the projection and construction of railroads on the north and south of us, drawing . . . men to the Northwest . . . it plainly was not in the power of the Wabash and Erie Canal to save Fort Wayne from impending stagnation."[11]

Thus by 1851 it was becoming apparent that Fort Wayne had to have a rail connection with the East, and with Chicago, if possible, in the West. As early as 1847 Jesse L. Williams predicted that Chicago would surpass all other cities of the Northwest and Fort Wayne could be the link between Chicago and Pittsburgh.[12] Eventually Williams was to use the knowledge he gained from the construction of the canal to complete the building of the Pittsburgh, Fort Wayne and Chicago Railroad. Later he was to be responsible for the construction of the Grand Rapids and Indiana Railroad. Pliny Hoagland, who had been chief engineer of Ohio's section of the Wabash and Erie Canal before coming to Fort Wayne in 1845, was also very instrumental in bringing the first railroad to Fort Wayne. William Mitchell, one of the early contractors for the plank

[10] The author is not speaking in terms of the canal's financial success in which it undoubtedly failed the investors, but rather in its relation to the city of Fort Wayne.

[11] Address of Joseph K. Edgerton on the occasion of the death of Samuel Hanna, delivered June 12, 1866, and quoted in the Fort Wayne *Daily Gazette,* June 14, 1866.

[12] Scrapbook of Jesse L. Williams in Allen County—Fort Wayne Historical Museum.

roads, likewise played a significant role in this project, as did Joseph K. Edgerton, who, as a lawyer in Fort Wayne after 1844, had represented the interests of eastern land speculators and, therefore, had contacts with eastern capitalists. However, as Edgerton himself admitted, "no man . . . took a more active or influential part . . ." in bringing the railroad to Fort Wayne than Samuel Hanna.[13] The difficulties that he encountered were many; at times the project collapsed almost completely. However, the experience that Hanna had gained in promoting internal improvements during the previous quarter century served him well in his new task.[14]

Unlike the canal, the railroads which were built to Fort Wayne in the 1850s received no government assistance, state or Federal. They were built by private corporations, while the canal was state owned. This still leaves the very interesting question, "Why did the generation of the 1850s finance its own improvements rather than look to the government for help?" Their decision may have been due in part to the failure of the state system of internal improvements, but the principal reason was that by 1850 the people were better prepared to carry out their program without public assistance. Capital was still scarce, but eastern financiers now were more willing to invest. Fort Wayne and the surrounding area were sufficiently settled and producing income from agriculture and some industry to insure a reasonably safe return on these investments. In commenting to his brother on an article in the Fort Wayne *Times and Press* about the city's increasingly favorable pros-

[13] Address of Edgerton quoted in the Fort Wayne *Daily Gazette,* June 14, 1866.

[14] The Ohio and Indiana Railroad was the first company organized principally under the direction of Samuel Hanna. The second was the Fort Wayne and Chicago Railroad. These were consolidated in 1856 under the title Pittsburgh, Fort Wayne and Chicago Railroad. Griswold, *Pictorial History of Fort Wayne,* 1:410. Later the railroad became known as the Pennsylvania. The company soon established its principal machine and repair shops at Fort Wayne because of its centralized location and the availability of skilled labor in the area.

pects for a railroad, G. W. Ewing noted that the New York capitalists were now interested because they "want their fair share of trade from the [Wabash] valley."[15] It is true that a type of public assistance was permitted in building the Ohio and Indiana Railroad, in that the county was permitted to purchase stock in the company.[16] This was really a revitalization of Hanna's former suggestions regarding the plank roads. At a mass meeting the citizens of Allen County authorized the county commissioners to raise $100,000 for this purpose.[17] The county then sold bonds the interest on which was to be paid through additional property taxes. Again, as they did for the plank roads, the residents of Fort Wayne and Allen County subscribed privately for stock in the railroads with promises of labor and materials. Farms and town lots were also mortgaged. As in the case of the canal, land was the principal means used to finance the construction of the railroads. The chief difference was that by now the land was privately owned and was for the most part under cultivation.

The actual problems in the construction of Fort Wayne's first railroads provide a fascinating subject almost as insidious in its tendency to sidetrack the historian as the Indian and fur trade of the earlier period. Nevertheless, it is not the purpose of this study to go into the railroad era, but merely to show how the methods used to meet the difficulties of the canal era helped to provide some answers to the problems of the later decades or to caution the builders of the railroads against adopting certain expedients. The coming of the rail-

[15] G. W. Ewing to W. G. Ewing, May 11, 1853, Ewing Papers.

[16] *Laws of Indiana,* 1851-52 (general), p. 258. See also Fort Wayne *Sentinel,* January 18, 1851, for a description of the joyful reaction to the passage of this act.

[17] Fort Wayne *Times,* April 10, 1851. It should be realized that $100,000 was usually enough to cover the ordinary expenses of a state government for an entire year at this time.

road was to introduce a new period in the history of Fort Wayne, but one that was closely related to the past.

A number of events—some symbolic, others more significant in reality—mark the years which saw the decline of the canal and the opening of the railroad era. The actual construction of the Ohio and Indiana Railroad began in 1852. The same year saw the destruction of the remaining timbers of the old fort—the last relics of the pre-canal era. The *Laurel Wreath,* Fort Wayne's literary publication, protested in a verse entitled "'Spare Wayne's Fort," which began:

> Why tear it down and spare it not?
> Are other days so soon forgot?
> Are other scenes no more to be
> Brought back to sweet, blessed memory?[18]

Despite the efforts of those interested in preserving the monuments of the past, today only an old cannon and a plaque mark the site of the bygone fort.

Municipal progress was made in a number of fields during the years 1853-54. Public improvements were to be seen in the new city market as well as in the planking of Columbia Street. The Fort Wayne Gas Light Company, a privately owned corporation, was granted a franchise in 1853, and within a few years gas lights were to appear on the main streets of the city, thus providing greater safety for its citizens at night. For those who could afford it, gas lighting was also made available for private homes and business establishments.[19] Also in 1853 the night watch was reorganized and three policemen were appointed to patrol the streets after sunset.

These advancements in municipal affairs undoubtedly led the average person of Fort Wayne to pay more attention to his city government. This interest was also stimulated to a certain extent by the four revisions of the city charter which

[18] Griswold, *Pictorial History of Fort Wayne,* 1:236.

[19] City ordinance printed in the Fort Wayne *Sentinel,* October 10, 1855.

took place between the years 1850 and 1854. As we have noted, the city officials were seeking by the end of the 1840s more extensive powers of taxation.[20] In 1850 they secured from the state legislature six amendments to the charter which in general increased the city's power to equalize, levy, and collect taxes.[21] Armed with this new authority, the Common Council voted to increase assessments and to levy a special tax of 25 cents per $100 of assessed property value in order to improve the city's streets.[22] While many of the more progressive merchants supported this tax in keeping with the efforts to build the plank roads in the county, a number of property owners rebelled and in 1851 secured a second series of amendments to the city charter. While these amendments (thirteen in all) went far in restricting the city's power to tax, they also provided for a number of fundamental changes in the structure of the city government. These included the abolition of the city offices of treasurer, assessor, and collector and the assumption of their duties by the respective county officials. While this was in part an economy measure, it was also a clear concession to the rural elements of the county. Section VI of the act which required the Common Council to pass, without delay, an ordinance to provide for a "well regulated and general market or markets, to be held at least two days a week . . ." was definitely in accord with the desires of the farmers. Section VII of the act provided for the annual election of the mayor, thus making the office more responsive to the popular will. The most notable restrictions on the power to tax were contained in Section II, which limited the Common Council from borrowing money or levying taxes in excess of 15 cents on each $100 evaluation unless authorized by the voters of

[20] See above, pp. 119-20.

[21] *Laws of Indiana,* 1850-51 (local), pp. 449-50.

[22] Records of the Common Council, March 15, 1851, p. 101, in Fort Wayne City Hall.

the city to do so in a special election, and in Section IV which required the Common Council to lower the existing road tax from 25 cents to 15 cents on each $100 valuation. Other provisions of the 1851 amendments indicated a growing interest in the role of municipal officials, such as that which required the mayor and the county treasurer to post security bonds. The final three sections of the 1851 act, which pertained to taxes derived from city licenses, were repealed by the Indiana legislature in 1852, thus changing the charter three times in three years.[23]

Actually these changes were but specific instances of legal revisions which resulted from the problems municipal governments throughout the state were facing. In general the expanding cities needed greater regulatory powers, but above all they required broader powers of taxation, especially since the cities were then endeavoring to establish public schools as well as to provide greater services. The Indiana legislators took cognizance of these facts in June, 1852, when they passed a general act for the incorporation of cities of three thousand or more population.[24] Under the terms of this emergency act the regulatory and taxing powers of the municipal governments were spelled out in greater detail. While taxes were still limited to three fourths of 1 per cent on each $100 of property subject to state and county taxes, this still permitted a rate of 75 cents per $100 evaluation as opposed to the previous 15 cents in the case of Fort Wayne. Other changes, when applied to Fort Wayne, provided for the re-establishment of the offices of city assessor, treasurer, and collector. Finally, by the terms of the act, the citizens of each city were free to decide by a special election whether or not they wished their particular city to come under the provisions of the new legislation. In a refer-

[23] *Laws of Indiana,* 1851 (local), pp. 314-16.

[24] *The Revised Statutes of the State of Indiana* (2 vols. Indianapolis, 1852), 1: 203-21.

endum held in conjunction with the city elections of 1854 the voters of Fort Wayne accepted the above revisions to the city charter.

Certainly these numerous revisions contributed to the intensification of political activity in city affairs during the early 1850s; whereas before 1850 it was difficult to find qualified men interested in running for municipal office, in 1853 there were eight candidates competing for the position of mayor.[25] The contest was actually between Charles Whitmore and William Stewart, however, with Whitmore winning in a close election. In 1854, for the first time in city elections, the two major parties endorsed individual slates of candidates.[26] Heretofore the parties had not considered it worth-while to become involved in the campaigns. One of the major reasons for the interest in the election of 1854 was the referendum on the charter, but other issues were also before the public, including the candidates' position on prohibition. It should not surprise us to learn that the question of taxation was paramount. As the *Sentinel* put it, "an exorbitant tax can be levied this year, and it is advisable to have such a board as will expend it economically and satisfactorily."[27] It is difficult to determine just what the majority of the Fort Wayne voters wanted in 1854; while they supported the revised charter they elected the Whig candidate, Charles Whitmore, who had received strong support from Dawson's *Times* which did not favor the new charter.[28] Furthermore, the election was sufficiently close for the Democrats to call for a new election on the grounds

[25] Letter of Charles Whitmore, printed in the Fort Wayne *Morning Gazette*, February 25, 1882.

[26] Fort Wayne *Sentinel*, February 11, 1854.

[27] *Ibid.*, February 18, 1854.

[28] Fort Wayne *Times*, February 22, 1854. Unfortunately a number of issues of the Fort Wayne papers, especially the *Sentinel*, are missing for these months; therefore it is difficult to reach any definite conclusions about the exact positions of the candidates and in particular the Democratic candidate James Worden.

that the revised charter invalidated the previous election.[29] Significantly, this was the first time the results of a city election were challenged.

Behind the question of taxation in 1854 there was the deeper problem of support for a free school system in the city. In the state-wide referendum of 1848 the people of Fort Wayne had voted overwhelmingly in favor of establishing a public school system.[30] Now after the adoption of the new state constitution in 1851 and the enactment of appropriate legislation authorizing the creation of a public school system to be supported by the townships, it was possible for the advocates of free schools to act. In 1853 Fort Wayne along with Indianapolis took the lead throughout the state in establishing a free school system.[31] Hugh McCulloch, Charles Case, and William Stewart were named as the city's first board of school trustees. With only $330.72 available, they did their best by hiring two men to teach in rented buildings for three months, beginning in October. The board realized that this was not a satisfactory nor by any means a permanent solution; consequently, they proposed a school tax of 50 cents per $100 evaluation. As required by the amendments to the charter in 1851, the issue was presented to the voters in a special election. When the tax was rejected by a vote of 325 to 130 the board resigned.[32] The fight had only begun, however. The question of free schools became a political issue in the succeeding years, and was further complicated by the demand of the German population that they be permitted to establish a separate

[29] Fort Wayne *Times,* March 15, 1854.

[30] See above, pp. 195-96.

[31] Walter G. Herrling, "Early Education in Fort Wayne," in *Old Fort News,* 5: nos. 1-2 (March-June, 1940): 5-6.

[32] Charles E. Slocum (ed.), *History of the Maumee River Basin* (Vol. 1 of 3 vols. Indianapolis, c. 1905), 1:230; Fort Wayne *News-Sentinel,* June 19, 1926 (Progress Edition), p. 4.

system.[33] A small tax of two mills on each dollar of assessed property plus private donations permitted a new board of trustees to start construction of a school building in 1855, which was dedicated as "Clay School" two years later.[34] Thus, although the final outcome was still uncertain, the public school system had been definitely launched in Fort Wayne by 1855.[35]

While the battle over public schools was still being fought as the era of the railroad began, other cultural advancements were being achieved more easily. Fort Wayne's first theater, Colerick Hall, was opened in 1853. Although by no means adequate, it was a definite improvement over the old courthouse, where most of the entertainment had taken place until then. We have previously mentioned the formation of the Workingmen's Institute and Library during these years, as well as the appearance of the two literary papers, the *Laurel Wreath* and the *Summit City Journal*. The former weekly newspaper was first published in May, 1852, by Thomas Cook. Amazingly Cook gained for a short time enough subscribers

[33] The issue was primarily an ethnic one although the religious question entered in. While the Lutherans and Catholics both had their own schools they were probably distressed by the fact that public money was being used to support a system largely under the control of the Presbyterians. Such appeared to be the case if one considers that the first superintendent of the public school was the Presbyterian minister, the Reverend George A. Irvin, and that most of his staff were likewise Presbyterian. Griswold, *Pictorial History of Fort Wayne,* 1:421.

[34] Fort Wayne *Sentinel,* February 4, 1857.

[35] In 1857 Samuel Morss was elected mayor on the "Free School Program." His opponent was Louis Wolke, a German. After Morss's election concessions were made to the German element in that they were permitted to rent their own school buildings and hire their own teachers. This arrangement continued throughout the remainder of the nineteenth century. Until 1865, nevertheless, the school board faced continuous financial problems which at times forced them to close the schools temporarily. Griswold, *Pictorial History of Fort Wayne,* 1: 441, 443.

to challenge the leading papers, the *Sentinel* and the *Times.*[36] The reason for this was primarily political and religious. When Dawson's *Times* began attacking immigrants and Catholics in the spirit of the Know-Nothing movement, Cook called for a more objective analysis of the problem and thus gained the support of the moderate Whigs and the newly created Republican party. Cook's entry into political issues led him far from his literary purpose, but apparently he had no real taste for the political arena, for he sold out to D. W. Burroughs in June, 1854. Burroughs renamed the paper the *Standard* and in November began publishing a daily paper which leaned decidedly toward abolitionism under its editor, Charles Case.[37]

Actually the *Standard* was the second daily paper initiated in Fort Wayne in 1854. In July John Dawson had started the publication of the *Daily Times,* and while attempts were somewhat premature, lasting only two years, Dawson revived the *Daily Times* on a permanent basis in 1859. In the years between 1852 and 1858 a number of short-lived weekly papers appeared in Fort Wayne—the *True Democrat,* the *Jeffersonian,* the *Journal,* and the *Weekly Republican*—emphasizing the changing political scene in the nation.

Religious progress, while not spectacular, was steady in the early years of the fifties. Some of the older societies, such as the Presbyterians and the Methodists, were establishing their third congregations. In 1852 the *Times* claimed the title "City of Churches" for Fort Wayne on the grounds that the city had twelve churches or one for every 417 people.[38] All of these churches had regular pastors. By 1855 the German Catho-

[36] Fort Wayne *Times,* February 22, 1854. John Dawson had acquired an interest in the Fort Wayne *Times and People's Press* in 1853 and changed the title to the *Times.* Dawson admitted the *Laurel Wreath* had up to seven hundred subscribers.

[37] Harold Hopkins *et al.,* "Hoosier Professional Backgrounds," in *Old Fort News,* 23: no. 1 (January-March, 1960), p. 47.

[38] Fort Wayne *Times,* June 24, 1852.

lics had firmly established a home for orphans. Two years later Fort Wayne was selected as the seat of a new Catholic diocese which included forty-two counties, virtually all of northern Indiana.

Some progress was apparent in almost every field in the years 1852-1855. In one respect these years were similar to those of the period 1829-1832. They were years of transition and expectation, but unlike the earlier years, these were times of optimism. With the city of Fort Wayne established commercially and industrially, with the hard lessons learned in the promotion and construction of the canal and the plank roads, the people could look forward to the future and to the coming of the railroads. Fort Wayne was no longer a simple village bewildered by the loss of the Indian trade, but a community assured of its continued life in the newly emerging industrial America. It was to be the central point of the Pittsburgh, Fort Wayne and Chicago Railroad.

In November, 1854, when the eastern half of the above line reached Fort Wayne the editor of the *Times* wrote:

> There can be no place justly entitled to the appellation "city" unless she has a Railroad, and now that Fort Wayne has a completed Railway, this with her vast wealth, her central position, her water power, manufacturing facilities and fertility and extent of adjacent territory, and her population of 8000 justly entitles her to the name.[39]

[39] Fort Wayne *Daily Times,* November 2, 1854.

APPENDIX

Regulatory Powers of the Common Council
Contained in Section 28 of the 1840
Charter of the City of Fort Wayne

Petitions and remonstrances may be presented to the Common Council. The Common Council shall have the management and control of the finances and of all property, real and personal belonging to the corporation, and shall have power within said city to make, establish, publish, alter, modify, amend and repeal ordinances, regulations and by-laws for the following purposes:

1st: To restrain and prohibit all descriptions of gaming and every kind of fraudulent devise and practice in said city.

2nd: To restrain and prohibit the selling or bartering of any spiritous liquors or ardent spirits to be drunk in the shop, store, grocery, outhouse, yard or garden of the person selling the same, unless licensed so to do by the city authority.

3rd: To restrain and prohibit the selling, giving away or bartering of any ardent spirits or intoxicating liquors to any person already drunk or known to be in the habit of intoxication or to any child, apprentice or servant without the consent of his or her parent, guardian, master or mistress, or to any Indian.

4th: To regulate and prohibit all exhibitions of natural and artificial curiosities and all shows, exhibitions and amusements whatsoever, which in the opinion of said Council are demoralizing to society or calculated to detract from the peace and good order of said City.

5th: To prevent riot, noise, disturbance and disorderly assemblies.

6th: To suppress and restrain disorderly houses and groceries, houses of ill fame, billiard tables, nine or ten pin alleys or tables and ball alleys.

7th: To compel the owner or occupant of any piece of ground, grocery, cellar, tallow chandler's shop, soap factory, tannery, barn, privy, sewer or other place to cleanse the same from time to time as often as it may be deemed necessary for the health, comfort and convenience of said city and to remove or abate or otherwise destroy the cause which renders such house unhealthy or uncomfortable.

8th: To direct the location of all powder houses, slaughter houses, tallow chandler's shops, soap factories and other houses that may be an annoyance to the health and comfort or safety of said city, and if thought necessary to prohibit the erection or continuance altogether of such establishments within the limits of said city.

9th: To regulate the keeping and conveying of gun powder and other combustibles and dangerous materials and the use of candles and lights in houses and stables.

10th: To prevent horse racing and immoderate riding or driving in the streets.

11th: To prevent the encumbering of the streets, sidewalks, lanes, alleys or wharves with carriages, carts, boxes, lumber, timber, firewood or any other substance or material whatsoever.

12th: To regulate and determine the times and places of bathing and swimming in the rivers and canals in or adjoining said City.

13th: To restrain and punish vagrants, mendicants, street beggers, habitual drunkards and common prostitutes.

14th: To regulate and restrain the running at large of cattle, horses, swine, sheep, goats, geese or other animals and to authorize the distraining, impounding and sale of same for the penalty incurred and the costs of proceedings.

15th: To prevent the running at large of dogs and to authorize the destruction of the same when at large contrary to the ordinances.

16th: To prohibit any person from bringing or depositing or having within the limits of said City any dead carcass or other unwholesome substance and to require the removal or destruction by any person who shall have the same upon or near his premises by his own act or consent, if any such substance or any putrid or unsound beef, pork, fish, hides or skins of any kind, or other unsound or unwholesome sustenance whatsoever and on the default of such person to authorize the removal or destruction by the proper officer of said City.

17th: To prohibit the rolling of hoops, playing at ball or long bullets, using of firecrackers or flying kites or other instruments or practice having a tendency to annoy or endanger persons passing the streets or to frighten teams or horses within said City.

18th: To compel all persons to keep the snow, ice and dirt from the sidewalks and to cleanse and to keep clean the gutter and street in front of the premises by them owned or occupied.

19th: To prevent the disorderly ringing of bells, blowing of horns and bugles and crying of goods and other things within the limits of said City to the disturbance of the citizens.

20th: To abate and remove nuisances, to declare what shall be deemed nuisances within said City and abate the same or punish by suitable penalties the person or persons causing or continuing the same or both abate and punish at discretion.

21st: To regulate and restrain runners and carriers for boats and stages.

22nd: To license and regulate carts, wagons, drays and carriages which may be kept in said City for hire.

23rd: To survey, mark and establish the boundaries of said City.

24th: To regulate the burial of the dead, purchase and provide common burying grounds, hearses and other things necessary to burial and to appoint one or more sextons and prescribe his duties.

25th: To direct the keeping of bills of mortality and to impose penalties on physicians, sextons and others for any default in the premises.

26th: To regulate gauging, the place and manner of selling and weighing hay and of selling and measuring lumber and woods, lime, grain and coal, the inspection of flour, salted pork, beef, butter and lard.

27th: To regulate the quality of bread and to provide for the seizure and forfeiture of bread baked contrary thereto.

28th: To establish, make and regulate the public pumps, wells, cisterns and reservoirs and to prevent the unnecessary waste of water.

29th: To provide for the watering of said City.

30th: To establish and regulate public pounds.

31st: To prevent the firing of guns and pistols and all other firearms or fireworks within said City.

32nd: To prevent the erection of wooden buildings in such parts of said City as they may think proper.

33rd: To erect market houses, a hospital, a council house, and a city jail, and to regulate and govern the same and to erect houses for common schools.

34th: To prevent and restrain forestalling and regrating.

35th: To guard against damage by fire, to organize companies and regulate and govern the same and regulate the duties and conduct of the citizens in relation thereto.

36th: To regulate the police of said City.

37th: To diminish or increase at any time otherwise alter the number and the limits of the wards of said City but no such change in the wards of said City shall in the least effect the present council or vacate the seat of any alderman for his present term or authorize the election of an alderman for any new made ward until the next annual election.

38th: To borrow money for the use of said corporation.

39th: To regulate auction of horses and other domestic animals in the streets and appoint and license auctioneers.

40th: To levy and collect the revenue for the use of said City in the manner hereinafter described.

41st: To prevent injuries to the inhabitants of said City from thieves, robbers, burglars and all other persons violating the public peace.

42nd: To establish a board of health for said City, to invest it with such power and to impose upon it such duties as shall be necessary to secure said City and the inhabitants thereof from the evils, distress and calamities of contagious, malignant or infectious diseases, provide for its proper organization and the election or appointment of the necessary officers thereof and make such by-laws, rules and regulations for its government and support as shall be required for the prompt performance of its duties and the lawful exercise of its powers.

43rd: To establish a city watch, define its duties and prescribe its powers.

44th: To license and regulate all taverns and all porter shops and houses and all other places where spiritous liquors are sold by a less quantity than a quart and all other houses of public entertainment within said City, all theatrical exhibitions of whatever name or nature to which admission is obtained on the payment of money or other reward.

45th:To regulate the construction of chimneys, fireplaces, hearths and stove pipes so as to prevent damage from fire.

INDEX